SHEFFIELD CORPOR
TRAMWAYS
AN ILLUSTRATED HISTORY

Kenneth Gandy

Sheffield City Libraries

First Published 1985.

Published by Sheffield City Libraries,
Central Library, Surrey Street,
Sheffield S1 1XZ.

ISBN 0 86321 032 5

Printed in Great Britain by City of Sheffield Printing Services

Contents

Introduction

It is generally believed that the high point in the development of the United Kingdom tramway systems was around 1927. In March of that year Sheffield had 421 passenger cars in service—out of a total of over 14,000 in the country as a whole.

At the turn of the century electric tramways were generally supplanting horse-drawn trams and in the years following 1927 the motor bus (or trolley bus) was in turn gradually replacing the electric tram, so that by the end of the 1950s only three tramway systems remained—and one of them was Sheffield's, where the last tram ran in October 1960.

In the tramway heyday virtually every city and large town in the land had a tramway system; even some comparatively small localities had one or were part of an inter-urban network extending out from a neighbouring centre.

So Sheffield was in the mainstream of urban passenger transport in this country. What singled it out as an *outstanding* tramway system?

Firstly, the Sheffield trams were superbly maintained so that the frequency and reliability of both day and night services were exceptionally good. Despite operating in what was then a grimy industrial city, the cars were of elegant design and displayed a memorable livery of dark blue and cream (in later years predominantly cream) which was generally kept in splendid condition and was a pleasure to see.

Secondly, the fares were cheap compared with other systems, and thirdly the passenger seating was extremely comfortable—far better, in fact, than the buses that were eventually to replace the trams.

The system had very substantial public support despite opposition from motoring interests. It is therefore all the more surprising that among the numerous publications on tramway topics that have appeared in the last twenty-five years or so, few have dealt in any detail with the Sheffield system, especially as Sheffield's was one of the largest and almost the last to disappear.

The aim of this work is to fill the gap and attempt to amplify the record; to set down the history of the Corporation tramway system from start to finish, and to chart the routes, the services and above all the cars, so that it can be seen and appreciated as the outstanding undertaking that it undoubtedly was.

The form is that of a reference work rather than an anecdotal one, hence the use of detailed appendices and index.

Chapter 1

Setting the Scene

The growth of Sheffield from a very small town in the Middle Ages to a city large enough to support one of the country's leading tramway undertakings is mainly the result of its physical geography and natural resources.

Sheffield's communications have always been based on the valleys of the rivers. The principal river is the Don which rises in the moors west of Dunford Bridge and flows into Sheffield from the north-west. In the City below Lady's Bridge the river changes direction and leaves on a north easterly course towards Rotherham.

The Don has numerous tributaries but as far as transport is concerned the most important are the Sheaf which flows from the south-west to the Don, where the latter changes direction; the Loxley from the west to Owlerton; and the Porter from a westerly location to the Sheaf near Suffolk Road.

A continuous moorland ridge of millstone grit stretches down the west side of Sheffield, not more than five to six miles from the centre of the City, at an altitude of between 1000 and 1500 feet, or even higher. The highest point in the County Borough boundary is 1502 feet at High Neb on Stanage Edge; the lowest is about 100 feet at Blackburn Meadows. The south and south-east of the City are also enclosed by hills of 600 feet or higher, on the south-east no more than one and a half miles from the centre. It was this terrain which caused George Stephenson to decide that it was impracticable to enter Sheffield by rail from the south when the North Midland Railway was built and opened in 1840.

In addition to the hills already mentioned, a shoulder of high ground projects into the centre of the City from the west, diminishing in altitude from 800 feet at Lydgate to 265 feet at the Town Hall, only one and three quarter miles away.

When the tramway system was constructed these geographical characteristics had a considerable effect on route planning, tramcar design and operation.

The presence of iron ore, timber and suitable stone for grinding wheels, together with water power from the swift flowing streams, led to the development of the cutlery industry, silver plating and, later, special steels. Because of the plentiful supply of water power, habitation and industry became centred around the confluence of the rivers Don and Sheaf and grew along the valleys enclosed by the comparatively high hills.

In 1624, the Fellowship and Company of Cutlers, formed in 1565, was superseded by the Company of Cutlers in Hallamshire, the latter being one of the few ancient guilds which is still active. At the time of its formation the population of Sheffield was about 5000.

Because of the abundance of water power already referred to, the use of steam came slowly to Sheffield (the first steam grinding wheel was not in use until 1786), but when steam was adopted the presence of local coal was an asset. Coal exists east of a line through Wincobank, Pitsmoor, Shalesmoor, Brook Hill, The Moor, Norfolk Park and Gleadless, i.e. below the centre and the north-east quarter of the City. Immediately to the west of the coal measures there is ganister, used in furnace processes.

By 1800 the population had increased to about 45,000 but up to that time none of the present roads out of the town existed, there being only rough tracks. There had been a stage waggon service to London for goods since 1710, and a stage coach service for passengers since 1760. The sole local transport was by hackney coaches, introduced in 1793, but this was only within the means of the rich.

About 1750 improvements to the River Don made it navigable to Doncaster for vessels of up to thirty tons and to Tinsley for those of up to twenty tons, the remainder of the journey to Sheffield being by road. Prior to this there had been a pack horse route to Bawtry, the inland port of those times on the Trent-Humber navigation and on the trade route between the West Riding and London (the Great North Road). A significant improvement in Sheffield's communications system occurred with the opening in 1819 of the canal from Tinsley into the City.

The railway reached Sheffield in 1838 with the opening of the Sheffield and Rotherham Railway, the terminus of which was at The Wicker (Savile Street). This line connected at Rotherham (Masborough) with the North Midland Railway from Derby to Leeds, which opened in 1840, so providing a service to London.

Then in 1845 the line from Manchester via Penistone, with its terminus at Bridgehouses, was opened. It was scon extended eastward to Retford, Lincoln and Grimsby. This system, which became the Manchester, Sheffield and Lincolnshire Railway in 1847, opened the Victoria Station in 1851, Bridgehouses then becoming a goods station. Lines into the colliery areas of South Yorkshire soon followed and on the 1st February 1870 the Midland Railway opened its direct line to Chesterfield via Bradway Tunnel, with a new station at Sheaf Street. The Wicker Station then became a goods station, as Bridgehouses had done nineteen years before. The construction of this direct line to the south became possible because of the improvement in locomotive engineering which had occurred since the time when Stephenson declared it to be impracticable on account of the steep gradients. With two notable exceptions (i.e. Dore and Totley to Chinley in 1893 and the Great Central, London Extension in 1899) the railway system in the Sheffield area was thus virtually complete by the time the horse tramways came into existence in 1873.

During the latter half of the nineteenth century the local Council took over control of several public utility undertakings and in 1864 became a highway authority.

The rapid growth of residential and industrial suburbs resulted in development beyond the toll-bars of the turnpike trusts, once located in the country. These tolls consequently became irritating barriers between residents and the centre of the town. Slowly, by petition to Parliament or by negotiations, the Council removed the inner bars. In 1875 they were removed from the Chesterfield and Langsett Roads and in 1879 from the Worksop Road. The last to be used was Hunters Bar on the 31st October 1884, but in 1900 part of Wincobank came within the City boundary and this area included the Meadow Hall Road toll-bar, not abandoned until 1907.

Between 1875 and 1900 several new streets were constructed in the centre of the City, and a number of existing ones were widened and improved. Much of this work was soon to facilitate tramway construction.

Apart from the hackney coaches already mentioned, public urban transport commenced with the horse buses to Heeley, Attercliffe, the Barracks, the Botanical Gardens and Broomhill in 1852, and later to Carbrook, Brightside, Nether Edge, Upperthorpe and elsewhere.

In the period of railway construction between 1838 and 1870, besides the central stations already mentioned, suburban stations were opened at Wadsley Bridge, Neepsend, Darnall, Attercliffe, Broughton Lane, Tinsley, Attercliffe Road, Brightside, West Tinsley, Heeley, Millhouses and Beauchief.

By the time the Tramways Act of 1870 became law, the population of Sheffield had grown to about 225,000. Before the end of the century, manual workers who had previously lived close to their work found it necessary to live further away due to the expansion of population and industry. An improved system of local transport therefore became essential. This need was met in the first instance by the horse tramways and afterwards by the electrified system.

The horse tramways were mainly confined to the valleys but the electric system extended into the higher ground around the City and negotiated steeper gradients. The highest point on the Company's horse tramways was 325 feet at Sharrow Lane on the Nether Edge route, whereas the Corporation's horse car route reached 400 feet at Harcourt Road. The highest location on the electric system was in Northfield Road on the Crookes route at 729 feet above sea level just south of Netherfield Road. Few tramway systems in the United Kingdom reached anything near this altitude, but the Outlane route at Huddersfield reached a much higher level of 1245 feet near its outer terminus.

Besides the abundance of gradients in Sheffield, most routes included considerable curvature; only the Intake route and the routes in the valley of the Don had appreciable straight sections. It was usually claimed that these conditions prevented the use of bogie cars and this local prejudice continued throughout the electric tramway era despite the introduction of much improved braking systems. Scarcely any other tramway undertaking would have employed four-wheeled trucks under cars as large as Sheffield's post-1918 fleet.

Another important feature which restricted tramway development was the dramatic difference of levels at some locations, such as 215 feet at Hillsborough Bridge and 520 feet at Walkley terminus only half a mile away (an average gradient of one in 8.6) and 630 feet at Crookes terminus, a quarter of a mile from Walkley; in all a difference of 415 feet in three quarters of a mile.

The altitudes of important central points, suburban termini and intermediate summits are shown on the 1936 system map (inside back cover).

A. D. Packer.

The elevated Crookes terminus at Heavygate Road showing the view beyond the valley of the Don on 29th April 1956.

Chapter 2

The Company Tramways

The Tramways Act 1870 provided for provisional orders empowering local authorities and private companies to construct tramways. The local authorities, however, were expressly precluded from working them. This meant leasing to private concerns or permitting private individuals to work their own vehicles on payment of authorised tolls.

In 1872 Sheffield Tramways Company secured powers by a Private Act which received the Royal Assent on 25th July 1872, to construct and work nine route miles of track, but a proviso in the Act allowed the Corporation to elect to construct the tramways themselves, and this they did. The cost of construction of the permanent way of the Attercliffe, Carbrook and Brightside routes was £41,090 and that for Owlerton, Nether Edge and Heeley £40,422. In turn the Company agreed to pay interest on loans raised by the Corporation to cover the cost of construction together with a rent of £100 per annum per street mile of track. In addition the Company had to maintain the track and the highway to the extent of eighteen inches either side of the tracks, to the satisfaction of the Borough Surveyor.

This commitment was a continual source of trouble and dispute, each party accusing the other of neglect of its respective part of the highway. In August 1879 the Borough Surveyor reported on the bad state of the track on the Attercliffe, Carbrook and Brightside routes, and similar complaints were made in March 1881 and October 1883.

The Company operated the following five routes, opened on the dates shown:

Lady's Bridge	—	Attercliffe "Golden Ball"	6.10.1873
		extended to Tinsley (then called Carbrook)	7.5.1874
Lady's Bridge	—	Brightside "Wellington Inn"	26.5.1875
		extended to Brightside Bridge	about 1885
Snig Hill	—	Hillsborough (Holme Lane Corner) (then called Owlerton)	19.5.1877
Moorhead	—	Heeley (Albert Road)	29.10.1877
Moorhead	—	Nether Edge	24.12.1877

Construction commenced at the "Twelve o'Clock Hotel", Savile Street Junction on 30th March 1873.

The Owlerton route was connected to Lady's Bridge via Bridge Street to give access to the Tinsley workshops, but the authorised line connecting Moorhead and Lady's Bridge via Union Street, Norfolk Street, Fitzalan Square, Haymarket and Waingate was never built, and at no time was there ever a tramway in Union Street and Norfolk Street.

A turning loop was constructed in 1873 via Blonk Street, Exchange Street and Waingate for the Attercliffe cars but the curves proved too tight and the loop was never used by the horse cars; it was later removed. At that period Exchange Street was narrow and ran straight from Castle Street to Wharf Street.

The workshops for the two southern routes were at Nether Edge. There were depots at each suburban terminus, as follows: in a yard behind the "Golden Ball' Attercliffe (until Tinsley Depot was fully operational); "Bridge Inn" Brightside; Hillsborough (Holme Lane); Heeley (Albert Road); and Nether Edge (Machon Bank Road). The horses employed on the Attercliffe route were stabled at Tinsley Depot from the beginning.

During 1873 and 1874 the Company placed twenty cars in service, and a further twenty-five in 1877. Only eight more were built in the period 1884-1887 and three of these were replacements for withdrawn cars of the original twelve (Nos. 1, 12 and one other*—see page 13).

The following is a summary of the Company fleet as it is believed to have been:

(a) The first twelve cars, built by Starbuck Car and Wagon Co. of Birkenhead, were double deck two-horse cars for the Attercliffe route.

(b) The same Company supplied the next eight, Nos. 13-20, in 1874 for the Brightside service and the Attercliffe-Carbrook section. They were single deck one-horse cars (No. 16 was rebuilt as a double deck car in 1882-3).

(c) A further one-horse single decker, No. 21, came into use in 1877. Little is known of this car, but it was on the Tinsley section when withdrawn on the electrification of that service in September 1899.

(d) Ten forty-four seater double deckers, Nos. 22-31, were built by Starbuck in 1877 for the Hillsborough service.

(e) In the same year nine double deck two-horse forty-two seater cars, Nos. 32-40, were acquired for the Heeley service.

(f) Soon after, five single deck two-horse twenty-two seater cars, Nos. 41-45, went into service on the Nether Edge route.

(g) The next cars did not arrive until 1884; these were four one-horse single deckers, Nos. 46-49, for the Attercliffe route, possibly to replace some of the original 1873 cars. They were rebuilt as double deckers in 1889. It is believed that No. 1 was withdrawn in 1885. Before the Corporation took over, Nos. 6-9, 14, 30 and one other car* had been withdrawn.

(h) In 1886 two double deck two-horse reversible type cars were supplied by the Ashbury Co. of Manchester for the Nether Edge route. They were numbered 1 and 50.

(i) Soon afterwards, what are believed to be the last two cars placed in service by the Company were purchased. No. 12 was a double deck car with garden seats on the top deck and the number* of the other is subject to doubt.

In 1877 and again in 1878 the Company was involved in steam trials and it is believed that at least two other such trials took place in Sheffield in the period to 1888 but the Company may have had no part in them.

Nothing came of the experiments. Following the first trial on 24th January 1877, the Borough Council declined to approve an application by the Company for a Provisional Order authorising the use of mechanical power.

As long ago as 1887 a suggestion was made that the double track in West Bar, Gibraltar Street and Infirmary Road be replaced by a single line to facilitate the passage of other traffic; it was not done. The following year a further suggestion was made for a new route from the bottom of The Moor to Hunters Bar to be constructed as single line, but nothing came of this suggestion in the time of the Company.

Almost throughout the years of the Company's existence street improvements in the centre of the City were under consideration or construction, but it was the Corporation's tramway system which was to benefit from them, rather than that of the Company. The Provisional Order of 1875 provided for the widening of the Moorhead from Backfields to Cambridge Street (then called Coal Pit Lane); the whole lengths of Pinstone Street and Fargate; Church Street from St. James' Row to Townhead Street; and part of Attercliffe

A. D. Packer.

Nos. 233 and 285 approaching Twelve o'Clock junction. The hotel stood on the central corner site. Norfolk Bridge can be seen to the right on the Tinsley route.

City Museum.

No. 16 one of the eight single-deck horse cars built in 1874. This car was rebuilt in 1882-3 as a double-decker and is shown at the Moorhead on the Heeley service.

Single-deck horse car No. 44 built in 1877. The photograph was taken at Nether Edge terminus. ***Lens of Sutton.***

Science Museum.
No. 1 one of the last cars placed in service by the Company, in 1886. It was a double-deck two horse reversible car and is seen in Moncrieffe Road facing Montgomery Road.

THE HORSE TRAMWAYS IN 1893 SHOWING THE CONNECTING LINE via Bridge Street BETWEEN THE SNIG HILL TERMINUS FOR HILLSBOROUGH AND THE LADY'S BRIDGE TERMINUS FOR BRIGHTSIDE AND TINSLEY

Reproduced from the Ordnance Survey Map 1893

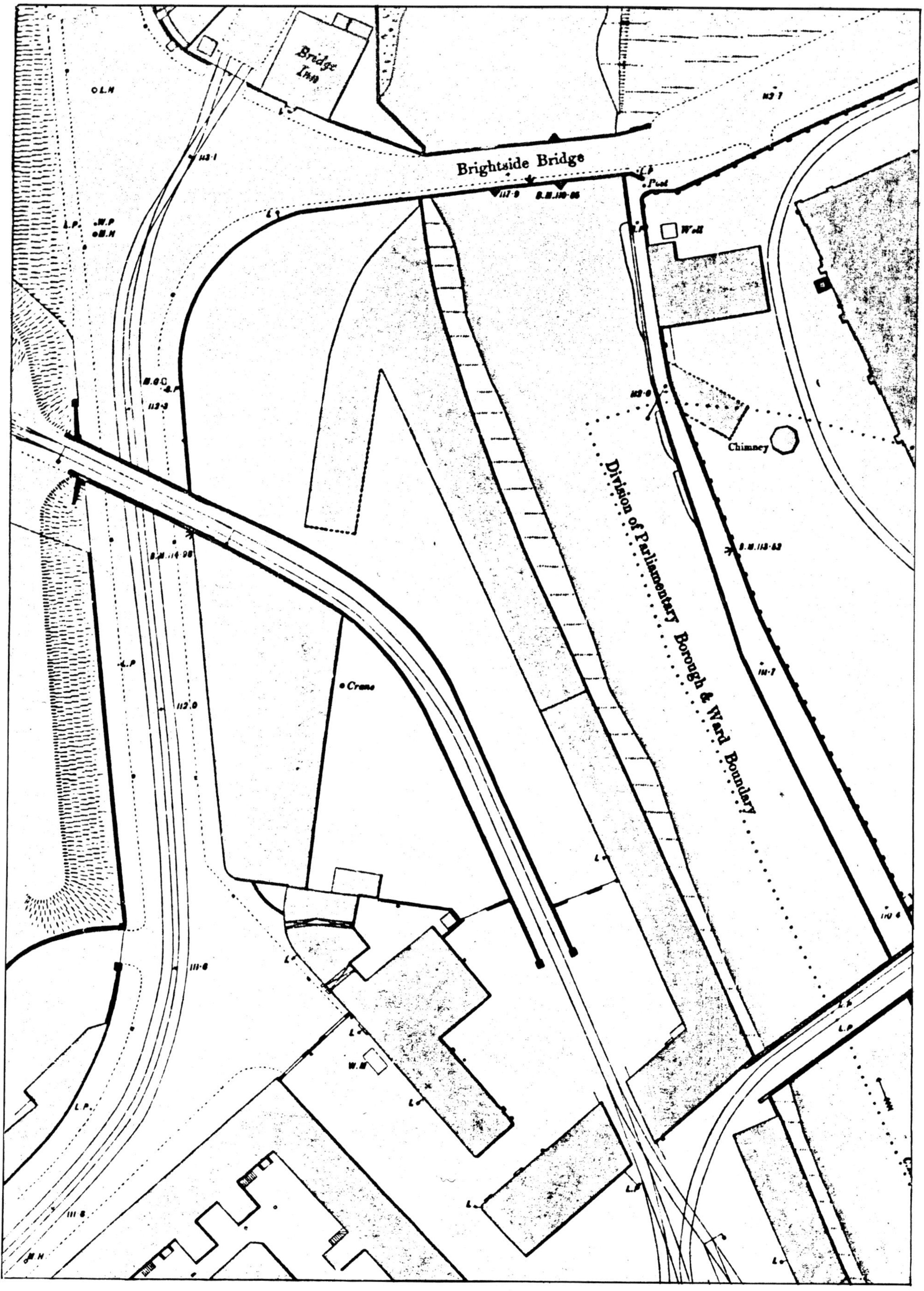

BRIGHTSIDE HORSE CAR TERMINUS AND DEPOT AS AT 1893

Reproduced from the Ordnance Survey Map 1893

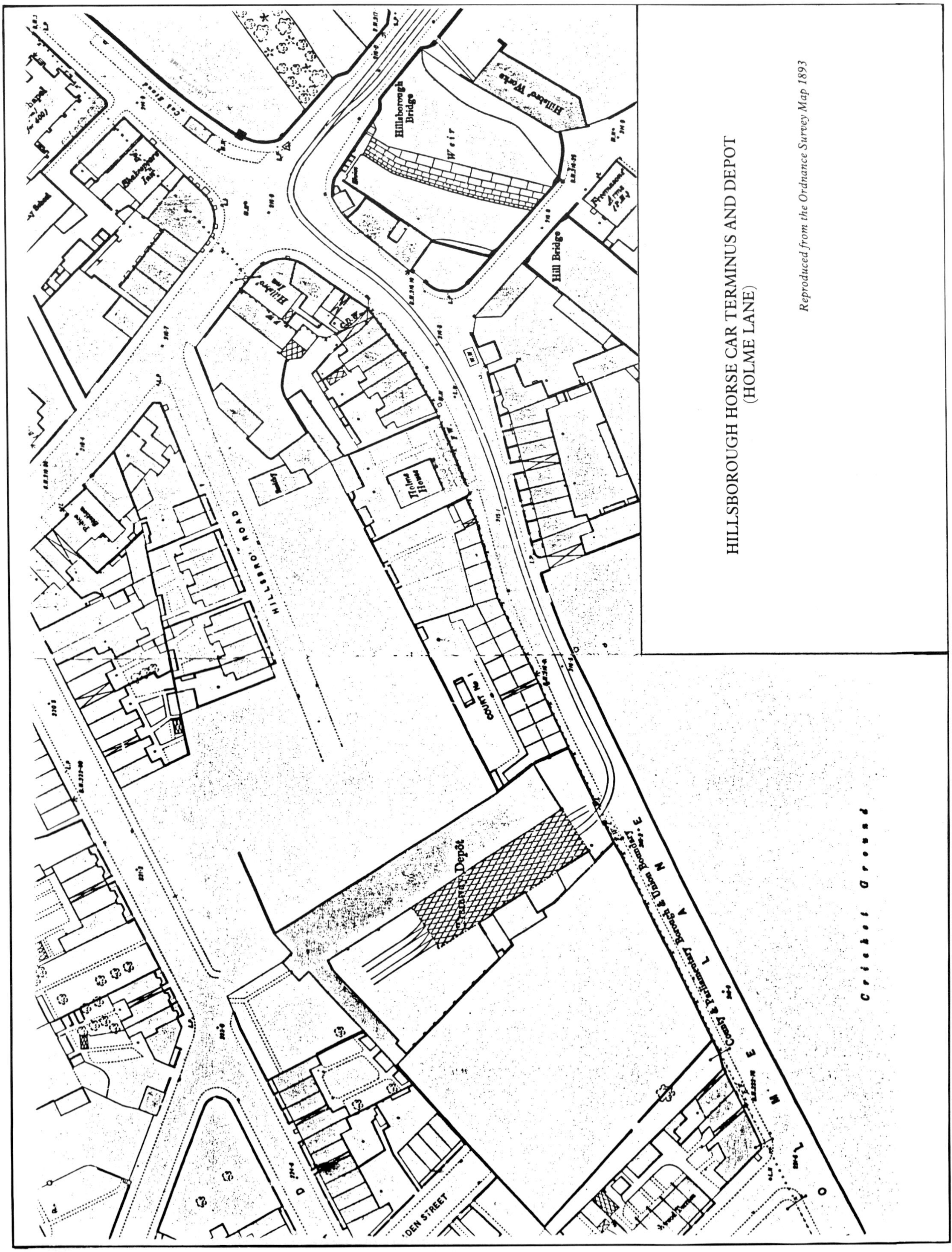

HILLSBOROUGH HORSE CAR TERMINUS AND DEPOT
(HOLME LANE)

Reproduced from the Ordnance Survey Map 1893

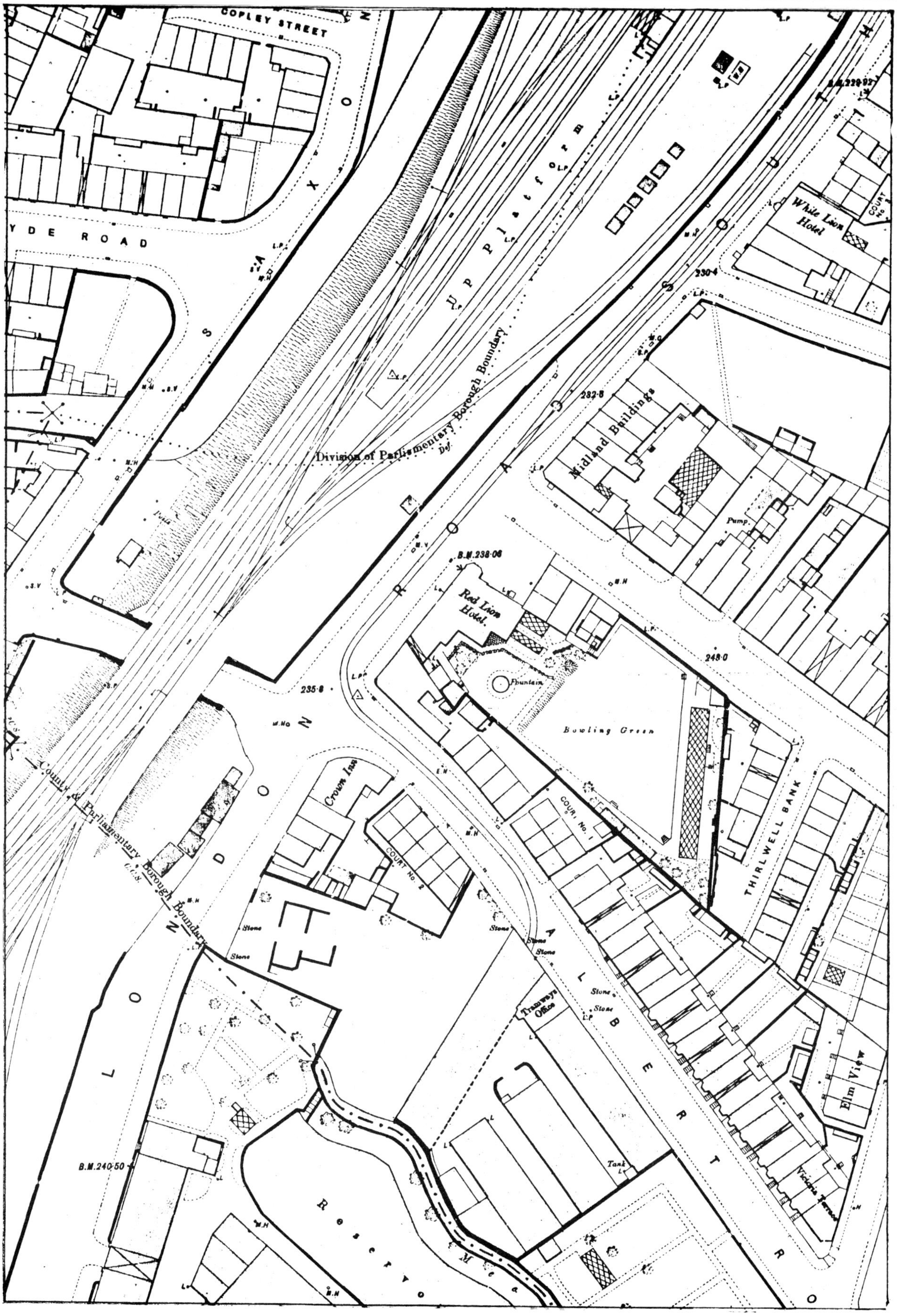

HEELEY HORSE CAR TERMINUS AND DEPOT

Reproduced from the Ordnance Survey Map 1893

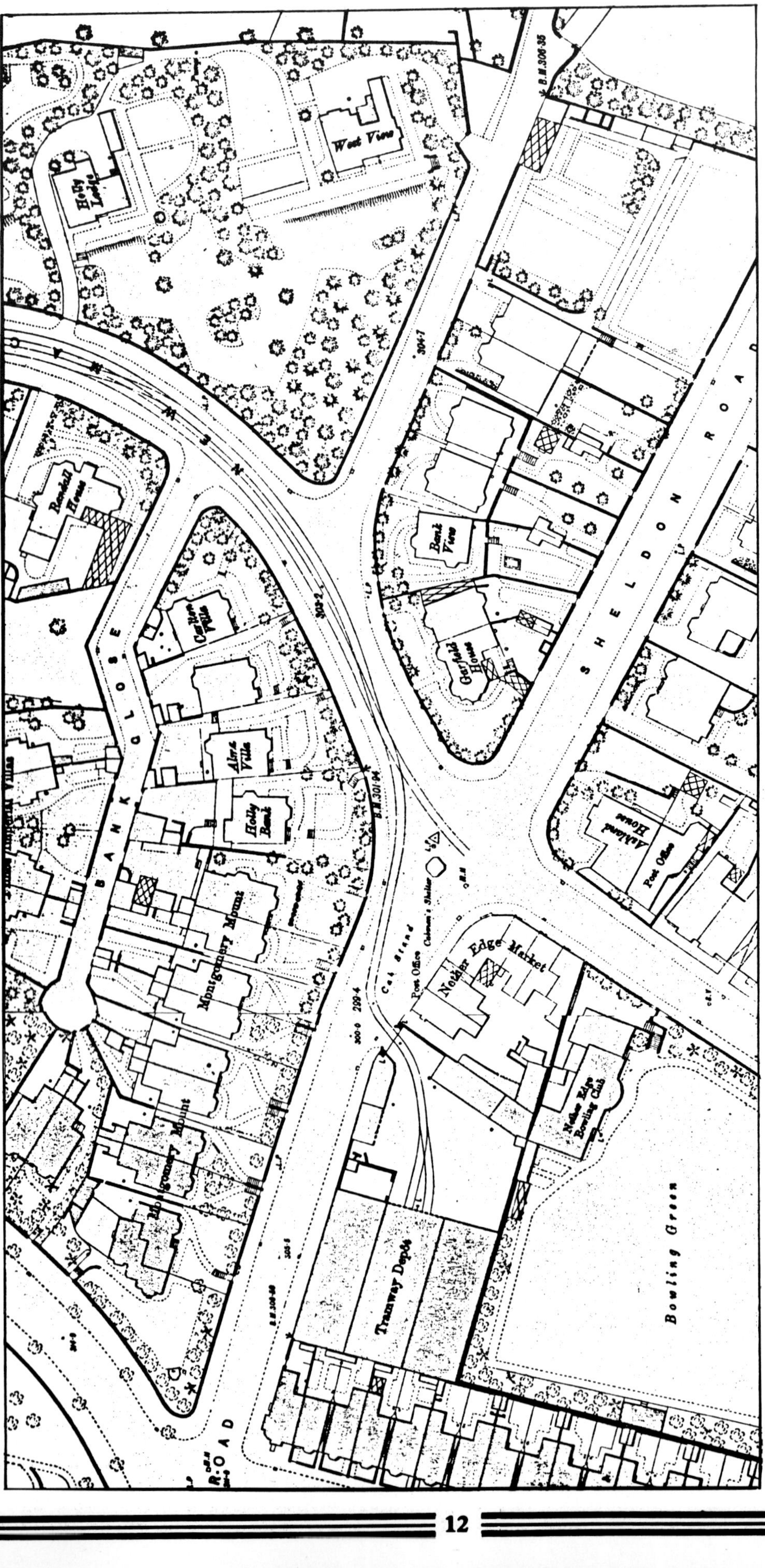

NETHER EDGE HORSE CAR TERMINUS AND DEPOT

Reproduced from the Ordnance Survey Map 1893

Road (then High Street, Attercliffe); and for the construction of Surrey Street and Leopold Street which were completely new.

From 1875 many deliberations took place on the widening of High Street, which was extremely narrow. Finally the Report of the High Street Committee, which had been formed to examine the matter, was adopted by the Council in October 1892 and the following month negotiations for the purchase of several properties began. Authority to carry out the proposed works was obtained in the Sheffield (Street Widenings) Act 1893. In addition, at this time the Improvements Committee had works on hand for the widening of Bridge Street and Snig Hill, and part widening of West Bar, Gibraltar Street, Shalesmoor and Infirmary Road, and also the building of the Town Hall. The site for the latter had been purchased in 1886 and the foundation stone was laid by Alderman W. J. Clegg on 9th October 1891. The completed building was opened by Queen Victoria on 21st May 1897 in excellent weather.

*May have been 2, 3 or 11.

Chapter 3

The Corporation: Pre-electrification Period

In December 1895 the City Council resolved to promote a bill to authorise the taking over of the working of the tramways on the expiry of the Company's lease in 1896.

In February 1896, although it was still not certain that the Sheffield Corporation Tramways Bill would receive parliamentary approval, the Council's Parliamentary Committee appointed a sub-committee to prepare a scheme for tramway extensions to be presented to Parliament later in the year.

On 10th June the Council approved the appointment of a Special Tramways Committee to administer and operate the tramways. At its first meeting on 16th of the month, Alderman W. E. Clegg (who later became Sir William Clegg) was appointed Chairman, a post which he held for thirty years. H. Mallyon Esq., the Company's Manager, was appointed temporary manager. The Committee also sought to take over the scheme for extension of the system and the arbitration proceedings with the Company.

At its second meeting on 24th June the Committee decided to continue various standing contracts entered into by the Company for advertising, the conveyance of Post Office officials, the supply of forage and stable requisites, the removal of manure and for the issue of tickets for pupil teachers. Twenty-four additional horses were purchased and a veterinary surgeon was appointed. It is noteworthy that all these matters, among other things, were attended to before the take-over day.

The Corporation superseded the Company on 11th July 1896 and acquired forty-four Company cars including five of the original twelve cars of 1873. The whole fleet was between nine and twenty-three years old, and carried the Nos. 1-50, excepting 6-9, 14 and 30. There were thirty-two double and twelve single deckers; the latter were numbered 13, 15, 17-21 and 41-45. Some cars were drawn by one horse but the majority required two.

The Corporation took over a route mileage of about nine and a quarter, nearly all double track except at termini. There were few crossovers, the Brightside route having only one, at Newhall Road, whereas exceptionally between Snig Hill and Hoyle Street, a distance of five eighths of a mile, there were both facing and trailing crossovers totalling nine! In addition there were four horse omnibuses which provided a service between Fitzalan Square and the tramway routes which commenced at the Moorhead. 310 horses and 182 employees were also transferred to the Corporation as well as the depots at Tinsley, Holme Lane (Hillsborough), Nether Edge and Heeley.

The Tramways Committee prescribed obligatory stopping places for horse car services as follows:

On 10th August 1896:

Attercliffe Section.

Lady's Bridge Terminus, Wicker Points, Wicker Arches, "Twelve o'Clock Inn', Norfolk Bridge, "Halfway House", Washford Bridge, "Green Dragon", Pinfold Lane, "Victoria Hotel", Attercliffe Church, "Golden Ball" Terminus.

Brightside Section.

As Attercliffe Section to "Twelve o'Clock Inn", "Cricket Ball", John Brown & Co.'s Gates, "Norfolk Arms", "Steam Clock" Terminus.

Hillsborough Section.

Snig Hill Terminus, Post Office (No. 47 West Bar), Corporation Street, Bowling Green Street, "New Inn"*, St. Philip's Road, Portland Street, Wood Street, Greaves Street, Barracks, Hillsborough Terminus.

*Hoyle Street substituted for "New Inn" in November 1898.

Heeley Section.

Moorhead Terminus, Prince Street, Brunswick Chapel, Lansdowne Road, "Coffee House", Sharrow Lane, Queen's Road, Heeley Station Approach, Well Road, Thirlwell Road Terminus.

Nether Edge Section.

Moorhead Terminus, Prince Street, Ecclesall Road, Cemetery Road Vestry Hall, Lansdowne Road, Sharrow Lane, Steade Road, Kenbourne Road, Rundle Road, Points near Bank Close, Terminus.

On 25th October 1898:

Walkley Section.

Church Gates Terminus, Leopold Street, Carver Street, Westfield Terrace, Regent Street, Hounsfield Road (bottom), Winter Street (Brookhill end), Weston Street, Mushroom Lane, Harcourt Road Terminus.

On 22nd November 1898, consequent upon the extension of the Heeley and Nether Edge Sections to High Street (at or near George Street) from 1st December 1898:

Moorhead, Charles Street, Monolith, Church Gates and George Street.

On 10th October 1899:

Ecclesall Road Section.

Ecclesall Road (bottom), Hanover Street, Summerfield Street, Plumpton Street, Collegiate Crescent, South Grove Road, Wadborough Road, Botanical Road, Hunters Bar Terminus.

In 1896 horse bus services from the centre of the City to the suburbs were being operated by private individuals or firms under licences granted by the Watch Committee. As late as 1901 licences were granted for services to Heeley via Shoreham Street and Endcliffe Vale via Clarkehouse Road.

Almost immediately after they acquired the tramways the Corporation commenced investigations concerning the improvement and expansion of the system. The Tramways Committee formed a sub-committee of six to visit English and continental towns and cities for the purpose of seeking advice on the most suitable form of traction.

The Sheffield Corporation Act 1897 authorised the construction and use of additional routes to be worked by electrical, mechanical or other power.

In August of that year it was decided to convert to an electric overhead system throughout, and immediately after this decision the Committee resolved to proceed at once with the electrification of the Tinsley-Nether Edge route. In October orders were placed with Barrow Haematite Steel Co. Ltd. for 4000 tons of rails and with British Thomson Houston Co. for cars, trolleys, wires, poles and electrical equipment at a total cost of approximately £74,380. Work commenced on the Nether Edge Section in February 1898 and a month later on the Tinsley section. In the summer of that year the City Council authorised the temporary closure of The Moor from Moorhead to Ellin Street for track relaying in readiness for electric traction. The Council also sanctioned the extension to Ellin Street of the Fitzalan Square-Moorhead horse bus service for the closure period.

After some hesitation as to whether it would be cheaper to obtain power from the Electric Light Company (then being acquired by the Corporation) the Council accepted in January 1898 the Committee's decision to acquire Kelham Island for the purpose of erecting a generating station. It was envisaged that eventually eight engines and thirteen boilers would be installed to energise the system at 650 volts D.C. In the first instance only three boilers, engines and dynamos were put into use, and further equipment was added contemporaneously with the construction of new tracks. The foundations were put down in May 1898 and by August 1899 the Electrical Inspector reported, "The generating plant is substantial and efficient".

In June 1900 the plant was sufficient to operate sixty-four cars. On the coming into use of the second 500 kW unit a further fifty-one could be worked. The station was in full use by 1902, but additional plant was added from time to time to meet increasing load.

The extensions authorised by the 1897 Act were:

(1) Moorhead to Lady's Bridge via Pinstone Street, Fargate, High Street, Haymarket and Waingate.
(2) Ecclesall Road to Hunters Bar (Rustlings Road).
(3) Wicker Arches to Firth Park (Bolsover Road).
(4) High Street to Walkley and Crookes.
(5) Wicker to Intake.

In the first instance the Corporation had no intention of extending the horse drawn system nor of building any new horse cars, but rapidly increasing demand for services caused a change of mind. Three more horse car services had to be provided as a temporary measure, though in each case the lines were constructed for electric working as soon as electric trams became available.

These additional horse car services were:

High Street — Walkley (Harcourt Road)
High Street — Hunters Bar (Rustlings Road)
High Street — Abbeydale (Woodseats Road)

In 1897 twenty-four horse cars were built for the Corporation by Milnes[1]—they were the last new horse cars for Sheffield; twelve were double deck cars and twelve were single deck covered "toast-rack" cars. The latter were for use in fine weather, but except for the purpose of enjoying warm summer evenings they found little favour with the public and they were disposed of at considerable financial loss before the end of horse car operation. The twelve double deckers were eventually converted for other uses with the electric system, as were three of the ex Company cars (see chapter four).

The new cars were as follows:

Numbers	Type	Seats	Entered Service	Route Allocation	Livery
6, 7 & 8	Double Deck	52	1st May 1897	Attercliffe	Crimson Lake
9, 14 & 30	Double Deck	46	1st May 1897	Hillsborough	Dark Blue
51-54	Double Deck	34	1st May 1897	Nether Edge	Royal Blue
55 & 56	Double Deck	46	1st May 1897	Heeley	Carmine
27*, 57 & 58	"Toast rack"	32	June 1897		
59-67	"Toast rack"	40	September 1897		

*No. 27 replaced an older car of 1877 condemned by resolution of Tramways Committee dated 4th May 1897.

From completion of these deliveries the Corporation was therefore running forty-three double deck and twenty-four single deck cars, a total of sixty-seven. They worked the five ex Company routes, and High Street to Walkley (Harcourt Road) which was opened on 7th November 1898, worked by the old Nether Edge single deckers Nos. 41-45 at a twenty minute interval, and from 1st December the inward extension from Moorhead to High Street of the Heeley and Nether Edge routes. This was the position until the first electric cars entered service.

In 1898 it was decided that the dominant colour of the cars would be royal blue with no advertisements. At this time route colour schemes similar to the latest horse cars were suggested but not adopted. The decision concerning advertisements was reversed in 1903 and a contract was entered into which provided for cars to carry advertisements from 2nd November.

In consequence of the Tinsley-Nether Edge electrification in 1899, four of the Attercliffe cars Nos. 46-49 (which had been rebuilt from single to double deck ten years earlier) were transferred for use on the Heeley service and, later, the Abbeydale service. The conversion of the Tinsley, Nether Edge and Walkley horse car routes to electric operation had already taken place before the introduction of the last two horse car routes—to Hunters Bar and Abbeydale. Both of these were short lived, and Hunters Bar had been replaced by electric cars before the Abbeydale horse car service started. The programme of conversion which commenced in 1898 was completed by 30th May 1903.

Particulars of the change-over are shown overleaf.

[1]Tramway Committee Minutes of 5th January, 4th May and 7th September 1897 refer.

ROUTE	HORSE SERVICE Commenced	HORSE SERVICE Ended if not at time electric service commenced	ELECTRIC SERVICE Commenced
Company:			
Attercliffe	6th October 1873		5th September 1899 (Attercliffe and Tinsley)
Tinsley	7th May 1874		
Brightside (Hawke Street)	26th May 1875		26th November 1900 (Brightside routes)
Brightside Bridge	1885		
Hillsborough (Holme Lane)	19th May 1877	11th November 1902	30th May 1903
Heeley	29th October 1877	5th May 1900	1st August 1900 to Lowfields; 1st November 1900 to Albert Road (Heeley)
Nether Edge	24th December 1877		5th September 1899
Corporation:			
Walkley (Harcourt Road)	7th November 1898	Ran for a time to Harcourt Road after electric service commenced.	18th September 1899 to South Road
Moorhead to High Street	1st December 1898		5th September 1899
Hunters Bar	1st October 1899*		13th April 1900
Abbeydale	6th May 1900+		28th July 1900

*Nether Edge double deck cars used.
+Heeley cars used.

Horse cars ran on Sunday mornings for some time after change-overs of 1899-1900 so that the power station could close for maintenance.

In contrast with developments in Sheffield, electric traction had been introduced at Blackpool in 1885, Leeds in 1891, Walsall in 1893, Bristol and Coventry in 1895. No electric tramways operated in the London area before the turn of the century.

Chapter 4

The Early Electric Period 1899 to 1904

On 3rd May 1898 the City Surveyor presented plans to the City Council for the alteration and extension of the existing horse car depot at Tinsley to accommodate a hundred electric cars. The scheme involved the purchase of 1,100 square yards of land between the existing southern boundary and Weedon Street as well as the demolition of the foreman's house on the south-west side of the depot and the stables on both sides. The Surveyor was authorised to negotiate for the purchase of the land and to proceed with the work.

In later years when the fleet consisted mainly of large cars the depot was capable of accommodating eighty passenger and eight works cars. This depot, which continued in use throughout the tramway era in Sheffield, was the first to accommodate electric cars. It ceased to be an operational depot in October 1959 but remained in use until December 1960 for storage of tramcars withdrawn for scrapping.

The first electric service—the through route from Tinsley (Weedon Street Junction) to Nether Edge—opened on 5th September 1899, but through working was discontinued after the first day because of trouble with the track at the Fitzalan Square junctions. This was quickly followed on 18th of the month by the whole route to Walkley (South Road) and on 27th to Pitsmoor (Bolsover Road) via Burngreave Road.[1]

The Walkley and Pitsmoor services were provided by the original single deck electric cars, but so great was the demand that for a time the horse cars to Harcourt Road on the Walkley route had to remain in service as well.

Upon electrification the Board of Trade denoted certain compulsory stops and for the first four routes these were:

Nether Edge Section.
Change Alley, Moorhead, Fitzwilliam Street, Cemetery Road (bottom), Lansdowne Road (top), Sharrow Lane, Kenbourne Road, Crescent Road/Rundle Road.

Tinsley Section.
Castle Street, Blonk Street, Pinfold Lane (i.e. Staniforth Road), Carbrook Board School.

Pitsmoor Section.
Castle Street, Blonk Street, Spital Street, Ellesmere Road.

T.M.S.

The experimental smoking car No. 51. The enclosed central saloon was for non-smokers. This car was converted to a snowplough in 1913.

[1]Following inspection of the route, horse traction to Firs Hill School was authorised on 24th August 1899 but horses were never used on this route. A trial trip with a single deck electric car took place on 26th September.

Walkley Section.
Bow Street (bottom), Hounsfield Road (bottom)[d], Western Bank, Weston Street, Crookesmoor Road, Barber Crescent[d], Barber Road (top), Heavygate Road[d], Fulton Road (Howard Hotel), Hadfield Street.
'*d*' indicates downhill direction only.

In November 1899 the Committee decided to use part of the depot at Tinsley to build cars, and one single deck body was built, but, although apparently a success, it was destroyed by fire in August 1900 before entering service. It is understood that this was a case of arson. Compensation amounting to £610-11s-2d. for damage to the depot and destruction of the car was received from insurance companies.

The car had cost £233-5s-11d. to build. The Committee decided to use part of the Nether Edge depot for further building.

double deck cars made redundant by electrification of the Nether Edge route. This service did not last long and on 13th April 1900 electric cars took over.

The Abbeydale service was provided by the horse cars switched from the Heeley service which ceased operation on 5th May 1900 to enable conversion work to proceed. The period of operation of the Abbeydale horse cars was even shorter than in the case of Hunters Bar. The route was electrified on 28th July after only twelve weeks.

During the conversion period there was no service from Highfield to Heeley. On 1st August 1900, only four days after the opening of the Abbeydale electric service, electric cars commenced running to Lowfields (and thence to Queen's Road Depot, but not for passengers). The continuation to Albert Road followed on 1st November. With the opening of electric services on the Heeley route, cars ran to Tinsley, and the Nether Edge service was linked with Pitsmoor.

Sheffield City Libraries.
No. 52, one of the twelve double-deck horse cars built for the Corporation in 1897, seen in High Street about 1900 on the Heeley service.

At this early stage the Committee complained of obstruction by loading and unloading of vans and drays, and sought police assistance to minimise the obstruction.

After the initial electric services came into use the last two horse car services commenced operation: on 1st October 1899 to Hunters Bar and on 6th May 1900 to Abbeydale (Woodseats Road). The Hunters Bar service was worked by

Between the opening of the horse car services to Hunters Bar and to Abbeydale, a further new electric route was opened on 10th January 1900 to Norfolk Park (Manor Lane) via Blonk Street. Single deck cars were used on this service.

In the same month the proprietors of the Owlerton horse bus service suggested that it be taken over by the

Corporation, but the Tramways Committee declined, saying that "It is no part of the policy, nor does it come within the duties and functions of the Tramways Committee to be the proprietors of omnibus services in any part of the City".

The Brightside route was electrified from 26th November 1900, leaving only Snig Hill to Hillsborough Bridge horse operated, and this remained so for almost two years. As electric trams replaced the horse cars the depots at Heeley and Brightside were closed but the other depots were retained.

It had been decided in May that, in view of the early conversion of the remaining horse car routes, the services of H. C. Mallyon Esq. as General Manager should be dispensed with, and his appointment was terminated by three months' notice. He had been the Company's General Manager and was retained temporarily when the Corporation took over in 1896. A. L. C. Fell Esq., who had been Electrical Engineer since 1897, was appointed to replace him, but did not remain long in the service of the Corporation. He resigned in November 1903 to take up an appointment with London County Council. From a long list of applicants to fill the vacant post of General Manager, the Council confirmed the appointment in January 1904 of Mr. A. R. Fearnley, who had had previous experience at Bradford and Shelf, and Birkenhead. He was to serve in that office for over thirty years.

Towards the end of 1900 tram routes were operating to and from several central termini, and this resulted in complaints to the Council of considerable obstruction of streets. At the time there were two main proposals for dealing with the problem. The first involved taking over part of the Fitzalan Market for the purpose of constructing a central tramway station. The *Sheffield Daily Telegraph* of 13th November 1900 published a plan and description of a scheme to utilise the ground floor of the site bounded by Market Place, King Street, Haymarket and Market Side (now the lower part of High Street). It was an elaborate scheme which provided for two tracks for each direction and four facing crossovers serving both pairs of tracks (eight in all), and five loading points for each direction as follows (front to back):

Northbound (all tracks leading down Haymarket):
Brightside, Intake, Tinsley etc., Firth Park, Hillsborough.

Southbound:
Ecclesall Road, Nether Edge, Heeley, Abbeydale, Walkley.

In addition, there was to have been a central discharging platform.

The scheme was rejected on the grounds that the site was too valuable for the purpose, that the cross slope on the proposed tramway docks was too great, and also on traffic grounds.

The second proposal, as contained in a report by Alderman Clegg, involved a scheme of through running with the need for certain routes to terminate at Fitzalan Square. This was adopted and proved successful throughout the electric tramway era.

A Council Minute of 19th September 1899 stated that the Tramways Sub-Committee recommended that the City Surveyor be instructed to lay tram lines with a crossover in Fitzalan Square in front of the "Bell Hotel" so that cars from Attercliffe, Tinsley, Brightside and Pitsmoor could cross over without having to ascend High Street. These tracks were constructed adjacent to the kerb of the central pedestrian area in the Square, terminating in a single line stub on the curve at the end of the Square just beyond the "Bell Hotel".

The original track layout at Fitzalan Square when completed comprised a double track crossing: High Street to Commercial Street, and Haymarket to the Square, along with curves from Haymarket to High Street and Commercial Street to the Square, as well as a line on the upper side of the Square (formerly named Market Street) and turning the corner round "Marples Hotel". A minute of 10th July 1900 recommended that this line should be used for turning cars for Nether Edge, Abbeydale Road and Ecclesall Road as from the closing of the Abbeydale Road horse car service, but no evidence has been found that it was ever completed and so used. In due course it was removed.

The points for the double track terminal sidings on the lower side of the Square were located on the curve from Haymarket into High Street and this formation gave much trouble which resulted in damage to track and wheels.

At an early date the double track curve from Commercial Street to the Square was removed and replaced by a curve from Commercial Street into Haymarket. This alteration to the junctions, which did not eliminate the Haymarket-High Street problem, did not last long, and in the autumn of 1901 the junctions were completely redesigned and relocated. The Commercial Street-Haymarket curve was disposed of and the whole junction layout was formed nearer to the top of Commercial Street, enabling the Haymarket-High Street curve to be eased. The points serving the Fitzalan Square terminal siding were located on the straight at the top of Haymarket. This layout became permanent apart from the later reinstatement of the Commercial Street curve into the Square referred to later.

The Weekly News of 22nd December 1900 published particulars of a scheme for a tramway station in Fitzalan Square which was remarkably elaborate. It comprised eight parallel tracks in the square and junctions so intricate that by comparison the actual junctions at the top of Commercial Street were simple. Nothing came of it.

In the years following the Sheffield (Street Widenings) Act, 1893, powers were obtained in numerous subsequent Acts and Provisional Orders for the widening of many streets and radial roads to facilitate double track tramway works. They included West Bar to Hillsborough Bridge, Ecclesall Road from Summerfield Street to Sharrow Vale Road, Abbeydale Road from Archer Road to Millhouses Lane, and partial widenings of Penistone Road, City Road, Owler Lane and Upwell Street, and the renewal of bridges over the railway and canal in Staniforth Road.

The expansion of tramway route mileage between 1899 and 1904 was so rapid that land acquisition for necessary proposed street widenings under the slow and tedious procedure required by the Lands Clauses Act of 1845 could not keep pace with developments. In addition, under the 1897 Streets and Tramways Act no tracks could be laid closer to the kerb than nine feet six inches if a third of affected frontagers formally objected.

For these reasons, whereas practically the whole of the original horse tram routes and most of the additions to them were double track, the earlier electric extensions to that system abounded in single line with passing loops, even near the centre of the City in a few cases, and none of the new routes constructed in the initial electrification period was entirely free from single line sections, which in all totalled about eight and three quarter miles.

The following is a summary of single line sections with passing loops in the electric system as originally constructed between 1899 and 1904.

Walkley beyond Crookesmoor Road, also West Street and Glossop Road.
Crookes (School Road) and *Nether Green*, beyond Northumberland Road, also West Street and Glossop Road.
Hunters Bar to *Nether Green*.
Woodseats beyond Derbyshire Lane.
Intake beyond City Road Cemetery.
Darnall between canal and railway (Staniforth Road).
Pitsmoor beyond Firs Hill.
Owlerton, Nursery Street, Neepsend Lane and Penistone Road between Owlerton Bridge and Parkside Road.

Isolated short sections:
Hillsborough near Wood Street.
Hunters Bar early part of Ecclesall Road.
Millhouses, Archer Road, Marriott Road.
Furnival Street Line.
Queen's Road Route, Suffolk Road.
Shoreham Street Route before St. Mary's Road.

In addition, the Rotherham to Tinsley route was single track with eight passing loops. (All Rotherham routes were single line with passing loops at the time.)

Even the routes constructed or extended in 1908 and 1913 to Malin Bridge and Middlewood respectively had single line sections, although by these dates some of the earlier single line sections on other routes had been doubled. Fuller details of single lines appear in Appendix E.

Trackwork was laid out on an ambitious scale and at several places turn-out points were installed for authorised lines which were never completed or never built. Principal among these was the double track junction at the bottom of Hounsfield Road leading into Glossop Road, thence single line, with loop round the first left hand bend and terminating in about thirty-seven yards of double track at the crossing of Clarkson Street and Wilkinson Street. Double track points facing the City were also installed at Fulwood Road into the top of Glossop Road.

Similar double track facing points were provided in City Road into the top of Granville Road and at the bottom of The Moor into Ellin Street and later at Banner Cross. In addition, when the Crookes route was extended to School Road the original terminus at the bottom of Lydgate Lane formed a straight turnout which could have been used for

H. B. Priestley.

On the single track in Neepsend Lane on 4th July 1952. The tramway signals can be seen attached to the standards.

future extension up the latter road. Nevertheless when the extension to School Road became operative, that junction was taken out.

City Council Minutes of the period stated that work commenced on 11th August 1902 at Jessop's crossing on the proposed half mile line through Weedon Street to link Brightside and Tinsley. By 29th September seven and a half chains had been completed from the Tinsley end to Carbrook Street including 150 yards of double track. A month later it was reported that work had started on the Brightside side of Jessop's crossing though track through the crossing was not complete. By 27th January 1903 the curve from Weedon Street to Tinsley Depot had been constructed. Work progressed slowly and the Minutes of 28th April reported two furlongs 4.9 chains completed. No record of further work has been traced and it appears that one furlong 5.1 chains of track at Brightside was never laid. Only the long terminal siding along the outside of the depot was ever used and this formed the Tinsley terminus until the last day of tramway operation in 1960.

By the time the last horse cars ceased to run the following new lines or extensions had come into use:

Lady's Bridge to Owlerton and Parkside Road (top) via Nursery Street on 26th January 1901.

Abbeydale Road to Woodseats Road, Bannerdale Road and Millhouses Lane on 17th April 1902.

Winter Street to Nether Green on 14th October 1901 and Crookes Junction to School Road on 28th April 1902.

Staniforth Road Junction to Darnall (Main Road) on 11th April 1901.

Hunters Bar to Hangingwater Road on 28th October 1901.

Manor Lane to Intake (Woodhouse Road) on 17th April 1902.

Attercliffe to Pitsmoor via Newhall Road and Upwell Street on 20th October 1902.

Heeley (Albert Road) to Woodbank Crescent on 1st November 1902.

The Market Place, Moorhead and Batley Street sidings (the latter possibly in the Spring of 1902, though one report stated that construction started in February 1902 and that the siding was brought into use in August).

When the horse cars finally went out of service on 11th November 1902 there were no trams along Infirmary Road and Langsett Road whilst conversion took place, but passengers could travel to Hillsborough via Nursery Street, Neepsend and Owlerton, and from 12th February 1903 via West Bar and Penistone Road. A report by the Tramways Committee dated 28th October 1902 stated that latterly the Hillsborough horse cars had been losing £70 per week due to competition from the electric cars on the Owlerton route

Lea Collection/Sheffield City Libraries.

No. 148 at Broomhill before fitting of top cover in 1904. The track leading into Glossop Road (which was never used) can be seen.

Lens of Sutton.

One of the first open top cars built with improved lower saloon ventilators in 1902, seen at Rustlings Road at the site of the future turning circle.

HORSE CARS CONVERTED FOR ELECTRIC OPERATION

Horse Car No.	Built	Purpose as Electric Car	Converted	Electric Car No.	Renumbered	Withdrawn
6	1897	Passenger	1904	244*		July 1926
7	1897	Passenger	1904	245*		July 1926
8	1897	{ Salt Car	1906-7			
		{ Stores	1919	279	373 in 1937	February 1951
9	1897	Snowplough	1906-7	274	353 in 1937	March 1952
15‡	1874	Breakdown	1902	166	375 in 1933	1946
Two of Nos. 41-45‡	1877	{ Stores	1901	199		1922
		{ Salt	1904 }	280	374 in 1937	March 1952
		{ Stores	After 1918 }			
51	1897	Salt Trailer/Snowplough+	1906-7	273*		August 1926
52	1897	Salt Trailer/Snowplough+	1906-7	275*		February 1915
53	1897	Salt Trailer/Snowplough+	1906-7	277*		February 1915
54	1897	Salt Trailer/Snowplough+	1906-7	278*		February 1915
55	1897	Snowplough	1906-7	276	355 in 1937	March 1952

‡Ex Company Cars
*Renumbered, not necessarily in order shown.
+It appears that after running as salt trailers for a time cars Nos. 51-54 were converted to snowploughs in 1906-7.

Three unnumbered salt trailers and car No. 30 were converted from horse cars in the period 1904 to 1912. In October 1912 the last three salt trailers were sold.

which had been opened in January 1901 and had later received an augmented service.

On 2nd February 1903 the Intake service was re-routed via Commercial Street instead of via Blonk Street. Track alterations at the Sheaf Street/Broad Street junction were necessary before this change could be made.

The direct route to Hillsborough via Infirmary Road, Langsett Road and Holme Lane corner to Parkside Road came into use on 30th May 1903 and so the whole horse tramway system had been electrified, except the approach tracks to the depots at Heeley and Brightside together with a short section under the low railway bridge at Brightside.

Following the withdrawal of the last passenger horse cars, all the twelve double deckers built by Milnes for the Corporation were stored in Holme Lane depot for later conversion to electric cars for various purposes, as shown on page 22.

Most of the other horse cars are believed to have been broken up but in 1903 two unidentified cars were sold to Chesterfield Corporation.

The period of rapid expansion continued until December 1904. On 6th April 1903 the extension from Woodbank Crescent to Chantrey Road had been opened, followed by Spital Hill to Petre Street (Canada Street) and Hangingwater Road to Nether Green on 24th September of that year. The following link lines had also been completed:

Sheaf Street (bottom of Commercial Street) to Paternoster Row and Furnival Street to Moorhead on 25th January 1904.

Shoreham Street to Havelock Bridge on 19th May 1904 including Cherry Street siding on 30th May.

Snig Hill to Bridge Street on 4th August.

Leadmill Road to Queen's Road Depot (which was not then complete) on 4th November and finally Wolseley Road on 25th December 1904.

With the exception of the Sheffield-Rotherham link referred to later, there were no more new lines for almost three and a half years. This is therefore a convenient point to consider certain other matters concerning the earlier years of Corporation administration.

At the end of 1904 the basic system was complete. In the centre of the City all that remained to be laid down were the lines in Leopold Street, Flat Street-Pond Street, Exchange Street and Tenter Street. The suburban termini had reached out to: Darnall (Main Road), Tinsley (Weedon Street), Brightside, Petre Street, Pitsmoor (Bolsover Road) via Burngreave and via Upwell Street, Owlerton (Parkside Road) via Nursery Street and via Shalesmoor, Hillsborough (Parkside Road), Walkley (South Road), Crookes (School Road), Nether Green via Broomhill and via Hunters Bar, Nether Edge, Millhouses (Springfield Road), Woodseats (Chantrey Road), and Intake (Woodhouse Road).

During the years of extensive track laying between 1898 and 1904 there was considerable disruption of streets as well as temporary closures. In the central area centre standards

H. B. Priestley.

Brightside terminus showing the low railway bridge which prevented double-deck electric cars reaching the previous horse car terminus.

Open top car built in 1904 standing at Hunters Bar. This car received a top cover in 1909. T.M.S.

with double cantilever brackets were used to support the overhead power lines in The Wicker, Haymarket, High Street, Fargate, Pinstone Street and The Moor, and also on parts of the Attercliffe and Brightside routes, but they were replaced at a later stage by roadside standards with cross bearer wires, except in The Wicker where the central standards were never replaced apart from for a few at both the Arches and Blonk Street ends of the street. In later years all the bracket arms were removed, standards were placed on both sides of the street and span wires were strung from the centre poles to the roadside poles. It is noteworthy that in lower High Street (Market Side) the tracks were never resited after the removal of the central standards and it was always safe to stand or walk between trams moving on both tracks. The central standards on The Moor were replaced in 1906[2] and electric street lighting was installed.

The superiority of the system in both equipment and efficiency began to show in these early years of the electric tramways. On 1st October 1902 the provision of postal boxes on late evening services began[3]. Then in 1904 power operated automatic facing point switches and overhead switches were introduced and became standard over the whole system but there were several exceptions: (1) at the top of Hounsfield Road where the gradient was too steep for satisfactory operation and where there was a pointsman throughout the years until the closure of the Walkley route, (2) at the bottom of The Moor where the Ecclesall Road junction was immediately followed by the Cemetery Road junction for Nether Edge and (3) at the turn-off from Fitzalan Square to Commercial Street. The arrangements at these places are dealt with more fully in Appendix G. In general therefore, hand operated portable point levers carried on tramcar platforms became unnecessary in normal service in Sheffield, except on entry to the Furnival Street line[4] and at certain non-sprung crossovers. They were also used when automatic points were tripped by mistake. A number of English systems which lasted into the 1930s never adopted automatic point switches, nor did many of them have sprung trailing points at crossovers which were a standard feature in Sheffield for many years.

Returning to rolling stock matters, the first double deck cars to be rebuilt with covered tops entered service in 1903, in the first instance on the Abbeydale and Nether Edge routes. This was the commencement of a rebuilding programme which lasted until 1927, as described in chapter eight. In contrast, no system in the West of England ever had a closed

[2] They were not removed from Savile Street until late 1909 and from the Twelve o'Clock junction-Tinsley section until 1911.
[3] Postal collection by tramcars was pioneered by Huddersfield Corporation in 1893, with hourly collections from 8.30 am to 9.30 pm and at 11 pm.
[4] Automatic points were installed here during the Second World War.

R. J. S. Wiseman.
Nos. 276 and 72 in Winter Street on the last day of operation of the Walkley route. Use of the pointsman and his hut at the top of Hounsfield Road ceased on that day.

upper deck car although Bristol and Plymouth operated tramways into the 1940s!

The rapid development of route mileage in the first five years of electrification was matched by the growth of the fleet of tramcars; by the end of 1904 241 electric passenger cars and four works cars had been placed in service. The passenger cars were of three main types: (1) the short open top non-canopy double deckers, (2) the long single deckers for the Crookes, Walkley, Intake, Brightside and Pitsmoor via Upwell Street services, and (3) the short non-canopy double deckers rebuilt with closed tops. Particulars of the fleet at this time are shown in Appendix B(1).

The single deck cars were required for the hilly routes and for the low railway bridges in Brightside Lane and Upwell Street. In the first instance the Board of Trade did not consider double deck cars to be safe on steep hills. This applied to Walkley, Pitsmoor via Burngreave Road, Intake and Crookes. It was anticipated that the extension from Hangingwater Road to Nether Green would also require single deck cars, as this extension included the steepest gradient on the whole system, which for a short distance of about thirty-three yards was one in 9.3[5]. The extension from Brightside to Tinsley would have required single deck cars had the line been completed, because of another low railway bridge at Brightside terminus.

However, when the line from Hangingwater Road to Nether Green was opened on 14th May 1904 double deck cars were utilised. The Brightside-Tinsley line was never completed, as previously stated, but the track remained in position until 1914 when it was taken up except for 200 yards at the Tinsley end which was retained as a siding. Furthermore the short-lived City circular service which was worked by single deck cars was withdrawn. At the same period the use of double deck cars was authorised on the Pitsmoor via Burngreave Road and Crookes services.

Finally, in 1904 the two low bridge routes to Brightside and Pitsmoor via Attercliffe were reorganised. The direct service to Brightside was rerouted via Attercliffe using double deck cars, and the Pitsmoor service was switched to the direct line via Savile Street East, so bringing the three low bridges on to one single deck car service. The need for single deck cars was thus substantially reduced, leaving only Intake, Walkley and Pitsmoor via Savile Street to be so worked. The first consequences of these changes are referred to in the next chapter.

During the initial years of electric operation there were no snowplough cars. The ploughs fitted to passenger cars for the first winter snow of early 1900 were unsatisfactory and horse

[5]These figures were quoted at the Conference of Tramway Managers in 1913 but when the Crookes route was extended later in that year a section almost as steep (one in 9.5) in Northfield Road came into use. By comparison the steepest part of Barber Road, Walkley was one in 10.7.

T.M.S.

Original open top car fitted with plough life guards, at Nether Green, showing single line section in Fulwood Road.

cars had to be utilised to provide a service as the electric cars became immobilised. On Sunday 11th February, and for several succeeding days, there was a general stoppage of all electric cars due to heavy snow. Subsequently eighty-eight passenger cars were fitted with V-shaped plough lifeguards, but on 8th March 1904 the Committee reported that the Board of Trade had objected to the use of this equipment on the few cars on which it was still employed.

By the end of March 1905 plough lifeguards had been removed from all cars. This made the provision of special cars for snow clearance essential, and as a result Sheffield became one of a small number of British tramway systems which operated a fleet of snowplough cars to undertake the whole job of snow and ice clearance.

T.M.S.

The same car rebuilt with top cover in 1903, photographed at Nether Green several years later.

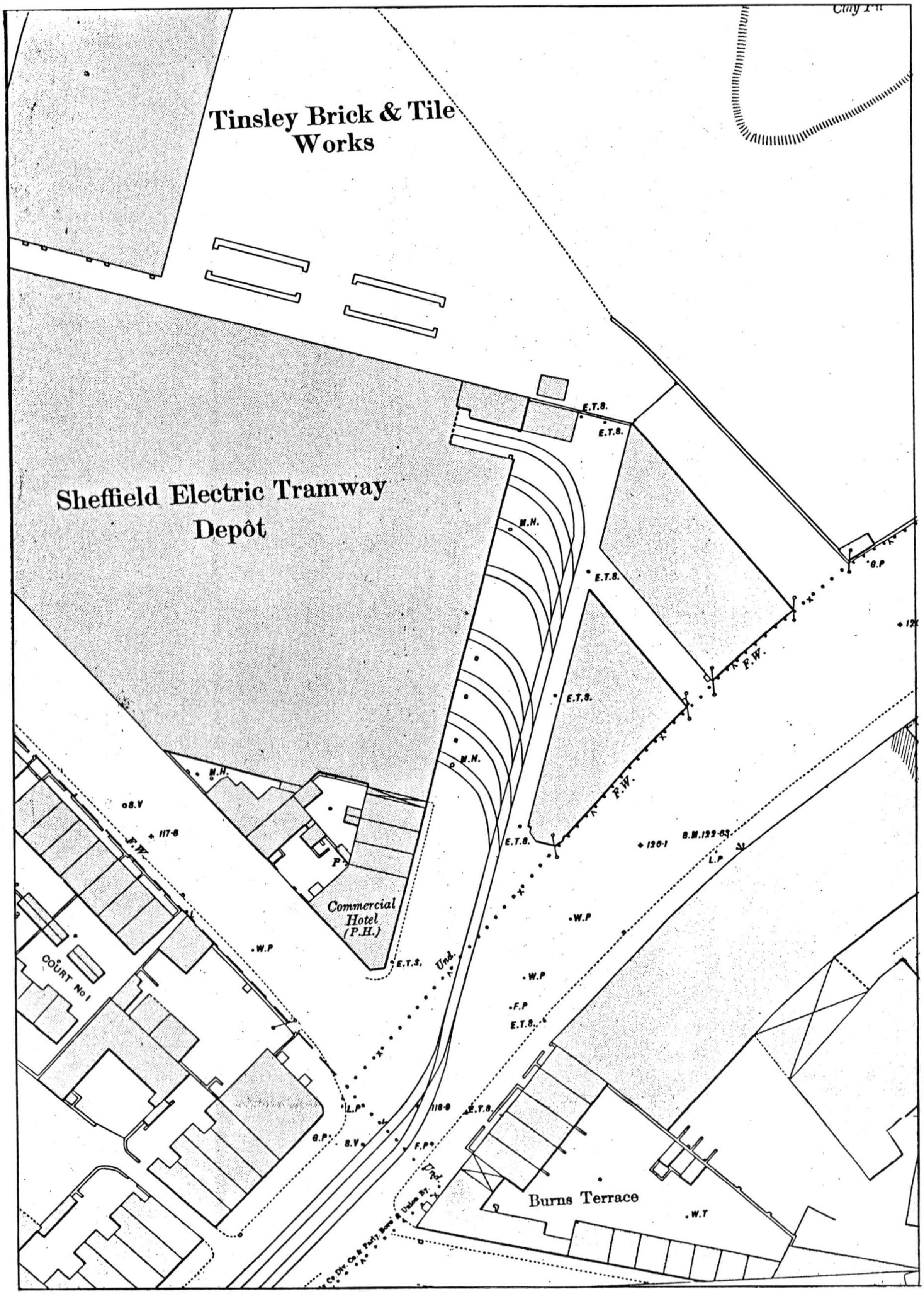

TINSLEY TERMINUS AND DEPOT AS AT 1902
before the construction of the Weedon Street Siding, the curve from the depot approach track into Weedon Street and the Rotherham Corporation route to Tinsley.

Reproduced from the Ordnance Survey Map 1903

Chapter 5

Edwardian Domination 1905 to 1914

The Sheffield and Rotherham termini at Tinsley Depot before the two systems were linked in 1905. *Sheffield City Libraries.*

One of the most significant characteristics of the period was the programme of rebuilding most of the earlier electric cars, but in 1905 several other important events took place.

The offices of the undertaking had been located at several places in the centre of the City: at the Town Hall, at the Prudential Buildings, the Traffic Department at Mulberry Street and the Ticket Department in West Street. At this time, however, all departments were transferred to the premises known as Cambridge House in Division Street which had previously been occupied by the Water Department. They remained the Headquarters of the Tramways Department for all the remaining years of the tramway era.

The lines of Rotherham Corporation which had reached Tinsley in 1903 were connected to the Sheffield system at Tinsley Depot on 20th June 1905, and through running between Sheffield (Fitzalan Square) and Rotherham commenced on 11th September. The through service resulted in increased tramcar traffic which made necessary the doubling of the Tinsley-Rotherham section. The work, which lasted over a year, was completed on 25th July 1909, but the line remained single under the Bessemer Bridge and over the old Bow Bridge near Rotherham. At a later date the track under the Bessemer Bridge was interlaced.

The permanent buildings at Queen's Road Depot also came into use in 1905, and in that year twelve new short covered top double deck cars numbered 246-257 were built at Nether Edge Works. They were the only cars of this style to be built with closed tops when new.

Towards the end of the year, No. 130, the rail watering car, was fitted with snow sweeping gear. This was the first vestibuled car in Sheffield.

The following year the lower part of Church Street was widened by reconstructing the footpath behind the Church railings.

In view of the reduced need for single deckers the surplus cars of this type were advertised for sale in 1906. Enquiries were received but no transactions resulted at that time.

In that year and in 1907, twelve single deckers were rebuilt as double deck cars and at the same period the first fleet of snowploughs was constructed. These matters are described in chapter eight. The workshops at Nether Edge were so busy with the rebuilding programme that in 1906 it became necessary to look elsewhere for additional new cars.

This led to the Corporation ordering fifteen cars of a very advanced design from the United Electric Car Company at Preston. They were double deck vestibuled platform extended canopy cars with open balconies. They had seats for fifty-eight passengers, and went into service between 18th June and 1st August 1907, bearing the numbers 258-272 in a new and improved style of large unshaded numerals.

Their height (almost exactly the same as the much later "Roberts" cars) was about five inches less than was normal

T.M.S.

At Crookes, School Road terminus. Built by the Corporation at Nether Edge in 1905-6, this car remained in service until 1931. The lower saloon indicators were double sized and showed legends such as "Crookes–Midland Railway Station–Queens Road–Heeley". This descriptive indication was a unique feature of this route.

in Sheffield and was achieved mainly by lower and flatter upper deck ceilings. It was commonly thought that these cars were designed for operation under low bridges but in their early years of service they were used principally on the Nether Edge, Fulwood via Broomhill, and Petre Street routes where there were no such bridges. They came to be known as the "Preston cars".

In 1907 the main junctions at Fitzalan Square were relaid and the double track curve between Commercial Street and the terminal siding on the lower side of the Square was reinstated. At the same time the terminal lines were relocated nearer to the "Bell Hotel" and at a minimum of twelve feet from the kerb of the old central island. The double track was extended round the curve at the south end of the Square and terminated facing Norfolk Street. Three crossovers were installed, opposite the "Bell Hotel", on the curve and near the bottom of Norfolk Street.

In June 1908 it was proposed to extend the siding into Flat Street with a crossover at the side of the General Post Office. In consequence the Norfolk Street crossover was eventually removed. (A Tramways Committee Minute of 23rd June 1908 refers.) In addition a single line terminal curve was constructed round the south end of the Square. Like the earlier siding at "Marples" corner, no evidence of use has been traced, and after a time the points were taken out, but the curve remained into the 1930s. No more track changes took place at Fitzalan Square except the removal of the crossover opposite the "Bell Hotel" during the 1940s.

On 8th December 1909 the new central island in the Square was opened by the Lord Mayor, the Earl Fitzwilliam. This island comprised a rectangular paved area with curved ends, a stone balustraded central area surrounded by pavements which on the east side were laid adjacent to the relocated tramway tracks, and underground lavatories. The old Clock Tower and shelter had been removed.

During 1908 and 1909 a further series of route extensions came into use as follows:

19th May 1908: Holme Lane junction to Malin Bridge.

1st August 1908: Rustlings Road junction to Banner Cross.[1]

29th May 1909: Darnall (Main Road) to Handsworth (Finchwell Road).

25th August 1909: Pitsmoor (Bolsover Road) to Firth Park (Bellhouse Road).

In February 1909 the Tramways Committee resolved to extend the Nether Green terminus by fifty yards, to a point

[1]Powers for this extension had lapsed, but in response to demand from residents of Ecclesall a clause to renew them was inserted in the Act of 1907, which also authorised the Darnall to Handsworth extension.

T.M.S.

The unique purpose-built "water car" constructed by the Corporation at Nether Edge in 1901.

just beyond the top of the gradient. This was a valuable safety measure.

Surprisingly, following these extensions no more new passenger tramcars came into service until 1912, a period of about five years. It seems likely that improved efficiency, and in particular the progress with doubling of single line sections, produced better utilisation of cars. Another feature which helped to eliminate the need for new cars was the fitting of top covers, which made the early double deckers an "all weather" fleet. Also the trade depression and unemployment in the period 1903 to 1910 probably reduced service requirements below what they might otherwise have been.

An event of 1908 was the division of the City Engineer's Department into two sections, and the appointment of Mr. W. J. Hadfield as Surveyor of Highways and Deputy City Engineer with responsibility for all highway work, construction of sewers, and construction and maintenance of tramway track.

The Leopold Street tracks, authorised by the Corporation Act 1901 as a siding, and as a through route only in emergency, became operative on 31st August 1908.[2] The reason for this restriction was "for the protection of the Guardians of the Standard of Wrought Plate in Sheffield". Passing trams might have caused electrical interference with functions carried out at the Assay Office. In 1906 the Tramways Committee had proposed that this double track be constructed as a siding dock for trams out of use in slack periods of the day. The proposal was defeated in the Council on the insistence of the Highways Committee. That it should have been suggested at all is a striking commentary on the dominance of the tram as a means of transport at the time, and also on the comparative lack of other traffic. In this latter connection it is of interest that a traffic census taken over the period 26th August to 8th September 1910 inclusive, between the hours of 8 am and 9 pm on Abbeydale Road South, Chesterfield Road, Ecclesall Road South, Manchester Road and Middlewood Road, showed daily averages ranging between thirty-two and 129 motor vehicles and 279 and 719 horse drawn vehicles on the different routes.

The small amount of other traffic made possible from mid-July 1909 a huge programme of track renewal including High Street, Fargate, Pinstone Street and the whole of The Moor. The work involved the laying of temporary duplicate tracks adjacent to the kerbs (and the consequent closing to all other traffic) in Pinstone Street and lengthy sections of The Moor at each stage of the operation.

In this way tram services were maintained along the temporary tracks while the permanent ones were replaced.

[2]As reported by General Manager on 24th November 1908.

No disturbance of the overhead wires was necessary, as the swivel trolley heads with which the cars were fitted were able to function with the booms deflected to one side of the cars.

Pinstone Street was the first section to receive attention, but in the case of Fargate and High Street, which were next dealt with, a different method was adopted. In order to accelerate the work, through services were suspended and temporary termini in Leopold Street and elsewhere were utilised. As a result, and aided by good weather, through running was resumed on 21st August 1909 after sixteen days' interruption, during which period 540 yards of double track, two double junctions and one crossover had been relaid.

Used ticket boxes on tramcars came into use in 1910. This was the year when the reconstruction of Fitzalan Square was completed with a central island and with lavatories below street level. The statue of King Edward VII was placed in the Square and unveiled on 28th October 1913.

Throughout the latter half of 1910 there were still forty-six cars in service without covered upper decks but all of them were rebuilt between 1911 and 1913 as described in chapter eight.

Several interesting developments occurred in 1911. The large depot at Shoreham Street[3] with twelve roads capable of accommodating approximately 108[4] of the longer cars was opened in February. This made possible the conversion of Queen's Road Depot into the Central Workshops and maintenance establishment, thus facilitating the closure of Nether Edge Workshops and Depot and the termination of building, repair and heavy maintenance functions at Tinsley.

The experimental rebuilding of "Preston" car No. 259 is also dealt with in chapter eight.

Another innovation of 1911 was the construction of the first passenger shelter in Sheffield, outside the Cutlers' Hall in Church Street. A member of the Tramways Committee thought the provision of shelters was coddling the community as the trams were so frequent that it was no hardship to wait in the open.

As the programme of fitting top covers to the original double deck fleet was coming towards its end, the Corporation resumed tramcar building in 1912. They built fifteen cars with extended canopies and open balconies and

Single-deck cars at Commonside on the Walkley route. ***Lens of Sutton.***

[3]This depot was small by London standards. The L.C.C.'s depot at New Cross held over 300 cars.

[4]A greater number of the shorter cars of which the fleet largely consisted at that time could be housed. This is true of the other depot capacities mentioned elsewhere.

platforms. These carried the numbers 281-295. Concurrently the last few open top cars were being rebuilt to similar design.

Nos. 281-295 were the first new cars built at Queen's Road and the first built by the Corporation for six years. A noteworthy feature of these cars was the open platforms five years after the delivery of the "Preston" vestibuled platform cars. Some drivers did not like the platform arrangements of the "Preston" cars. With the exception of No. 290 none of these 1912 cars was ever rebuilt or materially improved. The case of No. 290 is referred to in Appendix K (accidents)

The opening of the Rustlings Road turning loop at Hunters Bar on 21st December 1912 ushered in the last round of route extensions before the outbreak of war in August 1914. The routes extended at this period were:

(1) Parkside Road (Hillsborough) to Middlewood; firstly to Catch Bar Lane on 8th September 1913 and to Langsett Avenue on 26th November, the final terminus of the route.

(2) On the latter date, Crookes (School Road) to Heavygate Road, the final terminus of the Crookes route.

Practically all the routes which had been built by this time had been authorised either by the Sheffield Corporation (Streets and Tramways) Act 1897 or by the Sheffield Corporation Act 1900. Powers for some were allowed to lapse and were re-enacted in subsequent Corporation Acts. It seems that the Tramways Committee had contemplated a system in which trunk routes would be linked by interconnecting extensions.

Parliamentary powers were obtained in the period from 1897 to 1912 for a number of extensions of this kind in the localities of Broomhill, Hunters Bar, Sharrow and Banner Cross; The Moor (Ellin Street) to Norfolk Park; Heeley, Abbeydale and Nether Edge; and Kelham, Upperthorpe, St. Philip's and Crookes Valley. In addition, approval was obtained for lines from Broomhill to Crosspool, to Grimesthorpe via Carlisle Street, and Brightside to Meadow Hall. None of these proposed lines ever materialised except the Glossop Road line already mentioned, which was constructed as far as Clarkson Street but never used. A complete list of principal authorised lines which were never constructed appears in Appendix F.

The line to Banner Cross via Psalter Lane was first authorised by the Act of 1900. Authorisation was renewed by the 1907 Act along with an extension of the main line from Hunters Bar to Ecclesall Church, but because of local opposition the Psalter Lane proposal was abandoned in 1909. Nevertheless, double track points were installed at Banner Cross leading into Psalter Lane. They remained in situ until the mid 1920s. Whereas the line to Banner Cross from Hunters Bar had been opened in 1908, the extension to Ecclesall Church (and beyond) was deferred and did not materialise until after the First World War.

For some suggested routes parliamentary powers were never obtained. A proposal not acted upon was for a lengthy link between Malin Bridge and Broomhill via Rivelin Valley and Manchester Road. This was to be joined by an extension from Walkley to Rivelin Valley at Hollins Bridge, but was not proceeded with because of engineering difficulties which would have involved new road construction including gradients as steep as one in eight and a half.

Other proposals for which no parliamentary approval was obtained or sought were for the following lines:

Nursery Street at Bridgehouses to Pitsmoor Toll Bar.
Queen's Road Depot along Charlotte Road and Heeley Bank Road terminating at Myrtle Road.
Queen's Road/Suffolk Road to Duke Street via Shrewsbury Road and Talbot Street.
St. Philip's Road at Brook Hill to Glossop Road via Gell Street.
Church Street to Hounsfield Road via Pinfold Street, Trippett Lane, Portobello Street and Leavygreave Road.

It seems surprising that this latter route should have been considered in preference to the alternative of Townhead Street, Broad Lane and Brook Hill, the last two of which were much wider.

In 1913 and 1914 nine single deck cars were fitted with vestibuled platforms, and four were converted to snowploughs.

Valentines.
1907 "Preston" car at Hunters Bar before rebuilding as fully enclosed car in 1927. It was renumbered 339 in 1937.

The Tramway Conference was held in Sheffield in 1913 and in connection with this event one of the last three open topped cars, No. 6, was experimentally rebuilt. The alterations made to tramcars in this period are dealt with more fully in chapter eight.

In contrast to the five years up to 1912 when there were no new cars, the placing in service of Nos. 281-295 was quickly followed in 1913 by the first deliveries of a large order of fifty cars built by the Brush Company of Loughborough to Sheffield specification, along with ten

R. J. S. Wiseman.

Shoreham Street Depot entrance—track relaying on the night of 14th-15th May 1955.

Sheffield City Libraries.

Track relaying on the Moor in 1909 showing temporary tracks at either side of the road.

Sheffield City Libraries.
Track relaying in Fargate at a later period in the early 1920s. No. 398 is a Brush car of 1922 and No. 267 a "Preston" car before rebuilding in 1927.

Lens of Sutton.
Standard car in final livery about to leave Shoreham Street Depot. The Shoreham Street route is to the right and Queens Road route is in the left foreground.

Lens of Sutton.

One of the first cars built by the Corporation at Queen's Road in 1912. Seen at Cole's Corner when fairly new and before the demolition of shops on the future Telegraph Buildings site.

similar cars built by the Corporation. They were four side-windowed extended canopy open balcony cars with vestibuled platforms. This was the first class of car to be equipped with what became for many years the characteristic Sheffield front end design with "banjo-shaped" glass brake handle housing. (That description was generally used in Sheffield; it was in fact half banjo-shaped.) It was the absence of this feature which at least until 1927 singled out the "Preston Cars" as "foreigners".

These sixty Brush and S.C.T. cars were numbered 296-355. They were similar to the Queen's Road cars 281-295 except for the vestibuled platforms, and were the Sheffield equivalent of the "Preston" cars. Delivery was fairly rapid so that by 25th March 1914 all but fourteen were available for service[5] and the total fleet of passenger cars had risen to 325.

This large increase in the number of passenger cars (seventy-five in the years 1912 to 1914, except for the last one, in 1915) made necessary additional depot accommodation so that in 1914 the old horse car depot at Holme Lane was reconstructed with eight roads and a tramcar capacity of fifty-five.

The first automatic trolley reverser came into use in December 1915. This equipment was later installed at all regularly used reversing crossovers. Although bamboo poles were always carried, their use became limited to emergencies and to reversing movements at little used locations. In Sheffield, apart from the early years, trolleys were not equipped with the familiar and untidy rope employed on many other systems. Until the installation of trolley reversers, a trolley light had been affixed to the bracket arm of a standard at each terminus to permit the placing of the trolley on the correct wire after nightfall. Under Operating Rule 97 it was the duty of the driver of the last car of the day to switch off this light before leaving the terminus. The inverted hooks at each end of the car roofs for engaging the trolley when lowered out of use were introduced in the early 1920s and became standard equipment, but the short upper deck cars were not so fitted.

In the early years there were complaints from passengers of the jolting of tramcars over rail joints, but by 1913 the problem had largely been obviated by the introduction of thermite welded joints. In 1914 electric welding of worn rails was put in hand experimentally in lieu of renewal.

During the years up to this time much had been done in the matter of improved road surfaces. As long ago as 1894 there had been controversy regarding the use of granite setts and it had been agreed by the Highways Department that they would not be used where gradients were steeper than

[5]Nos. 330 and 351 entered service on 27th and 26th March respectively.

Sheffield City Libraries.

Brush built car of 1913 at Hillsborough followed by No. 3 of 1899 which was rebuilt in 1912.

one in thirty. Feelings ran higher when tramway extensions and relaying of old track for electrification were undertaken. Pressure for the use of wood paving was acceded to in general and especially in main streets. By 1905 tarmacadam was coming into use, and this resulted in substantially reduced highway costs. In consequence, it gradually replaced other materials and this process continued during the First World War.

With electric operation, much steeper gradients were encountered than that mentioned above. Granite setts remained the rule for the most severe, including parts of Duke Street and City Road, Hounsfield Road and Northfield Road, and the whole of the Walkley route between Harcourt Road and Cromwell Street, as well as certain City centre areas including Fitzalan Square and the Midland Station junctions. Wood paving, which had proved quiet for horse drawn traffic and iron-shod cart wheels, became dangerously slippery for pedestrians after rain. Perhaps the last place where it was used was in Fulwood Road in the Ranmoor area where it existed into the 1930s, not long before this tram route was abandoned.

Parliamentary powers had been obtained in the Sheffield Corporation Act 1907 to operate motor omnibuses but the first service between Broomhill and Lodge Moor did not commence until 15th February 1913. The delay was due to the search for a vehicle suitable for the hilly districts around the City.

Further omnibus services which commenced in 1913 were: Brightside terminus to Wincobank, Malin Bridge terminus to Rivelin Valley (Manchester Road junction), City to Heeley Green. Millhouses terminus to Totley, Middlewood terminus to Stocksbridge and Brightside to Tinsley were introduced in 1914.

Following a visit to Mulhausen and Vienna by a deputation from Sheffield in 1909, the running of trolley buses was authorised by the Sheffield Corporation Act 1912. The routes for which powers were obtained were: Rivelin Valley Road–Manchester Road–Fulwood Road, Fulwood Road (Broomhill)–Lodge Moor, and certain short lengths near the City centre.

A further proposal which was not included in the 1912 Act was Rivelin Valley Road–Wyming Brook–Redmires and Lodge Moor, there to join the authorised route. None of these schemes was proceeded with, and the Corporation never ran trolley buses.

In addition, the Act of 1912 authorised the widening of Exchange Street (along with twenty other widenings) and the work was well in hand at the outbreak of war. Around the same time the improvement of Waingate was also in progress.

Brush car of 1913 in Holme Lane Depot which became operational for electric cars in 1914. *Sheffield City Libraries.*

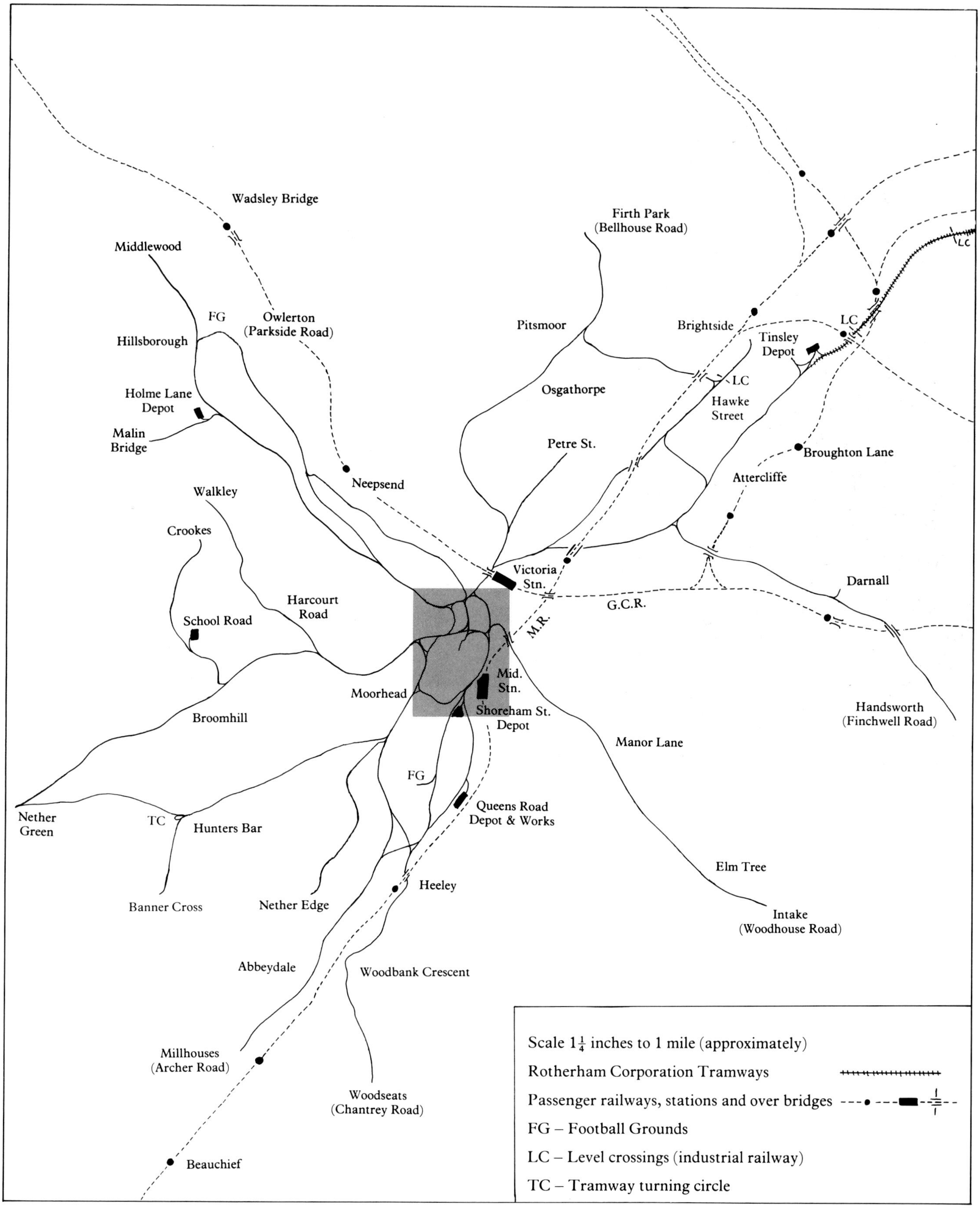

The Tramway System from 26th November 1913 until 1920

Chapter 6

The Period of the First World War 1914 to 1918

When war broke out on 4th August 1914 all tramway route development and tramcar building soon came to an end for several years but some rebuilding or improvement of rolling stock continued.

At the time the system comprised the routes to:

Intake (Woodhouse Road)
Handsworth (Finchwell Road)
Tinsley and Rotherham
Brightside
Petre Street
Firth Park (Bellhouse Road) via Pitsmoor and via Attercliffe
Owlerton (Parkside Road)
Middlewood
Malin Bridge
Walkley
Crookes
Nether Green[1] via Broomhill and via Hunters Bar
Banner Cross[2]
Nether Edge
Millhouses (Springfield Road)
Woodseats (Chantrey Road) via The Moor, via Queen's Road and via Shoreham Street

—and all lines in the City centre except Flat Street–Pond Street, Exchange Street and Tenter Street; the depots at Tinsley, Shoreham Street and Holme Lane, the Works at Queen's Road, the Power Station at Kelham Island, the underground Central Traffic Control Office at Fitzalan Square (opened in 1910) and headquarters offices at Division Street.

The tramcar fleet at the outbreak of war comprised:

138	short double deck covered top cars
43	short double deck extended canopy open balcony rebuilds
3	short double deck extended canopy open balcony vestibuled rebuilds
15	short double deck extended canopy open balcony built 1912
53	long single deckers
12	long double deckers extended canopy open balcony rebuilt from single deckers
14	"Preston" double deckers with vestibuled platforms and open balconies
1	"Preston" double decker rebuilt fully enclosed, No. 259
60[3]	Sheffield style "Preston" equivalent built by Brush and S.C.T.
339	

and sixteen works cars which were:

the rail grinder and snowplough	No. 130
the breakdown car	No. 166 (ex horse car 15)
the stores car	No. 199 (ex horse car)
the corrugation car	No. 212
the snowploughs	Nos. 273-280 (ex horse cars)
the snowploughs	Nos. 51, 52, 55 & 98 (ex electric SD)

[1]Known at the time as Fulwood if via Broomhill.
[2]Known as Ecclesall until route extended to Millhouses Lane.

[3]Included Nos. 354 and 355 which entered service on 24th September 1914 and 3rd February 1915 respectively.

In contrast with the fifteen years of electric operation which had gone, the four years of the First World War were a period of comparative inactivity especially until 1917. There were, however, some significant events. The first occurrence was administrative and was the transfer on 29th September 1914 of the Tramway Committee's power station at Kelham Island to the Electric Supply Department. Earlier in the year this power station had been connected to the Electric Supply Department's Neepsend Power Station. At about this time the use of energy from the flow of compensation water from the Water Department's reservoirs was suggested, but the Electrical Engineer reported that it was impracticable.

In 1915 three of the ex horse car snowploughs Nos. 275, 277 and 278 were withdrawn from service leaving nine for the remaining war years and until 1920. Their numbers were used again for later snowploughs during the 1920s.

On many systems the practice of queueing for tramcars originated in the war period. Milling crowds of waiting passengers had become intolerable so that queueing became an official requirement by Regulation of 1917. In Sheffield, however, queue barriers had been in use in the centre of the City for several years.

The use of the trams was greatly increased in the mornings and afternoons by munitions workers. The Report of the Tramways Committee for the year to March 1916 recorded an increase of 180,000 passengers per week on the Tinsley route alone.

At the end of the previous year a car mileage of 8,810,252 was reported on eighty-two miles of track measured as single line. The corresponding figures for 1900 had been 527,292 and twenty-six miles respectively.

The employment of women conductors commenced in 1915 and altogether a total of 680 were employed. 660 men in the service of the undertaking joined the armed forces to 11th November 1918 and sixty-one lost their lives. 465 men returned to duty by 25th March 1919.

The old depot and workshops at Nether Edge (closed in 1911) were used for storage by the military authorities until 1918 but ownership was transferred by the Corporation to a scrap metal merchant in 1917.

Used ticket boxes first fitted in 1910 were frequently used for collections for War Relief Funds.

Although no tramway extensions were made during the war, there was some development of omnibus services. Despite opposition from affected authorities outside the City boundary, the Sheffield Corporation Act 1914 authorised the running of buses to Ecclesfield, Mosborough, Grenoside and Stocksbridge, but the Corporation failed to obtain powers at that time to serve Dore, Fox House and Swallownest.

In the period 1915-16 services originating at the following tram termini commenced operation:
Intake to Mosborough (1915), Handsworth to Aston via Swallownest (1915), Firth Park to Ecclesfield (1916).

With the introduction of these services the Corporation was working ten routes with a total mileage of thirty. The number of buses in service rose from ten in 1914 to twenty-five in 1919.

With these events, in 1916 the title of the undertaking was changed from "Sheffield Corporation Tramways" to "Sheffield Corporation Tramways and Motors".

One of the few redeeming consequences of the First World War was the terminating at the end of 1916 of the contract entered into in 1903 for the display of advertisements on tramcars and buses[4]. For the following thirty-five years none of the trams and buses of the Corporation carried the unsightly advertisements so familiar on the vehicles of other undertakings. This contributed substantially to the elegant appearance of Sheffield's tramcars throughout the best years of the tramway system.

The Corporation was unable to purchase or build new tramcars because of wartime conditions, but some notable improvements were made in existing rolling stock, even though the workforce at Queen's Road was much reduced. Particulars of these improvements appear in chapter eight.

There was still urgent need, however, for additional double deck cars and so the Corporation acquired and placed in service the first of two batches of ten ex London County Council "B" class cars. These were double deck four wheelers with three side windows to the lower saloon. Whilst the upper deck was fully enclosed and had screened quarter turn staircases the platforms were not vestibuled.[5] Although this style of car was a familiar sight in London for many years, it was unique in Sheffield and unknown on many English systems.

T.M.S.

End view of ex-L.C.C. 'B' Class car leaving Queens Road Depot. The car was in service in Sheffield from 1919 to 1927.

They had an interesting history which seems worth detailed description.

One hundred cars of this type were built for the L.C.C. by the Electric Railway and Tramway Carriage Works at Preston in 1903, and were numbered 102-201. Originally they were double deck open top cars with reversed stairs, three side windows to the lower saloon, and were mounted on four wheeled trucks, being intended for routes carrying light passenger traffic or routes with steep hills. Further particulars appear in Appendix A. In the period 1906 to 1914 various stages of rebuilding were carried out in the following order:

(1) Open top with direct quarter turn stairs.
(2) Top-covers with open ends, retaining reversed stairs.
(3) Enclosed top-covers, retaining reversed stairs.
(4) Enclosed top-covers, with direct quarter turn stairs and draught screens.

By 1914 all the cars had been altered to the last mentioned type, though some of them did not pass through each of the intermediate stages.

At the beginning of 1917 nearly all the class were stored out of service due to staff shortage, and, at the instigation of the Ministry of Munitions, the L.C.C. was pressed to sell or hire them to other tramway undertakings which were in urgent need of additional cars. In 1917 and 1918, fifty-nine of the class were sold as follows: To Sheffield twenty, Bexley seventeen, Rotherham ten, Newport six and Southampton six.

Of the forty-one which remained in London, several were dismantled in 1922 and three became works cars, whilst twenty-one, which went into store in 1924, were converted to snowbrooms in 1927 and renumbered 016-036. The remainder were kept mainly for rush hour services until 1927.

Sheffield Corporation purchased ten in January 1917 for £450 each. They were L.C.C. Nos. 103, 108, 116, 119, 121, 126, 152, 156, 160 and 188, and entered service in Sheffield in the L.C.C. livery of deep purple lake with gold lining, and primrose with burnt sienna lining, and with trucks in red oxide. They received Sheffield Nos. 356-365. L.C.C. No. 188 had been supplied to Sheffield by mistake as it was one of the better cars of the class which the L.C.C. had already agreed to sell to Bexley.

Also in January 1917 Rotherham Corporation purchased at the same price ten of these cars, which were numbered 50-59 in the Rotherham fleet. They were later renumbered 39-48. Between April 1921 and the end of 1922 upper deck alterations were made to provide open balconies, in keeping with normal Rotherham standards. In this form eight of the ten, Nos. 40-47, were transferred to Sheffield along with the Tinsley–Templeborough section of route, on 1st January 1926.

In April 1918 Sheffield Corporation purchased, at £550 each, a further ten cars from the L.C.C., which were received in June and July. They were Nos. 149, 166, 170, 171, 173, 179, 181, 185, 186 and 193, which were similar to No. 188 purchased in 1917, having had their bodies practically reconstructed in 1912. Before these cars left London all their controllers and six of the trucks were sold by Sheffield Corporation to Preston Corporation, for fitting to Sheffield single deck bodies (Nos. 125, 129, 187, 188, 207 and 209) then being purchased by Preston. The remaining four trucks were retained by the L.C.C.

[4]Due to losses caused by introduction of universal one penny fares.
[5]Until 1931 the Metropolitan Police would not permit windscreens on London trams and buses, except for experimental vehicles.

These ten cars received Sheffield numbers vacated by single deckers which had been sold in 1918 to Glossop, Preston and Musselburgh: Nos. 56, 94, 125, 129, 187, 188, 203, 207, 209 and 210. They entered service in Sheffield between 17th July 1918 and the end of 1919 excepting No. 129 which came into use in 1920. Nos. 56 and 94 were renumbered 128 and 90 in 1925 and 1926 respectively.

All twenty of the cars purchased from London had been withdrawn from service before the end of 1931. No. 364 was the first to be scrapped on 16th June 1926, followed by Nos. 357, 362, 363 and 90 (previously numbered 94) in July and August. Nos. 361 and 210 went in March 1927 and Nos. 358, 359, 365 and 188 between May and September. Nos. 203 and 209 were scrapped in June and July 1928 respectively. The remaining "Sheffield Cars", Nos. 356, 360, 125, 128 (previously numbered 56), 129, 187 and 207 continued in service until 1931. Five of these survived until November or December, the last to be scrapped being No. 356 which was the first to enter service in Sheffield in March 1917.

The six ex-Rotherham cars (Sheffield Nos. 91-96) were all withdrawn between March and May 1931.

Finally, after twelve years' painstaking work at Bethnal Green, L.C.C. 'B' Class car No. 106 has been rebuilt and restored. It entered service at The Tramway Museum, Crich, on 15th May 1983 exactly eighty years after it was used for the opening of the Westminster Bridge to Tooting service, the inauguration of L.C.C. electric tramways.

The development of improved brakes resulted in authorisation by the Board of Trade for the use of double deckers on the steep hills of the Intake and Walkley routes. In this way the single deckers became redundant and their consequent sale commenced in 1918 and proceeded as follows: No. 56 to Glossop on 13th February 1918, Nos. 94, 203, 210 to Musselburgh on 10th June 1918, Nos. 125, 129, 187, 188, 207, 209 to Preston.

Accordingly, in 1918 and 1919 the above ten numbers were allocated to the second batch of 'B' class cars, as already mentioned.

R. J. S. Wiseman.
Standard car No. 103 on the steep gradient in Duke Street on 10th June 1955.

Further sales occurred in 1919 and 1920 as will be seen later.

When double deck cars were introduced on the Intake and Walkley routes, only the short-ended type was permitted and at least ten years were to elapse before larger cars were allowed, and then only those equipped with air brakes. Probably the most notable tramway event of the war period was the construction at Queen's Road, despite all the difficulties of the time, of the experimental car No. 366. It was a large fully enclosed car with twenty foot lower saloon having five side windows. The quarter turn staircases were completely screened from the upper deck saloon and each had a hinged door at the top. The lower saloon was equipped with longitudinal seats, whereas two per side transverse reversible seats were fitted on the upper deck, except in the end bays which had facing bench seats for four passengers per side.[6] The total seating capacity was seventy-six; all seats were of wood. The car had the now familiar Sheffield appearance with curved corner windows and "banjo-shaped" projection to accommodate the brake lever handle. It was mounted on a Peckham P22 eight feet six inch wheelbase four wheel truck. This car which went into service on 17th May 1918, was the last to be built for service in Sheffield with the headlamp above the car number on the dash at each end.

The superiority and elegance of No. 366 and the many similar cars which followed in the next nine years can be evaluated only by comparison with the tramcars and omnibuses of all other contemporary road transport undertakings in the United Kingdom. Although this exercise can now be carried out only by reference to illustrations, preserved vehicles in the museums and models, there can be little doubt that in 1918 No. 366 was the finest public service vehicle in the country.

Sheffield City Libraries.
The 1918 experimental car, the forerunner of a class of 154 cars, leaving Angel Street for Fulwood in the post Second World War period.

[6] Later cars followed this pattern with the notable exception of car No. 425 on which the bench seats backing on to the side windows at each end were extended into the upper saloon, providing six seats instead of four, thus taking the place of one transverse double.

Chapter 7

Post-War Expansion 1919 to 1927

The period following the end of the Great War was one of many economic and social difficulties, and this was particularly so in Sheffield. The bright hopes of the immediate post-war period quickly faded and by November 1919 disillusionment was rife. The return of unemployment, which had been a serious problem between 1903 and 1910, was made much worse by industrial unrest. The National Coal Strike, which lasted from 1st April to 27th June 1921, was disastrous to Sheffield and by its end there were 70,000 unemployed in the City. From March to June the following year there occurred an engineers' lock-out. Unemployment became an insoluble problem and remained so until the mid 1930s. Widespread distress resulting from prolonged unemployment caused violence in Sheffield, but this was no more than average in the country, and was mainly confined to 1921. In that year there were two demonstrations outside the Town Hall and at the second, in August, the trams were held up for three hours. The General Strike in May 1926 lasted only eight days, but it left much resentment and bitterness among workers. The Coal Strike continued until November 1926.

The Corporation endeavoured to alleviate the unemployment situation by organising schemes of public works in the form of new and improved roads. In this way the City obtained an improved road system many years in advance of what would have been a normal construction programme. The relief of unemployment resulting from these works was unfortunately far less significant, work being found for fewer than 1,000 men.

Over £900,000 was spent on works which were carried out during the six years to 31st March 1927, as follows:

1922 The construction of Prince of Wales Road[1] and Whirlowdale Road.
The widening of Abbey Lane from Camping Lane to Beauchief Station[1], and Abbeydale Road from Millhouses to Limb Brook[1].
Tramway extension costing £25,000.

1923 The construction of Herries Road (part).
The widening of Abbey Lane from Abbeydale Road to Whirlowdale Road.
Tramway extensions costing £22,000 and improved road surfaces, over £18,000.

H. B. Priestley.

Brush car in Attercliffe Road beyond Norfolk Bridge on 5th June 1939. The 'To City' track has been relayed but road surface not yet restored.

[1]These works were wholly or partially necessary for imminent or future tramway extensions.

1924 Further construction of Herries Road and the construction of Ridgeway Road.
Tramway extensions costing £38,000, and minor widenings on twenty-six roads.

1925 The improvement of Worksop Road from Handsworth to Woodhouse Mill[1], Abbey Lane from Whirlowdale Road to Ecclesall Road South, and Ecclesall Road from Banner Cross to Ringinglow Road[1] and from Bents Road to Croft Lane.
The extension of Rutland Road to Pitsmoor Road.

1926 The improvement of Richmond Road.
Tramway renewals (£45,000), and improved road surfaces.

1927 Improved road surfaces costing £13,000 within a reduced total of £49,086.

In addition to these works the following highway and transport matters are worthy of mention before considering purely tramway affairs.

By 1921 asphaltic paving had largely superseded granite and wooden setts, at half the cost or less, and by 1926 it was practically standard except on severe gradients and in other special conditions as outlined previously. Mr. W. J. Hadfield, the City Engineer, had gained a national reputation for his work on asphalt paving and surfacing. In spite of higher wages and cost of materials, mechanical aids and improved construction methods had made the cost per mile of highways lower in 1927 than in 1902.

It was reported that at 31st March 1927 the City had 1508 electrically lit street lights compared with only 300 in July 1924.

The traffic census of 1921 showed that on a number of thoroughfares, the average daily weight of traffic had increased by 150 to 200 per cent since 1913-14.

The Development Committee, formed just before the end of the war, wanted to modernise the canal and take it into public ownership. The canal has twelve locks between Tinsley and the City, eight of which, with a combined fall of forty-eight feet four inches, are located close together near Tinsley.

The Sheffield Corporation Act of 1920 authorised the purchase of the Government's aerodrome at Norton. These schemes were not proceeded with, nor was the suggestion of 1919 that passenger tube railways should be constructed as an alternative to, or to supplement, the tramway system.

Notwithstanding the economic and social difficulties already mentioned, as soon as the war was over, a period of intense activity commenced at Queen's Road Works, which continued almost until the outbreak of the Second World War in 1939. Most of the programme of work until 1927 was concerned with rebuilding tramcars built between 1899 and 1914 as described in chapter eight.

The basic types of car in service at the beginning of 1919 were:

125 Double deck, short covered upper deck built 1905 and rebuilds 1903-1910 numbered between 1 and 257

34 Long single deck, built 1899-1904 numbered between 39 and 211

21 Long double deck rebuilt from single deck 1906-1918, open balcony numbered between 48 and 208

15 Double deck "Preston" type open balcony built 1907 (including No. 259 rebuilt fully enclosed 1911) numbered 258 to 272

58 Double deck open balcony and platform built 1912 and rebuilds 1910-1913 numbered between 2 and 295

76[2] Double deck Sheffield equivalent of "Preston", built 1913-1915 numbered 296 to 355 and rebuilds 1913-1918 numbered between 6 and 238

14 Double deck open platform ex L.C.C. "B" class purchased 1917 and 1918 numbered between 56 and 365

1 Long double deck fully enclosed built at Queen's Road 1918 numbered 366.

In 1917 the Corporation purchased part of the site of the old Crookes Brickworks and quarry. The land had an area slightly exceeding three quarters of an acre and cost £1,117 for the freehold in possession. This purchase was in anticipation of post-war enlargement of the tramcar fleet and the consequent need for further depot accommodation.

They accepted a tender by the end of March 1919 for the construction of a new depot. The work progressed slowly and the building came into use in stages between mid 1920 and early 1921. When complete the depot had eleven roads capable of accommodating fifty-two large cars.

This depot had no frontage to the Crookes tram route; it was approached by an access siding along Pickmere Road, where it occupied an elevated and steeply sloping site. The track level at the rear of the depot was above the roofs of the houses behind it in Sackville Road and Fitzgerald Road.

A. D. Packer.
Stores car and Brush No. 416 in Pickmere Road outside Crookes Depot.

At about 690 feet above sea level it was one of the highest tramway depots in the United Kingdom. It is believed that only the original Halifax depot at Mile Cross at an altitude of 820 feet and the Bradford depot at Horton Bank Top at 942 feet occupied more elevated positions.

The only new cars built by the Corporation during the nine years covered by this chapter were the three large cars Nos. 367-369, which were generally similar to No. 366.

[2]The last rebuilt car of this type did not appear until January 1919. (No. 181.)

They were constructed between 1919 and 1921 and were the first cars to be built with the headlamp below the number on the dash at each end.

In October 1919, the Brush works at Loughborough commenced delivery of an order of fifty large cars, similar to Nos. 366-369. They were numbered 401-450 and delivery was completed in July 1920. By 31st March 1920 the number of passenger cars in service had risen to 373.

Between July 1921 and January 1922 the Brush Company delivered another twenty-five new cars, Nos. 376-400. They were of the same pattern as the previous order.

More single deck cars were sold in 1919 and 1920:

Nos. 40, 44, 45, 47, 49, 91, 93, 101, 103, 128, 204 and 211 to Yorkshire Woollen District Tramways in December 1919 and February and August 1920.

Nos. 58, 96 and 97 to Potteries Electric Traction Co. in October and November 1920.

No. 202 to Paisley District Tramways in October 1920.

Nos. 89, 90 and 95 to Preston Corporation in March 1920 in addition to the six cars already sent in 1918.

Nos. 41, 43, 100, 102, 126 and 206 to Barrow-in-Furness in September 1920.

These sales brought the total of single deck cars sold to thirty-five.

In 1920 and 1921 single deckers Nos. 39, 42, 46 and 99 were converted to snowploughs, leaving only four single deck cars Nos. 50, 53, 57 and 92 in passenger service. They were withdrawn from service before the end of 1921 and the bodies of Nos. 50, 53 and 57 were sold to the Corporation Parks Department. The history of the single deck cars is summarised below:

T. Elliott.

The last of the four cars built at Queens Road between 1918 and 1921, at the bottom of Parkside Road, Owlerton, on a football special.

No. of Cars	Fleet Numbers	Builder and Date	Rebuilt as Double Deckers 1906-1918	Converted to Snowploughs 1913-1921	Sold 1918-1920
12	39-50	Milnes 1899	48*	39, 42, 46	40, 41, 43, 44, 45, 47, 49
2	51-52	Milnes 1899		51, 52	
6	53-58	E.R. & T.C. 1899		54, 55	56, 58
15	89-103	Brush 1900		98, 99	89, 90, 91, 93, 94, 95, 96, 97, 100, 101, 102, 103
6	124-129	S.C.T. 1901	124, 127		125, 126, 128, 129
10	156-165	Cravens 1902	156-165		
6	187-192	Milnes 1902	189-192		187, 188
12	200-211	S.C.T. 1903-1904	200, 201, 205, 208		202, 203, 204, 206, 207, 209, 210, 211
Totals					
69			21	9	35

*Re-numbered 126 after withdrawal of single decker of that number. The number 48 was required for one of the 1924-5 cars 36-60.

Cars which remained single deck passenger cars until withdrawn by S.C.T. in 1921—50, 53, 57, 92.			
Cars purchased by other tramway undertakings:			
Yorkshire W.D.	1919 and 1920	40, 44, 45, 47, 49, 91, 93, 101, 103, 128, 204, 211	12
Glossop	1918 (February)	56	1
Potteries E.T.	1920 (October)	58, 96, 97	3
Preston	1918 and 1920	89, 90, 95, 125, 129, 187, 188, 207, 209	9
Musselburgh	1918 (June)	94, 203, 210	3
Paisley	1920 (October)	202	1
Barrow	1920	41, 43, 100, 102, 126, 206	6
		Total	35

Sheffield City Libraries.
Brush car of 1919 as originally built, at Middlewood terminus.

David Robins Collection.
Single-deck car built by the Corporation in 1903 seen in West Street at Westfield Terrace. Sold to Yorkshire Woollen District.

The first additional route development after the War was the Flat Street–Pond Street line which linked Fitzalan Square with the Midland Station junctions. The work was completed in 1921.

The Ecclesall route, which had terminated at Banner Cross for almost fourteen years, was extended almost to its final terminus at Millhouses Lane on 14th April 1922, and this was the first outward extension of the system since 1913.

The following further extensions soon followed:

22nd January 1923	Woodseats (Chantrey Road) to Abbey Lane (Mitchell Road)
12th July 1923	Nether Green (Storth Lane) to Fulwood (Canterbury Avenue)
7th June 1924	Owlerton (Parkside Road) to Wadsley Bridge
22nd September 1924	Exchange Street.

A very short extension was constructed in 1923 at Firth Park, from Bellhouse Road to North Quadrant.

The extension to Fulwood made necessary the construction of a short section of new highway between Stumperlowe Lane and Stumperlowe Hall Road. The Exchange Street line completed the terminal loop, inward via Blonk Street and outward via Waingate for several routes as described in chapter sixteen. The City terminus for these routes was located along the side of the old Norfolk Market Hall. The track for the opposite direction was not normally used. A composite list of routes extended between 1922 and 1935 inclusive also appears in chapter sixteen.

In 1922 the rail grinder or "water car" No. 130 was withdrawn from service. It had been built at Nether Edge in 1901 and converted to a snowplough in 1905.

1923 was significant in that it was the only year between the two world wars when no new tramcars were placed in service, but several cars were disposed of. The single deck car No. 52 which became a snowplough in 1913 was withdrawn, and replaced in November by No. 185, the first short ended double decker to become a snowplough. The

Sheffield City Libraries.
Brush car built in 1913 seen at Fulwood after rebuilding in 1922 with vestibuled balconies but before double end indicators had been fitted.

number of ploughs remained at twelve which it had been since the withdrawal of No. 130 the previous year. In addition three of the double deck cars of the same type as No. 185 were sold to Musselburgh and District Electric Light and Traction Co. Ltd., and were despatched on 4th August. Their numbers were 141, 170 and 252. Eight of these cars (Nos. 16, 35, 37, 38, 74, 176, 182 and 186) were sold around the same time to Gateshead and District Tramways Company.

Delivery of twenty-five more new cars from Brush began in 1924 and was completed the following year. These cars were numbered 36-60 and were generally similar in design to 376-450, but they incorporated several improvements. They were the first cars to be fitted with air brakes from the outset[3], which became standard from that time. Cars so equipped had a red triangle on the banjo-shaped end glasses. A further innovation which became a permanency was the arrangement of the reversible upper deck seating to provide for two passengers on one side and one on the other. This made possible more commodious seats though fewer of them, and wider gangways.

Double indicators were fitted at each end of the cars within the curved end panels above the upper deck floor. The upper deck end bays had roof ventilators in the form of an opening skylight, through which the trolley boom could be seen provided the overhead power line was fairly centrally positioned above the car[4].

M. J. O'Connor.

1904 car seen at Exchange Street terminus after second rebuilding in 1922. In the background is the City Stores of Brightside and Carbrook Co-operative Society which was destroyed in the air raid on 12th December 1940.

[3]No. 366 was the first car to be fitted with air-brakes, but not when new.

[4]This latter feature was to appear on later cars Nos. 451-500, No. 1 (Cravens), Nos. 131-155 (Hills), Nos. 3 and 4 (S.C.T.) and on the rebuilt "Prestons". Curiously, S.C.T. car No. 2 was so equipped in one canopy only, as was Brush car No. 421.

In order to make numbering space for these cars the following ten cars had to be renumbered as shown below:

Short ended double deck car No. 36 became No. 35
Snowplough No. 39 became No. 95
Snowplough No. 42 became No. 96
Snowplough No. 46 became No. 97
Converted double deck car No. 48 became No. 126
Snowplough No. 54 became No. 100
Snowplough No. 55 became No. 101
Ex-L.C.C. "B" class car No. 56[5] became No. 128
Short ended double deck car No. 59 became No. 87
Short ended double deck car No. 60 became No. 89.

All the other cars in this series of numbers had already been disposed of: nine single deckers including the original No. 56, and two short ended double deckers had been sold; three single deckers and two snowploughs had been scrapped.

The second of the snowploughs was No. 51, another single decker converted to a snowplough in 1913. This car was withdrawn and replaced in March 1924 by No. 111, one of the short ended double deckers which consequently became a snowplough.

In the years which ended in March 1925 and 1926 there was considerable activity in omnibus matters, some of which was wasteful in character. Several bus services which hitherto had commenced at suburban tram termini were extended inwards to the centre of the City, so duplicating services, a situation which did not make sense in terms of economical use of equipment and highway space. The replacement of three tram services by buses between 1925 and 1936 and the discontinuation of the through service to Rotherham in 1948 had similar results.

Reference has already been made to some proposed tramway extensions where sanction was either not sought or not given. The Petre Street route figured twice in proposals of this kind. A scheme of June 1911 would have converted the City's shortest route into one of the longest. It was planned to extend from the terminus at Canada Street across undeveloped land ahead past the top side of the Recreation Ground. It would then have turned east along a road already laid out (Scott Street) to join Carlisle Street East by the "Alexandra Hotel". Continuing thence it would have crossed the existing Upwell Street tramway and terminated at Wincobank by way of Holywell Road and Tyler Street, which included a further section of then unmade road. A Council minute of 11th June 1911 stated that if this scheme went ahead, powers for the Brightside and Wincobank extension would not be renewed.

An extension much shorter in length than that intended in 1911 was mooted in the summer of 1924 at a time when the existing track required complete renewal. In the first instance an extension was proposed of 800 yards to the boundary of the Government's wartime housing estate for munition workers at "The Brickfield", and then a further 160 yards across "The Brickfield" to Ludlow Street near Botham Street.

An examination of the immediate relative costs of these suggested or proposed extensions and the relaying of the existing tracks resulted in the decision to replace the tram route by buses. The tram service ended on 19th April 1925 and the replacing buses were the first double deckers in Sheffield to have covered tops except for one bus which had

[5]Second car to bear this number.

been in operation from July 1924. They were less comfortable than the trams and there were many protests by passengers. In addition the change caused the same duplication of trams and buses in the busy streets from Fitzalan Square to the junction of Burngreave Road and Ellesmere Road as occurred around the same time when suburban bus routes were extended into the City centre.

When the Petre Street route was converted to bus operation there remained an outstanding debt of £3,626 in respect of the original expenditure on this route. This was the only tram route in Sheffield to close with an outstanding debt.

Sir William Clegg stated in December 1925 that the Tramways and Motors Committee could do all that was necessary to provide for areas adjacent to Sheffield, and that in the interests of efficiency, expense and co-ordinated transport, the running of private companies' vehicles into the City should be resisted. In the light of the above tram/bus duplications, this does not seem very convincing. However, in reply to Sir William's statement, the Chairman of the Watch Committee said that whatever the policy of the Tramways and Motors Committee might be, his Committee had a statutory duty to grant licences to operators who had satisfactory vehicles and observed recognised standards of wages and conditions.

A Council minute of the period recorded that the tram and omnibus network comprised a route mileage of 170. There were 101 buses in service, twenty-four of which had their solid tyres replaced by pneumatic ones in 1925. There were forty-two bus routes.

On 1st January 1926 the Corporation took over the 1.28 route miles of track from Tinsley to Templeborough, along with eight ex-L.C.C. "B" class cars which Rotherham Corporation had converted to open balcony cars, bearing Rotherham Nos. 40-47. They were brought into service as follows:

Rotherham No.	Received by Sheffield	Entered Service in Sheffield	Sheffield No.
43	8th January 1926	30th January 1926	91
45	8th January 1926	22nd February 1926	92
42	7th January 1926	20 March 1926	93
46	19th January 1926	22nd March 1926	94
47	25th January 1926	21st April 1926	95
41	8th January 1926	5th June 1926	96
40	24th June 1926	Never used in Sheffield and were broken up.	
44	24th June 1926		

A. D. Packer.

At Vulcan Road terminal siding on 11th April 1960. The property in this street was entirely industrial.

Further renumbering of snowploughs took place in consequence: 95 became 102, 96 became 103, 97 became 275 and 98 became 277. In the event, the numbers 97 and 98 were not required because of the two withdrawals. In addition, ex-L.C.C. "B" class No. 94 became No. 90.

The Corporation quickly relaid the track taken over and at the same time constructed the Vulcan Road siding which was opened on 20th September 1927, and the Templeborough terminal kerbside siding, in Sheffield Road, on the Sheffield-bound side of the carriageway. The overall length of the siding was about 133 yards and the Sheffield end of it was fifty-seven yards east of Ferrars Road.

The General Strike of 1926, which lasted from 4th to 12th May, brought about a total stoppage of the City's tram and bus services.

On 31st July of that year the extension of the Millhouses route from Springfield Road/Millhouses Lane to "The Waggon and Horses" came into use. In the first instance the new terminus was equipped with a trailing crossover located at the commencement of the future Abbeydale Road reservation. This crossover was retained when the turning loop was subsequently constructed.

Delivery of fifty new cars by Cravens Railway Carriage and Wagon Co. Ltd. at Darnall commenced in 1926 and was completed early in 1927. They were similar to Nos. 36-60 except that the side indicators were built into the ventilator window space above the middle side windows. They were numbered 451-500 and although the numerals were similar in style to those which were standard at the time, they were slightly different in shape which gave the exterior of the dashes of these cars a distinctive appearance. This batch of cars brought the total of the handsome post-1917 new cars to 154. They were the last to be built for Sheffield with wooden seats.

During the Summer of 1926 the first five of the ex-L.C.C. "B" class cars to be withdrawn from service were scrapped.

Further developments took place in the snowplough fleet in 1926. The short ended double deck car No. 73 was converted to a plough in September, No. 273 (ex horse car) was withdrawn in August, and No. 100 (previously No. 54) was also withdrawn.

Two important policy changes took effect after the year ended 31st March 1927, which resulted from the coming to power of the Labour Party in the local elections of 1st November 1926. First was the cessation of the practice of the Tramways and Motors Committee of transferring part of its profits to the relief of rates. The Committee's finances had flourished continually and between 1900 and 1927 a total of £558,843 had been contributed in this way. There were contributions every year except 1920 and 1921. The

Lens of Sutton.

Cravens car No. 457 and Brush cars in High Street, seen from Coles' Corner about 1930.

largest was £41,856 in 1916 and the smallest £5,000 in 1902. The Labour administration decided that the benefit of transport profits should go to users of the services in the form of lower fares.

Secondly, with the notable exception of the Hills cars of 1929 mentioned later, no more tramcars were built by outside contractors after the Cravens cars of 1926-27, until 1950. The Corporation decided to build their own cars by direct labour at Queen's Road Works.

P. N. Williams.

Cravens car No. 500 of 1927 in Fargate on 6th August 1951. This was the highest numbered car until 1946.

Chapter 8

Tramcar Rebuilding 1903 to 1927

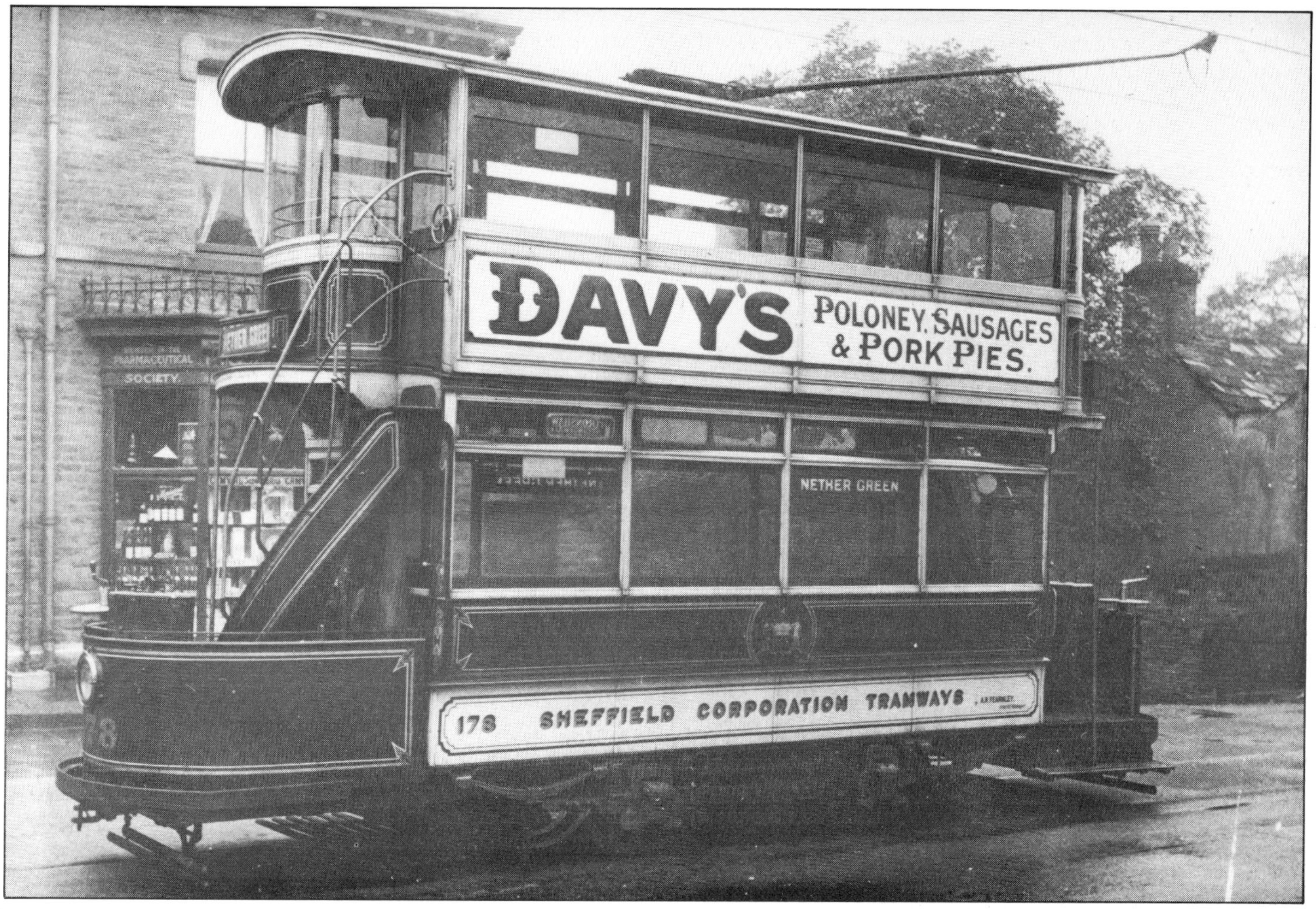

No. 178 at Millhouses Terminus following the replacement in 1904 of the ex Milnes Voss top cover. *T.M.S.*

The works undertaken during this period illustrate the desire of the Corporation to keep its fleet of tramcars up to date with the development of design technique and improvement, matters neglected by many English tramway undertakings.

The extent of the rebuilding programme can be appreciated when it is recalled that between 1903 and the end of 1927 a total of 292 cars were substantially rebuilt or materially improved. Forty-three of this total were rebuilt a second time and two a third time. Eighteen ex horse cars or early electric passenger cars were converted to snowploughs. Indeed of the pre-First World War fleet of 343 passenger cars, the only ones which escaped rebuilding by the end of 1927 were the twelve short covered top cars built at Nether Edge in 1905 (Nos. 246-257) and all but one of the fifteen open balcony and platform cars built at Queen's Road in 1912 (Nos. 281-295), and of course, most of the single deckers sold or withdrawn between 1918 and 1921.

This was not the only constructional work with which the Corporation was involved. When rebuilding commenced in 1903 they had already built twenty-two electric cars at Nether Edge Works and three were in hand at the time. Building of new tramcars continued in 1904 and 1905, when a further nineteen cars were constructed.

Following the opening of Queen's Road workshops, twenty-five new cars were built there between 1912 and early 1915, and another four between 1918 and 1921.

The rebuilding work undertaken between 1903 and 1910 comprised the fitting of top covers to 126 of the short open top double deckers, and the rebuilding of twelve single deck cars as long double deckers, as well as works car adaptations referred to later. This prodigious programme commenced with the fitting of an experimental Milnes Voss top cover to the short open top double deck car No. 178. This was the forerunner of the first batch of thirty Milnes Voss type top covers fitted to cars Nos. 131-155 and 34-38 between September 1903 and November 1904 inclusive. A further batch of thirty-one cars, Nos. 78-88 and 167-186, were so equipped in 1904 and 1905 including the top covering again of No. 178.

In addition to the fitting of top covers, the workshops were engaged on the conversion of two ex horse cars to electric short open top cars in May and September 1904. They received the numbers 244 and 245 respectively. In 1902 another horse car, No. 15, had been converted into a breakdown wagon and given the number 166.

Besides these tasks, the Corporation built twelve short double deck cars complete with top covers, Nos. 246-257, as mentioned in chapter five. They were placed in service between January 1905 and January 1906 inclusive.

There followed in 1906 the conversion of two single deck cars Nos. 200 and 208 into double deck open balcony extended canopy cars; they were fitted with half-turn staircases and the platforms were not vestibuled. This involved the greatest design transformation of the whole rebuilding programme by reason of the seating capacity being more than doubled—from twenty-eight to seventy-two, by far the largest at that time.

These two cars were also the first in Sheffield to have their headlamps fitted on the dashes instead of at upper deck floor level or on the canopy of single deck cars. Both cars returned to service in March, and in September Nos. 124 and 127 were similarly rebuilt. In the year from December 1906 Nos. 48 and 156-162 followed, bringing the total to twelve. These cars and the nine which were rebuilt during the First World War were until 1918 the largest cars in the City.

The original fleet of snowploughs was formed in 1905-7 by the fitting in 1905 of snow clearing equipment to No. 130 (the water car built in 1901), and the conversion in 1906-1907 of seven of the 1897 double deck horse cars which had been stored in Holme Lane depot since 1902. They received the numbers 273-279, as shown in chapter four.

As soon as these works were completed a start was made on the fitting of "Sheffield type" covered tops (a modified design of Milnes Voss type) to more of the open top double deckers, and in the two and a half years from December 1907 to June 1910 sixty-five cars were so dealt with. By this latter date a total of 126 had received top covers, leaving forty-six still with open upper decks.

At this time the Tramways Committee was investigating an improved design of upper deck for the rebuilding of the remaining open top cars. The first result was the experimental rebuilding of "Preston" car No. 259. It was fitted with upper deck vestibules but the bulkheads were altered to enclose the staircases, with a sliding door at the top of each staircase. The half turn staircases were retained and the car had a total of sixty seats. This was the first fully enclosed double deck tramcar in England and became known locally as "Kelly's Cottage". It went into service in January 1911 but the Tramways Committee was not satisfied and no more completely enclosed cars were introduced until 1918. In consequence the upper deck pattern of No. 259 remained unique in Sheffield.

From the beginning of 1905 cars entering service were fitted with roller blind destination indicators and during the years 1907 to 1910 the pre-1905 cars had their route letter panels replaced by destination indicator boxes containing roller blinds, and their headlamps at upper deck floor level (or roof level on single deckers) were removed and replaced by lamps on the dashes, making necessary the use of smaller numerals for car numbers.

Between January 1911, the month when No. 259 entered

No. 159 at Millhouses, Archer Road. Rebuilt in 1907 from single decker. Vestibuled platforms were fitted in 1915.

service in its rebuilt form as mentioned above, and July 1913 the remaining forty-six open top cars were rebuilt with full length upper decks and canopies. Forty-three of these rebuilds had open platforms and balconies and half-turn staircases; they were similar in appearance to, but shorter in length than, the 1906-7 rebuilt single deckers already described. These cars were Nos. 2, 3, 5, 7-12, 14, 15, 17-19, 21, 24-32, 64, 65, 70, 73, 75, 104, 105, 108, 112-119, 222, 235 and 243. In addition fifteen new cars of this type were built at Queen's Road in 1912, numbered 281-295. The remaining three open top cars Nos. 6, 22 and 33, rebuilt in 1913, were fitted with vestibuled platforms, though Nos. 22 and 33 were probably not vestibuled until a later date. No. 33 rebuilt in July 1913 was the last open top car in service in Sheffield.

No. 6, one of the original short open top double deckers, was rebuilt in March 1913 in connection with the Tramway Conference held in Sheffield in that year. It was fitted with vestibuled platforms and was the first such conversion of a passenger car, though the "Preston" cars had been in this general form since their introduction in 1907. It is believed that it had straight glass in the corner windows—the only car ever to be so fitted in Sheffield before the 1939-45 war. It was also the first car to have the banjo-shaped brake handle housing which later became familiar. However in 1920 this car reverted to the standard open platform type of the 1911-13 period.

In May 1913 four of the early single deckers, numbered 51, 52, 55 and 98, were converted to snowploughs, retaining their existing numbers and bringing the total to twelve ploughs. These conversions involved the shortening of the bodies by four feet, reducing the side windows from five to four. They were the first electric cars to go out of passenger service.

Between August 1913 and September 1914 nine other single deckers numbered 40, 41, 44, 45, 47, 49, 126, 128 and 129 were fitted with vestibuled platforms which, although of the Sheffield style which became standard in 1913, did not have the banjo-shaped brake handle housing. This vestibuling involved the lengthening of the platforms to six feet six inches on some of these cars.

In the period 1913-1919 thirteen of the short double deck cars were rebuilt for a second time as extended canopy open balcony and vestibuled platform cars similar to Nos. 22 and 33. These were Nos. 59, 60, 88, 107, 120, 167, 171, 173, 174, 181, 198, 225 and 238.

In addition sixty new cars of similar type to these rebuilds entered service between 1913 and 1915 bearing the Nos. 296-355, as mentioned in chapter seven.

Between 1914 and 1916 the twelve large double deck cars

Lens of Sutton.

Single-deck car No. 162 of 1902 rebuilt in 1907 into open balcony and platform double-decker, seen in High Street with open top cars.

Lens of Sutton.

One of the last batch of open top cars built in 1904, fitted with top cover in 1908 and withdrawn in 1930. At Millhouses terminus.

T.M.S.

The "Preston" car No. 259 experimentally rebuilt in 1911 to form the first fully enclosed tramcar in England.

Lens of Sutton.

One of the first open top double-deck electric cars placed in service in September 1899. This car was rebuilt in 1913 into an open balcony car, as shown. It is standing at the Banner Cross terminus then known as Ecclesall.

"Short ended" car in Firth Park Road after fitting of top cover in 1909.

T.M.S.

No. 107 at Chantrey Road terminus, Woodseats after second rebuilding in 1914. *T.M.S.*

Sheffield City Libraries.
1902 car fitted with top cover in 1905 and one of the first (and the lowest numbered) to be rebuilt in the form shown in 1919. It was the first of the type to be withdrawn in 1931. The car is standing in open country at Banner Cross.

rebuilt from single deckers in 1906-7 were fitted with vestibuled platforms, and in the period 1915 to 1918 a further nine single deck cars, Nos. 163-165, 189-192, 201 and 205, were similarly converted to double deckers with the addition of platform vestibules.

In the years following the war the rebuilding programme was devoted almost entirely to the provision of fully enclosed upper decks, and eighty-nine cars were dealt with in this way by the end of 1927, as described later.

Other work undertaken included the replacement of the trucks of the fifteen "Preston" cars, which commenced in 1918 and was completed in 1920. The original Mountain and Gibson eight foot six inch wheelbase radial trucks had been troublesome in service and were consequently replaced by Peckham P.22s with an eight foot wheelbase, which these trams retained for the rest of their long years of duty.

In 1919 the upper deck of No. 259 was altered again, when the sliding doors at the tops of the staircases were removed and the bulkheads reinstated. Around this time the salt trailer No. 279 was converted to a stores car.

The short upper deck car No. 179 was rebuilt for the second time in May 1919 with upper deck bulkheads with sliding doors, half turn staircases and vestibuled balconies. It was followed in October by similar car No. 177, and No. 290, one of the fifteen open balcony and platform cars built by the Corporation at Queen's Road in 1912. This latter car was severely damaged in the 1919 accident at Nether Green (Appendix K). It is believed that these three cars did not have the drop type opening end windows on the upper deck which became standard for later rebuilds in this style.

During the same year an experimental detachable screen was fitted to the Brush-built open balcony car No. 300 but in November permanent type upper deck vestibules were tried on No. 328 of the same class. This treatment was applied to No. 330 the following month, and by the end of 1922 fifty-five of the class of sixty cars Nos. 296-355 were similarly dealt with. No. 354 followed in 1924 and later No. 355 making a total of fifty-seven. Nos. 350, 352 and 353 remained open balcony cars until withdrawn in 1934-1935. The new vestibuled balconies were fitted with a centre upper deck window, as already referred to, which could be lowered or raised by passengers.

Between November 1921 and November 1925, eleven of the short upper deck cars, Nos. 194, 197, 214, 220, 224, 229, 230, 234, 236, 237 and 239, and two open balcony and platform cars Nos. 235 and 243 were again rebuilt with vestibuled balconies (and vestibuled platforms in the case of the latter two) to the same design, excepting detail, as the 296-355 rebuilds. In addition "Preston" cars Nos. 263 and 269 were similarly treated in May 1925 and December 1924 respectively.

Nos. 296-355 (including the three which remained open balcony cars) retained their original dashes, as did "Preston" car No. 263. The others were fitted with new dashes with lamps below the numbers. At the time of rebuilding or later, double end indicators were fitted to nearly all the other similar rebuilds, but No. 214 was an exception which retained single indicators throughout its rebuilt existence. In addition, most of the open balcony cars were provided with double end indicators to replace their original single ones.

In all, seventy-six cars were altered or rebuilt with vestibuled balconies, sliding door upper deck bulkheads and vestibuled platforms. This number included three "Preston" cars. The total diminished by two when No. 259 was again rebuilt in 1926, and No. 179 received the upper deck of No. 8 when the latter was withdrawn from service in 1928, so converting No. 179 into an open balcony car.

During the years 1920-1927 several more passenger cars were converted to snowploughs, as follows:

August 1920 single deck car No. 42
October 1920 single deck car No. 46
October 1921 single deck car No. 39
November 1921 single deck car No. 99
November 1923 short upper deck car No. 185
July 1924 short upper deck car No. 111
November 1927 short upper deck car No. 172
November 1927 short upper deck car No. 226.

These last four conversions involved the removal of upper deck and staircases.

In November 1923, short upper deck car No. 142 was converted to a water car and extended canopies were added in 1924.

The last major stage of tramcar rebuilding concerned the "Preston" cars of 1907. Late in 1925 work commenced on the rebuilding of the twelve cars which still had open balconies, and the third alteration of the upper deck of No. 259. These thirteen cars received new upper decks with quarter-turn enclosed staircases making them into a shorter version of the 1918-22 cars Nos. 366-369 and 376-450 but without the distinctive "banjo ends". Seats on the upper deck accommodated forty passengers comprising six double reversible seats on either side, and two facing bench seats for four passengers each in each end bay. All these cars also received new dashes with the lamps below the car numbers, with the exception of No. 259 which retained its original dashes. They were fitted with double end indicators and their side indicators were raised to the top ventilator position above the third side windows of the lower saloon.

The final item, in 1927, was the extensive rebuilding of No. 228, the short double deck car, originally open topped and fitted with top cover in July 1909. In appearance it became a shorter version of the Cravens cars of 1926-27, fully enclosed and with screened quarter-turn staircases. However, it retained double seats on either side of the upper deck and the Brill type truck and hand brakes. It was a handsome little car, and the only one of the original fleet to be rebuilt in this form. It was also the last car to be rebuilt in the inter-war years, and the last in Sheffield to be equipped with "banjo ends".

After the end of 1927 and until 1939 Queen's Road workshops became fully engaged on the building of new tramcars, running repairs and minor improvements to the fleet, and no further rebuilding of older cars was carried out except for three conversions to snowploughs, comprising cars Nos. 77 and 113 in 1929 and No. 225 in 1933.

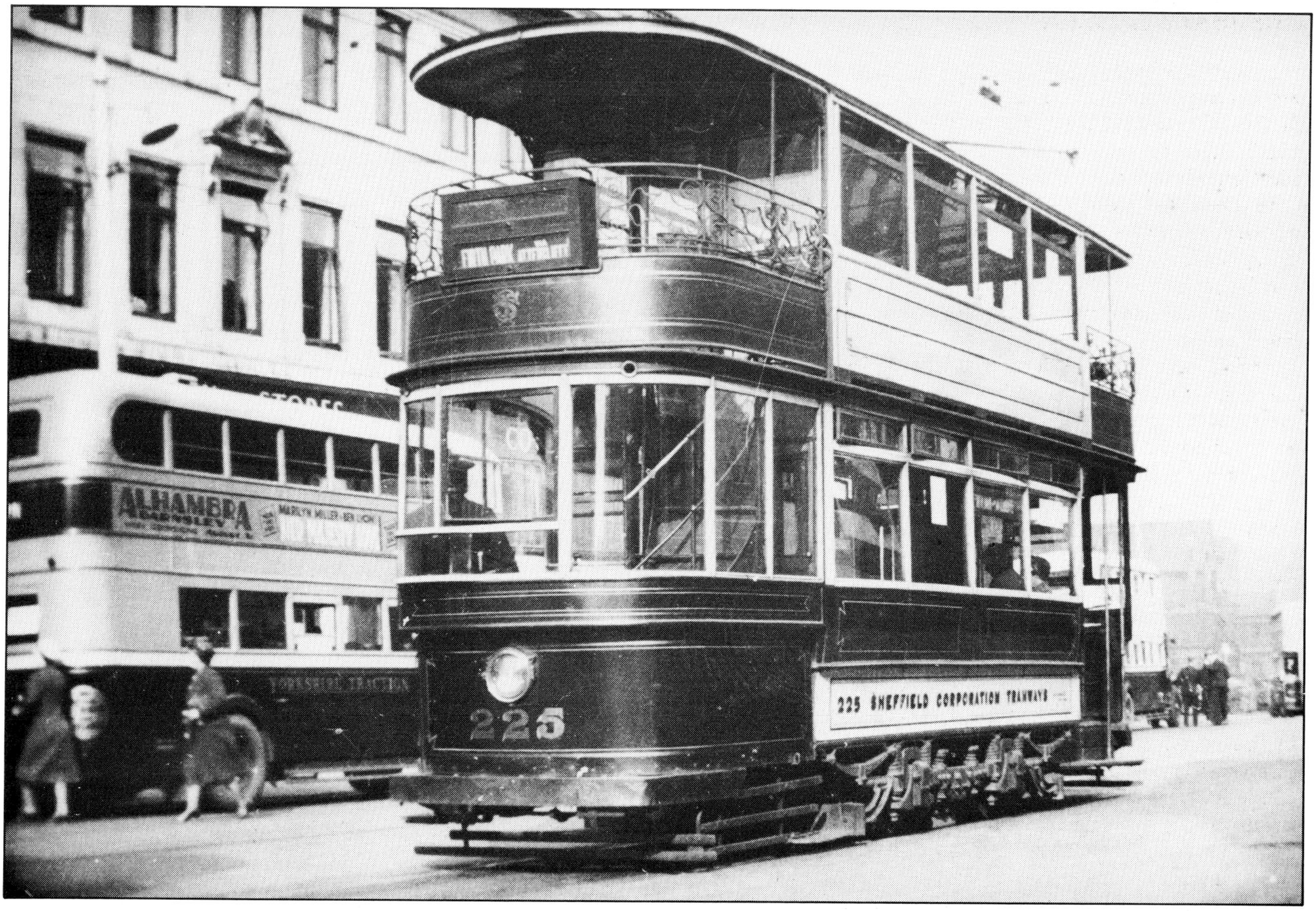

M. J. O'Connor.

No. 225 became an open balcony car in 1913. In 1933 it was converted to a snowplough and renumbered 278. It became No. 357 in 1937 and was scrapped in April 1960. The car is standing at the Exchange Street terminus with Yorkshire Traction bus and City Stores opposite.

M. J. O'Connor.

Originally single-deck car, converted to double-decker in 1907 and fitted with vestibuled platforms in 1916, seen outside Marples Hotel.

The late J. G. Parsons.

No. 190 was the last single-deck car to be rebuilt as a double-decker, in 1918. At Firth Park in the early 1930s.

T.M.S.
In Crookes Depot after second rebuilding in 1925. This car remained in service until 1938.

The late J. G. Parsons.
In Hounsfield Road after final rebuilding in 1926, but before being renumbered 337 in 1937.

Chapter 9

The Best Years 1927 to 1939

The period was one of continuous progress, and although no route extensions were carried out during the worst years of trade depression and heavy unemployment, the programme of renewal of the tramcar fleet went on unceasingly.

On 13th April 1927 a provisional order was granted by the Ministry of Transport to Sheffield Corporation authorising the construction of tramway tracks from Woodseats to Four Lane Ends, Norton, and along Prince of Wales Road connecting existing routes at Intake and Darnall.

The next day, in good weather[1], the line linking Millhouses ("Waggon and Horses") and Woodseats was opened. It was constructed on a stone paved roadside reservation along the whole length of Abbeydale Road South from "The Waggon and Horses" to Beauchief Corner; a right angled turn was made into Abbey Lane, where the track was in the carriageway over the River Sheaf bridge and L.M.S. Railway bridge at Beauchief Station and to the bottom of Dalewood Road. There a second reservation commenced, this time on a broad grass sward which extended to Strelley Road, where the track returned finally to the carriageway, and thence to Woodseats.

The opening ceremony was performed by Alderman Humberstone (Lord Mayor). It commenced at Millhouses, where a decorated open balcony car was used as a platform, and the new Cravens cars Nos. 500 and 496 were used to convey members of the Committee, Council and officials of the Corporation. The cars travelled out to Beauchief and Woodseats and then returned to Millhouses.

The normal service on the Millhouses–Woodseats route was from Tinsley to "Woodseats via Millhouses" returning to "Firth Park via Pitsmoor". In this direction the destination indicators were changed at Beauchief. Cars from Firth Park returned to "Millhouses via Woodseats" and thence to Tinsley, the indicators being changed at Woodseats. This pattern of service remained unchanged throughout the existence of the route, apart from certain adjustments at times during later years in northern terminal points. Some Tinsley cars continued beyond Weedon Street to Vulcan Road or Templeborough, (Vulcan Road after the closure of the Rotherham route). When Firth Park terminus

H. B. Priestley.

Brush car No. 422 on Millhouses turning circle on 30th June 1939. The passenger shelter can be seen to the right.

[1] 1927 was a year of extremes of weather in Sheffield. The very fine Easter, Whitsun and August Bank Holidays brought heavy traffic to tram, bus and train services. Severe gales on 28th January and 28th October and a thunderstorm on 5th July caused much damage to property. Heavy rain on 8th August led to floods in low-lying areas which interrupted tram services. Snow over Christmas disrupted traffic in the outskirts and the Castleton bus service had to be suspended on Boxing Day.

was extended to Sheffield Lane Top some cars ran to the latter point.

There was only one trailing crossover on the new line and this was located at Beauchief, where certain rush hour services outward via Millhouses terminated, and returned to the City. There was however no trolley reverser at Beauchief before the Second World War. It was not usual for cars which had travelled out via Woodseats and Abbey Lane to reverse at Beauchief. When the Abbey Lane route was opened the Woodseats crossover was moved from Mitchell Road to Camping Lane.

A few months after the opening, the Millhouses turning loop came into use. It was by far the best suburban terminal layout on the system, being located entirely within a grassed rectangular reservation. It was worked in a clockwise direction and the waiting and loading point was towards the end of the loop near Hartington Avenue.

Towards the end of 1927 the new vicar of St. Paul's Church adjoining the Town Hall, Rev. A. J. Talbot Easter, protested against the proposal to take part of the churchyard to widen Pinstone Street for the purpose of constructing a tram terminus. His objection was unsuccessful as the Highway Authority obtained sanction for the scheme. However the Pinstone Street widening did not materialise and the wall of the churchyard remained in its original position and formed the back of the tramway shelter which was subsequently erected.

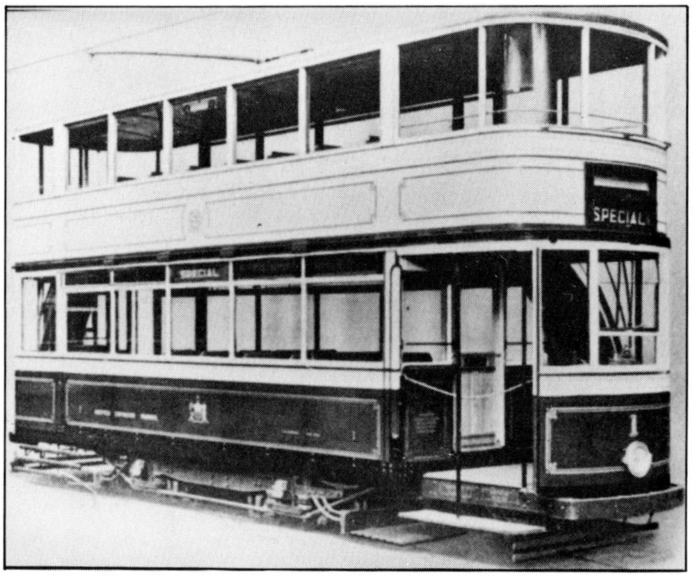

Cravens.

The experimental car No. 1 of 1927, the last built for the Corporation by Cravens Railway Carriage & Wagon Company.

Soon after the opening of the Abbey Lane route, the Corporation placed in service on 28th December the experimental tramcar No. 1 which was built by Cravens Railway Carriage and Wagon Company at Darnall. It was the last tramcar built by Cravens for service in Sheffield. Whilst in general design it was similar to the 154 post-war cars already referred to, the major internal improvements were the transverse reversible seats in the lower saloon, except those over the sandboxes at each corner which remained longitudinal; the upholstered seating throughout; the introduction of white painted aluminium ceilings in contrast to the birch veneer ceilings of the older cars; and the superior reflection of the electric lamps housed in concave spun aluminium reflectors. These were a great improvement on the old-fashioned brass lampholders hitherto installed.

External appearance differed materially from all earlier Sheffield cars. The rocker panels which were a traditional feature of English tramcars were replaced by vertical side panelling which was carried forward to form the dash of the same vertical depth. The radii of the hand brake lever handle and wheel were reduced and so the familiar Sheffield end design incorporating the "banjo" glass housing, which originated and became standard in 1913 with cars Nos. 296-355, was replaced by a much simplified pattern. These changes made necessary some modification of the exterior livery below the lower deck windows. The usual dark blue was retained, but a cream band about nine inches deep was provided below the windows. The normal style of lining-out, suitably adapted, was also retained, but the large block lettering "Sheffield Corporation Tramways" preceded by the car number, which had previously adorned the cream coloured rocker panels, was replaced by smaller gilt lettering and number on the blue side panelling. The Sheffield coat-of-arms which had for some years appeared on the sides of all cars was unaffected by the new design.

Shortly after the introduction of this car, the Cravens car No. 476 was re-seated on similar lines, soon to be followed in 1928 by Brush cars Nos. 445 and 447. The seat design and covering materials used on No. 476 were different from those of the other three cars, it having forty seats on the upper deck, compared with thirty-seven on the other three.

So successful was No. 1 that it formed the pattern for tramcar building by or for the Corporation over the period from 1928 to 1936. This building programme is described later.

Ten months after the opening of the Millhouses to Woodseats link a similar connecting line was opened on 24th February 1928 between Elm Tree, the summit point on the Intake route, and Darnall via Prince of Wales Road. This new section was on a continuous central reservation between the dual carriageways except for the short distance on single carriageway road between Halsall Avenue and Main Road at Darnall. There was a trailing crossover at Beaumont Road which was of far greater importance for short workings than that at Beauchief on the Abbey Lane route. Further crossovers were provided at the head of the reservation at Elm Tree, and in Prince of Wales Road near its junction with Main Road, Darnall.

The route ran through the whole length of the Manor Estate and services in both directions commenced and terminated at Fitzalan Square. The indicator descriptions, in contrast to those used on the Millhouses/Woodseats link which seemed to confuse some passengers, were "Intake (Elm Tree) and Darnall" and "Darnall and Intake (Elm Tree)", each being changed to "City (Fitzalan Square)" for the return journey. In addition to this basic service there were numerous journeys at busy periods of the day between Intake and the East End via Prince of Wales Road to meet the needs of industrial workers. Details are shown in chapter sixteen.

The new car No. 1 was used for the ceremonial opening journey on 24th February 1928, and open balcony car No. 284 was used for speech making purposes. It is believed that No. 288 of the same type was similarly used later in the year at the Woodseats (Abbey Lane) to Meadowhead opening ceremony on 12th July.

The junction at the end of Abbey Lane was constructed as a triangle, so that the new extension could be reached either via Heeley or via Millhouses, but in normal conditions the latter route was not used. At first the indicator description displayed was "Woodseats and Meadowhead via Heeley" but later this became simply "Meadowhead". The normal service was worked to and from Firth Park (later Sheffield Lane Top) via Pitsmoor.

With the exception of the 'non-public' tracks from West Bar to Tenter Street Depot, which made the latter operational on 23rd October 1928[2], there were no more route extensions for six years.

Tenter Street Depot had twenty-two roads and a capacity of eighty-six service cars. It was built on a sloping site with the tramcar entrance at the lowest point—the corner of Tenter Street and Silver Street Head. The slope facilitated the construction of an omnibus garage above with access from Lee Croft and Sims Street. The double tramway track to the depot included a triangular junction at West Bar and a scissors crossover outside the depot entrance.

It was in 1928 that the L.M.S. and L.N.E. railways obtained general powers to provide bus services and in order to avoid wasteful competition the Sheffield Joint Omnibus Committee, with headquarters at the Division Street offices of the Transport Department, was formed to control and operate services extending to and from places beyond the City boundary. In the earlier years the L.M.S. and L.N.E.R. placed in service single deck buses in their own colour schemes, in addition to those provided for the joint services by the Corporation which were in Sheffield livery, except for the coat of arms of the City, which was replaced by the lettering "Sheffield Corporation, L.M.S. and L.N.E. Railways". There were also railway owned buses in Sheffield livery which bore the title "L.M.S. and L.N.E. Railways".

In tramway matters the great event of the year was the resumption of tramcar building at Queen's Road—a prodigious programme of replacement which lasted for eleven years and produced probably the finest tramcar fleet in the country, worthy of great craftsmen and a credit to A. R. Fearnley Esq., the General Manager, and his staff.

Similar in style to No. 1 with only minor differences of detail, No. 2 was the first car to appear from Queen's Road Works. It went into service on 12th July 1928, and was followed by cars numbered consecutively up to No. 10 by the end of the year. At the end of 1929 new cars from Queen's

Lens of Sutton.

No. 219 leaving Tenter Street Depot. The omnibus garage is on the upper floor.

[2]Officially opened by Herbert Morrison Esq., on 20th September.

Road reached up to No. 29, but in that year the first eighteen cars of an order of twenty-five from W. & E. Hill Ltd. of South Shields-on-Tyne went into service. They carried the numbers 131-148 and the first to appear was No. 132 on 11th February.

A. D. Packer.
In the depot area of Queen's Road Works on 17th June, 1956.

At the end of 1929 that Company went into liquidation, a public hearing being held at Sunderland on the first Monday of 1930. The Receiver indicated his intention to complete the contract and there would have been no loss to Sheffield Corporation as the contract had been on an "on delivery" basis. The contract price for the twenty-five cars was £1,190 for each car, which was £400 less than the next nearest tender. The remaining cars Nos. 149-155 were delivered by the end of June 1930.

During that year the Corporation built a further eighteen cars at Queen's Road, Nos. 30-35 and 61-72.

In mid 1929 a noticeable variation in livery was introduced on new cars built at Queen's Road. A further cream band was provided along the foot of the dashes and side panels. The broad blue panels were thereby reduced in depth, whereas the car number, which had occurred twice on the blue side panels, was replaced by a single number in the centre of the new lower cream band, and for clarity the gilt numerals were edged in black[3]. The first car to be so treated was No. 20. The earlier cars 1-19 and all the Hills' cars 131-155 were dealt with in similar fashion when they became due for repainting.

As the programme of building progressed the older cars were withdrawn and their numbers taken by the new ones. The year 1931 brought the end of the numerous short upper deck cars, which were being withdrawn over a period of nine years. Nos. 248 and 250 were the last to go, in February. In addition the last of the ex L.C.C. "B" class, both the Sheffield and the ex Rotherham ones, were withdrawn.

The last of the shorter non-vestibuled open balcony cars was withdrawn in 1933 (excepting No. 289 which outlasted all other balcony cars, being scrapped on 10th August 1935), which exercise again had taken nine years. In 1934-35 the majority of the short vestibuled open balcony cars and the long vestibuled open balcony cars which were originally single deckers also disappeared[4], the earliest scrapping of these classes having started in 1921 and 1933 respectively. Although most of the short four-windowed fully enclosed cars were to remain in service for a few more years, a few of that type were also scrapped in 1933-34.

The replacement of the original Mountain and Gibson trucks under the "Preston" cars by Peckham P.22 trucks with an eight foot wheelbase has already been mentioned, as also has the similar but eight foot six inch wheelbase truck on which the 1918 car, No. 366, was mounted from new. This Peckham "Pendulum" type truck was used for all new cars built after 1918 except for the final thirty-six—see appendix A(1).

The trucks under the earlier cars had been a variety of Peckham Cantilever, Brill 21E, Brush and Milnes. By 1934, with two exceptions and excluding the Departmental cars, all the remaining cars built by 1915 were mounted on Brill trucks. The exceptions were the very long cars converted from single deck, by then mounted on Peckham "Pendulum" eight foot six inch wheelbase trucks and two cars of the series Nos. 296-355. No. 349 had an eight foot Peckham "Pendulum" truck and No. 355 a seven foot wheelbase Cravens truck.

From time to time refinements of detail and design were introduced on new cars being built at Queen's Road, and as far as practicable these improvements were in due course applied to the post 1912 Brush and Cravens cars.

New controllers and air brakes were fitted to Nos. 366-369 and to 376-450. Their single indicators at the car ends were replaced by double ones. These cars, as well as Nos. 36-60, also had their side indicators built into the ventilator panel above the centre side windows of the lower saloon.

After the Corporation and Brush-built cars of 1918-1922 had been in operation for ten years or more, the high seating capacity on the upper deck had been found to hamper the movement of the conductor, and cause passenger congestion. By December 1933 fifty-eight of these seventy-nine cars had their upper deck seating reduced from forty-eight to forty-seven by the substitution of a single seat instead of a double one on one side of the car, half way along the saloon; the seating on one car (No. 448) was reduced to forty and seven cars were equipped with thirty-seven upholstered seats each, leaving only thirteen cars (Nos. 402, 403, 413, 414,

[3] During the Second World War and possibly as early as 1942 the numbers on the side panels were altered to Gill Sans style.

[4] Whilst the last open balcony car disappeared from the Sheffield streets in 1935, cars of that type remained in service in Leeds during the war years and in Liverpool and Birmingham into 1949.

R. J. S. Wiseman.

Snowplough emerging from depot into yard at Tinsley, driven by depot employee on 14th April 1956.

Sheffield Transport Department.

The experimental Duralumin car photographed on Abbey Lane at Dalewood Road when new in 1931.

R. J. S. Wiseman.

From April 1932 single line working was adopted between Hillsborough and Middlewood whilst the 'To City' line was used as a siding for football cars during home matches at Sheffield Wednesday's ground. The scene was photographed on 20th February 1954.

I. R. Davidson.

Rotherham 'single-ended' car No. 5 at Exchange Street on 13th April 1947. The buildings in the right background are at the canal wharf and in the left background is the Park goods station.

417, 421-424, 427, 428, 449 and 450) with forty-eight seats, later also reduced to forty-seven.

In due course not only most of these cars but also many of the wooden seated cars of 1924-1927[5] had upholstered seats in replacement. Of the total class of 154 cars, only thirty-three retained wooden seats on both decks and a further eleven on the upper deck only.

The replacement seats were normally leather-covered longitudinal type in the lower saloon. On the upper deck they were standard transverse seats and bench type in the end bays, all in leather. The last two cars to be converted were Nos. 50 and 52 in July 1948.

By the end of the re-seating programme the following cars had been so treated:

Brush	36-60	Nos. 50 and 52
S.C.T.	366-369	All cars
Brush	376-450	All except No. 448. Nos. 402-411 and 415 lower deck only.
Cravens	451-500	All except nine cars, Nos. 481, 482, 484, 486-490 and 495. (It is not known whether No. 493, damaged in 1946, had been re-seated.)

No. 448 had its original upper deck wooden seats replaced by the type originally fitted to the Cravens cars, i.e. two on one side and one on the other. It seems probable that the seven Brush cars Nos. 441-444, 446, 449 and 450 received second-hand seats, possibly from another tramway undertaking.

The improved type end indicators without external access, which first appeared on new car No. 24 in 1929 and thereafter became standard, were fitted to many of the 1918-1927 cars. In addition, from 1939 bilateral driver's mirrors were fitted to all cars not already so equipped.

Around 1928 to 1930 the rebuilt Brush and S.C.T. cars Nos. 296-355 were provided with new controllers and the improved type side indicators. Earlier, the single end indicators fitted to these cars when they were rebuilt in the early 1920s had been replaced by double ones.

The building programme up to 1935 made necessary the following renumbering of existing cars:

1927	142 to 211 (Corrugation car)
1929	102 to 362 (Snowplough) 103 to 363 (Snowplough) 99 to 361 (Snowplough)
1930	73 to 364 (Snowplough) 77 to 365 (Snowplough)
1932	111 to 359 (Snowplough) 113 to 360 (Snowplough) 126 to 202 Open balcony (second renumbering)
1933	172 to 273 (Snowplough) 185 to 277 (Snowplough) 225 to 278 (Snowplough) 226 to 358 (Snowplough) 166 to 375 (Breakdown car) Open balcony cars Nos. 124, 127 and 156-165 to vacant numbers in the series 197-215
1935	211 to 371 (Corrugation car) (second renumbering) 212 to 372 (Corrugation car)
1935-6	Short enclosed cars between Nos. 214 and 243 to 281 upwards.

H. B. Priestley.
The last car to enter service in 1934 and the last in the old livery. At Middlewood terminus on 7th June 1938.

D. A. Thompson.
At College Square on the single track circuit in the centre of Rotherham on 6th August 1939. The car reflects the high maintenance standards of the period.

[5]Nos. 36-60 (Brush) and 451-500 (Cravens) which were built with forty seats on the upper deck.

Following the entry to service of No. 81 on 2nd April 1931 no more new cars appeared for over five months—the longest interlude during the 1928-1939 building programme. However, when No. 82 appeared on 11th September it was equipped with improved upper deck lighting, there being a lamp above each side window in the main saloon corresponding to the lighting arrangement in the lower saloon of previous standard cars. This increased the total of upper deck lights from eight to twelve. This improvement became standard and was applied in due course to pre-1928 cars but not the earlier standard ones.

By the end of 1931 numbering of new cars had reached 91, and in October of that year the experimental car No. 370 was placed in service. This car had a "Duralumin" (aluminium alloy) body of rigid construction. The car was generally similar in style to the post-1927 standard cars but there were several differences which included wider window posts and half-drop windows individually operated by the passenger (instead of wind-down), and lower powered motors of 40 h.p.

In 1932 numbering progressed to 121 and in 1933 new cars Nos. 122-130 and 156-170 went into service.

The total of thirty-one, Nos. 171-201, built at Queen's Road in 1934 was the highest number in any calendar year. These cars were the last in the old dark blue and cream livery.

On 9th July 1934 Rotherham's last internal tram service, to Canklow, ceased operation leaving only the joint route to Sheffield which had a terminal loop at each end: in Sheffield via Blonk Street, Exchange Street, Waingate and Lady's Bridge, and at Rotherham via Corporation Street, Frederick Street, Howard Street, College Square, College Street and High Street.

As Sheffield Corporation would not agree to Rotherham's request for the joint service to be operated by trolleybuses, Rotherham Corporation ordered six unique "single ended" double deck tramcars. The first went into service to Sheffield on the evening of 3rd October 1934. So successful were these new cars that five more were ordered in December, which incorporated some mechanical improvements. Passengers would wait for one of these cars in preference to travelling in the older Rotherham cars or even Sheffield standard cars which were working the route by this time! In general, for the joint service Sheffield seemed to use cars as nearly as possible equivalent in quality to those supplied by Rotherham.

In 1935 Rotherham Corporation constructed a reversing triangle at Temple Street, Templeborough to turn their new cars, when short working from Rotherham. They were fitted with rear controllers so that they could be driven in reverse with safety. In addition to running loops at Rotherham and Sheffield and the Templeborough triangle they could be

Bamforth & Co.

The first 1935 car, No. 202, in experimental pale blue and cream livery approaching along Fargate. This car was repainted in the normal new livery in May 1936.

turned at Tinsley depot by using the weighbridge line.

No. 202, the first new car to enter service in 1935, was in a new colour scheme of lighter blue on the panelling of both decks with bands of cream below the upper deck windows

H. B. Priestley.

No. 214 at College Square, Rotherham on 11th June 1935 only three weeks after entering service. Only the last thirty-four of this class of 210 cars received this livery when built.

and at the foot of the lower deck panelling. In addition there was a strip of cream below the lower deck windows; the window posts were also in cream on both decks and Gill Sans lettering and numerals were used for the first time. It appears that at this time the vertical type of hand-brake wheel was introduced, giving more space on the platforms. No. 203 was the first car to receive what became the standard livery of cream with three blue bands, two being top and bottom of the lower deck panels and the third below the upper deck windows, with simple horizontal red lining and gilt Gill Sans style lettering and numerals[6]. The blue was a lighter shade of royal blue than the navy blue used prior to 1935. All that remained of the old scheme was the coat of arms, and the monogram on the middle of the sides of the lower and upper decks respectively, together with the black fenders and red oxide coloured trucks and life guards. It was a handsome scheme which was standard for the remainder of the tramway era. No. 202 was repainted in this new standard livery in May 1936. In suitably modified form the new livery was adopted for the buses until the Sheffield undertaking came under the control of the larger local government authority in April 1974.

The style of this livery was not dissimilar to that adopted for the new Rotherham cars which preceded the new Sheffield livery by about three months except that the horizontal bands on the Rotherham cars were somewhat differently located and were in very dark blue.

Although power to close the Fitzalan Market had been obtained as early as 1901, the redevelopment of the site did not take place until 1930. When the market had gone, the City terminal point of the northern routes at the lower end of High Street continued to be known as Market Side.

By this time the question of control of traffic congestion was causing considerable concern to the authorities. For many years the City termini for cars to Woodseats, Millhouses and latterly Nether Edge had been in Fargate, the Woodseats terminus being opposite the end of Norfolk Row, and those for the other routes about two tramcar lengths respectively in the rear. Finally, behind all those was a stop for cars to Ecclesall, Nether Green and Fulwood via Hunters Bar.

The Chief Constable had been in consultation with the Watch Committee and at the meeting of that Committee on 20th March 1930 a motion was put and adopted. The two principal matters involved were the abolition of all tram stopping stations in Fargate and their removal to Pinstone Street, and the making of Pinstone Street into a northbound one-way street for all traffic except trams, which could travel in both directions. Additional points dealt with the siting of pedestrian refuges but only one was relevant to tramway passengers; this was for an island opposite the Town Hall adjacent to the "to City" track.

These arrangements came into force on 5th June 1930, the three City termini being located outside St. Paul's Church in the same order as had applied in Fargate. The Ecclesall, Nether Green and Fulwood via Hunters Bar cars continued to enjoy their previous facility of a stop outside the main door of the Town Hall.

A large 'No Entry' board was placed at the approach to Pinstone Street in the front of the Town Hall and directing arrows were painted on the carriageways.

On the former site of Queen Victoria's statue, a ten feet high flashing red beacon was erected. This scheme required the services of two point duty policemen, one near the head of Fargate and the other at the bottom of Barkers Pool.

At a meeting of the Tramways Committee on 16th December 1930 it was stated that the Chief Constable had reported on the scheme adopted six months earlier for a trial period, and had recommended its continuation subject to the construction of an island in Fargate opposite the Yorkshire Penny Bank (i.e. the junction with Surrey Street). The Committee accepted the recommendation but with the proviso that the island should be sited opposite the end of Norfolk Row and should be used for alighting tram passengers only. They also decided that at such time as this island came into use, the tram stop at Charles Street on the "from City" line should be abolished. Both these alterations became operative on 18th January 1931. Still with tram passengers in mind, the Highways Committee had on 16th January recommended the erection of a temporary island adjacent to the down track in Fargate at "Coles' Corner" and had specified that it should be only fifteen feet long. On 17th July the Highways Committee recommended that the "Coles' Corner" island should be made permanent and "slightly longer".

[6] During the war period (1939-1945) smaller end numerals came into use and became standard, and with the exception of the wartime grey cars and the 1952 green ones, the gilt colouring was replaced by blue.

The system of traffic control at the Town Hall junctions was replaced on 17th May 1931 by a police manned kiosk with two aspect colour lights with 'stop' semaphore arm signals and bells. The new arrangement was the patent of the Brighton Lighting and Electrical Co. Ltd. who provided similar equipment for a five way junction at Preston Circus, Brighton. The signals were operated between the hours of six am and eleven pm.

On the afternoon of 11th September 1933 a southbound kerbside loading siding became operative in Pinstone Street with three loading docks for the following services: (1) Meadowhead, Woodseats and Abbey Lane, (2) Millhouses, Beauchief and Abbey Lane, and (3) Nether Edge. This enabled Ecclesall and Fulwood via Hunters Bar services to pass without delay, having made their normal stop outside the Town Hall. At 11 pm that night use of the police operated traffic signals was discontinued and from 6 am on the following day Pinstone Street ceased to be one-way, a strange turn of events which brought road traffic into conflict with tramcars using the new siding, a situation which remained until the last day of tramway operation and at many times required direction by a tramway employee. A larger traffic island replaced the kiosk site and later this was superseded by a rock garden island.

The last series of route extensions occurred in 1934 and 1935. On 7th September 1934 the Handsworth route extension from Finchwell Road to Orgreave Lane was opened. This was followed on 18th November by Firth Park (North Quadrant) to Sheffield Lane Top. The Intake route extension from Woodhouse Road to Hollinsend Road opened on 8th February 1935, followed by the further extension to Birley Vale on 29th December. This was the last tramway extension in Sheffield.

All these final extensions were constructed in the carriageways. Sheffield's total of about three route miles of reserved track, built in 1927 and 1928 was short by comparison with twenty-eight miles at Liverpool and twelve miles at Leeds.

New car construction had reached No. 230 by the end of 1935.

Around this period two routes were closed and replaced by buses as follows: 24th March 1934—Nether Edge; 22nd August 1936—City (Leopold Street) to Fulwood via Broomhill.

These closures involved the withdrawal of trams from the bottom of The Moor to Nether Edge and along Fulwood Road from Crookes Junction to Nether Green. The Handsworth cars which had previously run to Nether Edge were re-routed to Fulwood via Broomhill for the two years and five months until the latter route closed. Thereafter they terminated in the City, travelling inward via Church Street to Leopold Street and returning via Fargate.

Sheffield Lane Top central terminal siding with passenger shelter at end. *A. D. Packer.*

David Robins Collection.

Cravens car at Market Side before the demolition of the Fitzalan Market around 1930.

H. B. Priestley.

The Pinstone Street loading siding opened in September 1933, photographed on 1st May 1955.

In Pinstone Street loading siding on 30th April 1957. The shelter survived until it was dismantled on 14th July 1985. **Mrs. A. R. Wiseman.**

At Handsworth terminus (Orgreave Lane) on 1st April 1938. The photographer's Sunbeam motor cycle is in the foreground. **H. B. Priestley.**

Considerations which probably influenced these closures were the need for track relaying, poor patronage and poor prospects of improvement because of low density housing, as well as the narrowness of the streets used. They did not indicate any policy of general or further replacement.

A novel feature on destination blinds disappeared with the Nether Edge closure. The first letter of each of the two words of the place name was red in colour, the rest of the indication being the normal white capitals on black background. It was said that the red letters were to emphasise the difference between Nether Edge and Nether Green.

On 17th October 1933 the City Council authorised the construction of an extension of the lines at Ecclesall to form an improved terminal siding located on a reservation to the east side of the top of Millhouses Lane. On 20th March 1934 the Council agreed to the purchase for £2,000 of freehold land and buildings situated at the junction of Ecclesall Road South, Woodholm Road and Millhouses Lane for this improved terminus. The Annual Report for the year ended 31st March 1936 stated that the works of track improvement and increased loading facilities had been completed. The improved terminus was required primarily for the safety of students attending the new secondary school at High Storrs, which had been opened in September 1933. A few years later the surplus land not required for the terminal siding was used for the erection of an Air Raid Precautions Decontamination Centre.

A proposed extension to serve Shiregreen Estate was authorised in 1935. Due to the narrowness of the estate roads the intended construction was to have been single line with six passing loops except for the section between Sheffield Lane Top along Barnsley Road to Hartley Brook Road which would have been double. The route would have been thence along Nether Shire Lane and Sicey Avenue to Firth Park, to form a circular route from the City back to the City. The extension was to have been two miles and 5.4 chains in length of which one mile two furlongs 0.4 chains would have been single line. The work was never undertaken and it was decided that Shiregreen Estate should be served by buses.

In the mid 1930s, Chesterfield Road was widened opposite Cobnar Road (Woodseats) at the point where the stream from Graves Park passes under the road. The scheme involved extended culverting of the stream and the tram tracks were slewed to the west and new part of the road, so easing the curve and straightening the approaches between Holmhurst Road and Bromwich Road.

During the 1930s a number of substantial passenger shelters were erected at terminal and other points such as Millhouses, Beauchief, Hutcliffe Wood Road and Middlewood. The shelter at Millhouses was brick built and

Intake terminus at Birley Vale looking away from the City on 14th August 1955. *A. D. Packer.*

was larger than the one which previously occupied the site.

By resolution of the City Council on 17th April 1934 the name of the undertaking was changed again, from Sheffield Corporation Tramways and Motors to Sheffield Transport Department and this title lasted beyond the existence of the tramways and until the local government reorganisation of 1974.

The General Manager, Arthur R. Fearnley, retired in 1936 after thirty-two years service, and so the Department and the Corporation lost a highly respected and experienced officer. Much of the excellence and efficiency of the tramway system resulted from his leadership. He was succeeded by Harris Watson Esq. Mr. Fearnley died at the age of seventy-one on 28th March 1943 at North Mimms, Hertfordshire.

A further important step in tramcar design materialised in 1936. The first twelve cars to enter service in that year, Nos. 231-242, were a modernised form of the 1928-1935 standard cars, referred to throughout this work as the improved standard cars. The main features were the individually opening five half-drop side windows on each side of the upper deck operated by spring clips which controlled pawls engaging ratchet bars, along with two similar windows (second and fourth) on each side of the lower saloon. (These windows are referred to again later.) All the upper deck windows were canted inwards and the roof was domed in shape. It was from this latter feature that this class of car was known in Sheffield as the Domed Roof class. On the lower deck the curved dashes were carried round practically to the full width of the body, giving more protection to the platforms, and the ventilation windows above the main saloon side windows were panelled over and replaced by air deflecting ventilators. The saloon destination indicators were within this panelling, over the centre window, an aperture allowing the crew a reverse sight of the screen. Adjustment of the opening windows by passengers frequently resulted in difficulty. The windows were heavy and the spring clips could not always be easily reached from a sitting position. This often resulted in one side of the window being lowered to a greater degree than the other and this distortion spoiled the appearance of the cars. In an effort to obviate this, wind-down handles were provided in later car building from about No. 251. Half-drop windows were retained and the winding mechanism was located at the half pane position. After limited use, body movements in these cars in motion caused the gears in the window mechanism to disengage. In consequence cars Nos. 274-303 were built with a third type of opening window but only on

H. B. Priestley.

Cravens cars Nos. 465 and 486 in a holiday scene at Millhouses on Whit Tuesday 30th May 1939. The bus in old livery is returning from Bakewell. In the centre background is Millhouses Station booking office, Laycock's chimney and Woodside Brickworks on the Woodseats route beyond. To the left is the Turner control box behind the railings (see page 169).

H. B. Priestley.

Standard cars Nos. 203 and 247 in the Ecclesall siding reservation, on 28th April 1940.

H. B. Priestley.

Improved Standard car in Infirmary Road on the 'To City' line on 7th June 1938.

D. A. Thompson.

Fitzalan Square on 6th August 1939. The C & A building behind No. 297 was destroyed on 12th December 1940, as was car No. 274 in the Wicker on the same night.

J. H. Meredith.

The car "reprieved" late in 1939 passing Victoria Station approach on 23rd August 1953.

the upper deck. This was a full-pane opening type, the winding mechanism being in the car frame between the seats. With seven seats and five windows each side it was necessary to locate the winding mechanisms off-centre of some windows. To facilitate easy operation, because of the weight of the whole window the handles for winding had to be larger than for the half-drop panes. It is believed that the opening windows in the lower saloon reverted to the clip and ratchet type of control. Wherever practicable all window corners were curved and the heads of the platform entrances were similarly treated. The 1935 colour scheme remained unchanged.

A final six cars of the earlier pattern numbered 243-248 followed, presumably to use up materials in stock. They were the last of the basic standard cars and brought the total, including the experimental 'Duralumin' car No. 370, to 212 cars.

Construction of the new type was resumed with No. 249 and progressed to No. 257 by the end of the year; to 279 by the end of 1937; to 299 during 1938 and finally to 303 in March 1939, making a total of sixty-seven of these fine cars. No further construction of new cars was contemplated for a few years.

In 1937 this stage of the building programme necessitated further renumbering, when the following cars were affected:

Preston cars Nos. 258-272 became 336-350 respectively
Snowploughs Nos. 273-278 became 352-357 respectively
Stores cars Nos. 279 and 280 became 373 and 374 respectively.

This renumbering brought the whole fleet of fourteen snowploughs within the consecutive numbering range of 352-365 and the other works cars 371-375, a process which had commenced in 1929.

By the end of 1938 all the sixty Brush and S.C.T. cars, Nos. 296-355 in the original numbering scheme, had been scrapped but there still remained in service five older rebuilt Brush and S.C.T. cars of similar type. They were as follows:

S.C.T. No. 290 renumbered 331 in March 1938
Brush No. 236 renumbered 332 in March 1938
Brush No. 237 renumbered 333 in March 1938
Brush No. 239 renumbered 334 in March 1938
Brush No. 243 renumbered 335 in March 1938

These cars were scrapped in 1939, No. 335 being the last to go on 27th December, almost four months after the start of the War. In addition, by this time four of the "Preston" cars had been withdrawn, and scrapped on the following dates:

No. 337 on 24th December 1938
No. 341 on 30th January 1939
No. 340 on 3rd June 1939
No. 338 on 30th June 1939.

Cravens car on Abbey Lane reservation on 6th August 1939 approaching Folds Lane, the stopping place for Beauchief Abbey. *D. A. Thompson.*

No. 339 had been withdrawn from service in April 1939 and by the outbreak of war some fittings had been removed from it. The remainder of the class was also listed for withdrawal, but the war brought about their reprieve and No. 339 was restored to service in December 1939.

The position at 3rd September 1939, almost forty years to the day since the first electric cars commenced service in Sheffield, was that there were 443 passenger cars comprising:

154 built between 1918 and 1926
206 built between 1927 and 1935
73 built between 1936 and 1939
10 built in 1907 and rebuilt between 1925 and 1927.

In addition there was No. 339 in store.

It follows that all the other pre-1918 cars as well as the second- and third-hand ex L.C.C. cars had been removed from passenger service, a total of 358 cars. Of these, forty-six were sold. Eighteen were converted to works cars and the remainder were scrapped.

During the period of twenty-one years from 1918 the whole fleet had been totally replaced with the exception of the remaining "Preston" cars, and 433 cars had been placed in service; one hundred were built by Brush at Loughborough, fifty-one by Cravens at Darnall, twenty-five by Hills at South Shields and 257 by the Corporation at Queen's Road Works.

D. A. Thompson.
Cravens car No. 458 on Prince of Wales Road service at Fitzalan Square on Sunday 6th August 1939. The buildings in the centre and left background were destroyed in the air raid on 12th December 1940.

Chapter 10

Interrupted Progress 1939 to 1945

When war broke out again in 1939 tramcar building had already ceased for the time being, and any further route developments had to be deferred as in 1914. The extension of the Meadowhead route to Dronfield planned in 1938-9 was placed in abeyance and never materialised.

The extension of the Wadsley Bridge route from its terminus beyond Southey Green Road to the City boundary just beyond Deerlands Avenue, a distance of about 1200 yards, had been authorised in 1937 and was to have been carried out when Halifax Road was widened. Plans for this widening were approved in 1944, but the war and its aftermath prevented the construction of this extension which was to have been on a central reservation. Like the Dronfield proposals, it was never done.

In war conditions it was no longer practicable to achieve any material benefit from the postal car services—they were withdrawn and were never reinstated.

Blackout regulations made necessary the removal of lens-shaped headlamp glasses and their replacement by masks. In 1940 a new type of mask was fitted which would show either a white or red aspect. After the war glasses were reinstated, but many of the original ones were no longer available and substitutes had to be provided. These were flat and of poorer appearance.

At the outbreak of war the black fenders of the cars were painted white and, as an aid to pedestrians in unlit streets, three white bands were painted round all tramway standards. Some of the interior lights of the cars were removed and the remainder were fitted with very low power bulbs and were also heavily shaded. Because of the fear of enemy invasion the word "Sheffield" on the sides of the cars was painted out, and because of the threat of air raids, the cream roofs of the Improved Standard cars were painted in a very dark shade of grey during the early months of 1940.

In addition anti-flash plates were installed on overhead frogs to conceal from enemy aircraft the light of arcing.

In the case of the older cars with rocker panels, a start was made during the war on replacing the large letters and numerals on the rocker panels with the smaller Gill Sans type, a process which was completed after the war.

In 1940 it became normal wartime practice to park some tramcars overnight outside the depots to minimise the risk of damage from air raids in the event of the depots being hit. One such parking site was Shoreham Street near Bramall Lane Football Ground.

A new shelter was erected in the autumn of 1939 at the top of Angel Street for use by Ecclesall and Fulwood passengers. During the war period a number of loading islands and shelters were constructed, and in 1940 the stopping place in Haymarket for northbound cars was moved to Waingate where the road was wider, and a loading island was provided. Between mid-July and 12th October 1941, because of heavy traffic in Haymarket, Waingate and Lady's Bridge, cars to Tinsley were rerouted at rush hour periods via Commercial Street, Sheaf Street and Blonk Street, making their loading stop in Commercial Street instead of Market Side. See chapter sixteen.

To facilitate even traffic flow and easier collection of fares, two stops for setting down only were prescribed in High Street. Around the same time steps were taken to secure economy of operation and speedier service by the elimination of some stops, as had happened in 1918 when fifty-nine request stops were cancelled, many of which were never restored.

H. B. Priestley.
At Wadsley Bridge terminus near Southey Green Road on 30th March 1958.

H. B. Priestley.
Second World War headlamp mask and white-painted fender on car leaving Pickmere Road, Crookes on 1st June 1940.

The old Heeley horse tram depot, which like Nether Edge had been used as a motor garage, was taken over by the Fire Service as an auxiliary station with number 3A 2Y.

The most significant event in tramway affairs of the whole war period took place late in 1940. Despite its war industries, Sheffield had remained immune from the air attacks which had struck other places in England following the withdrawal of the British Army from Dunkirk in the spring of that year.

On 14th November 1940 the great raid on Coventry took place, immobilising that city's remaining tram routes, and the system was not reinstated. At the next full moon on Thursday 12th December Sheffield was the target of the German bombers but even then it was not industry which suffered to a great extent but the shopping streets in the centre of the City. The raid commenced just before seven o'clock in the evening and lasted for over nine hours. In that time enormous damage was done, particularly in High Street, Angel Street and The Moor.

The first raid brought the whole tramway system to a standstill and the City centre was isolated. The track was torn up in twenty-two places; the worst damage occurred in The Wicker just north of Blonk Street, in Abbeydale Road at Gatefield Road and in Nursery Street where there were large craters in the carriageways. The overhead wires were broken in thirty places. Seven poles were destroyed on The Moor, and three more at Ecclesall Road junction. Three were destroyed in Angel Street, as were others in The Wicker and Blonk Street. Although enormous damage was sustained by buildings in High Street and The Moor surprisingly little damage was done to track in these streets where a number of tramcars were severely damaged or destroyed by fire.

The roof at Queen's Road Works was damaged as well as the roofs at Bramall Lane and Townhead Street bus garages.

H. B. Priestley.

At Beauchief on 1st April 1938; this car was destroyed in the air raid on 12th December 1940. The studded line marked the limit of overhang of cars approaching round the sharp curve from Abbey Lane.

John Walsh's store in High Street was burnt out and Cockaynes in Angel Street was destroyed along with many other shops and buildings.

Another raid took place on 15th December (three days later) but it was of lesser intensity. Thereafter Sheffield remained practically free from air attack for the rest of the war.

Censorship severely restricted the dissemination of news of war damage. However, on New Year's Day 1941, less than three weeks after the air raids, the local press published a photograph of burning cars in High Street[1] and not long afterwards a national newspaper published one of car No. 274 destroyed in The Wicker. Early reports from the

[1]See "Raiders over Sheffield" by Walton and Lamb.

Department that sixteen trams had been destroyed, eleven by fire and five by other means, were revised to fourteen as two of the latter were found to be capable of restoration. No. 16 received a new upper deck and No. 228 a new end platform and canopy.

In order to give relief to the consequent rolling stock shortage and provide temporary service where the tramways could not be quickly restored, 120 buses were borrowed from Bradford, Doncaster, Halifax, Huddersfield, Hull, Leeds, Newcastle, Todmorden and West Hartlepool. By the end of the severe snow in January 1941 all had been returned.

The work of clearance after the first raid commenced on Friday 13th December but work was delayed by the discovery of unexploded bombs in Queen's Road, and the detonation of one of them caused the death of a workman. The first streets to be cleared were Snig Hill and West Bar, Ecclesall Road and on the Abbey Lane reservation.

On the weekend of 14th and 15th December trams were operating again between Norfolk Bridge and Tinsley, Templeborough, Rotherham, Handsworth and Prince of Wales Road, and the overhead wires were restored for the route to Sheffield Lane Top via Newhall Road and Upwell Street, but the second raid on Sunday night, 15th December, blocked the lines from Norfolk Bridge and the services from there had to be temporarily withdrawn.

On Monday 16th December services commenced from Hoyle Street to Malin Bridge, Middlewood and Wadsley Bridge, but the latter had to be suspended until the 20th because of the discovery of an unexploded bomb.

The Intake route returned to use on Thursday 19th, and Walkley and Crookes on 20th December.

The overhead equipment was restored in The Wicker on

No. 201 wrecked at West Bar in the air raid of 12th December 1940. Beyond is damaged car No. 228.

followed by The Wicker. Crossovers and trolley reversers were installed where necessary, as near to the centre of the City as possible, in order to provide services to and from the suburbs until through working could be resumed.

Within a week all damaged cars had been moved to Queen's Road Works, but this task was interrupted by the unexploded bombs in Queen's Road mentioned above. Cars temporarily out of service were parked in Commercial Street, Pinstone Street (twenty-four cars), Crookes, Monday 23rd and on that day the Brightside via Savile Street service was resumed along with Firth Park via Pitsmoor.

On Christmas Day services to Ecclesall and Fulwood commencing at Ecclesall Road junction (where a trolley reverser was installed for the purpose—a crossover already existed) were restored, and following overhead restoration on The Moor and completion of repairs in the centre of the City on 29th, these services were working through to Snig

Hill from Monday 30th December. On that day working to Meadowhead was also resumed.

Woodseats via Queen's Road became operational again on Wednesday, 1st January 1941.

Trams returned to Abbeydale Road on 4th January, buses having used it from the 2nd, after an interruption of three weeks.

Three weeks after the second raid there remained closed only Shoreham Street, because of a crater, (reopened on 30th January) and the Neepsend route, where there were three craters (closed until mid February 1941).

The Regional Transport Commissioner complimented the General Manager on the efficient and expeditious restoration of services[2].

Particulars of the fourteen wrecked tramcars are shown in the table below. The loss of these cars, and for a while the larger number of cars out of service for essential repairs, led to serious problems at rush hour periods, especially as wartime conditions brought about increased passenger journeys. Compared with 1939, over 532,000 more journeys were made in the first quarter of 1940. A consequence of this situation was that a number of cars received temporary repairs and returned to service in a variety of strange guises. This state of affairs was not allowed to continue any longer than was necessary and, as soon as circumstances permitted, the damaged cars were totally restored.

There remained a pressing demand for more tramcars but new ones could not be purchased. The Corporation was, however, able to build replacements for the fourteen cars lost in December 1940. With minor modifications they were of the Improved Standard pattern of 1936-1939. They were mounted as far as possible on reconditioned trucks recovered from the destroyed cars.

Construction of these cars continued slowly during the remaining four years of the war. The vacant numbers were generally filled in rotation. Nos. 83, 85, 112 and 129 appeared in normal livery but the rest of these cars were finished in grey with horizontal red lining. As a wartime livery it was simple but pleasing.

Particulars of these cars were as follows:

Car Number	Type	Built By	Year	Replacement Entered Service
83	Standard 1928-35	S.C.T.	1931	7th November 1941
85	Standard 1928-35	S.C.T.	1931	12th November 1941
100	Standard 1928-35	S.C.T.	1932	29th April 1942
112	Standard 1928-35	S.C.T.	1932	29th April 1942
119	Standard 1928-35	S.C.T.	1932	24th April 1942
129	Standard 1928-35	S.C.T.	1933	21st July 1942
133	Standard 1928-35	Hills	1929	14th December 1942
192	Standard 1928-35	S.C.T.	1934	17th November 1942
201	Standard 1928-35	S.C.T.	1934	12th January 1943
227	Standard 1928-35	S.C.T.	1935	21st December 1942
261	Improved Standard 1936-39	S.C.T.	1937	31st March 1943
274	Improved Standard 1936-39	S.C.T.	1937	22nd November 1943
430	1919-1927	Brush	1920	3rd July 1944
483	1919-1927	Cravens	1926	17th November 1944

Apart from these replacements, the increased demand for additional cars had to be met by the purchase of second-hand ones as had been done in the previous war. In the latter part of 1941 fourteen cars were purchased from Newcastle. They were open platform top covered cars of Newcastle's Class A and they received the Sheffield numbers 311-324 as follows:

Newcastle 122 became Sheffield 311
Newcastle 124 became Sheffield 312
Newcastle 113 became Sheffield 313
Newcastle 129 became Sheffield 314
Newcastle 118 became Sheffield 315
Newcastle 117 became Sheffield 316
Newcastle 114 became Sheffield 317
Newcastle 116 became Sheffield 318
Newcastle 112 became Sheffield 319
Newcastle 119 became Sheffield 320
Newcastle 125 became Sheffield 321
Newcastle 126 became Sheffield 322
Newcastle 123 became Sheffield 323
Newcastle 128 became Sheffield 324.

In Sheffield they were converted to fully enclosed cars and six of them were re-motored. They were repainted in standard cream and blue but to the style of the pre-1928 Sheffield cars, apart from the use of the newer shade of blue and the omission of the old decorative lining out. End destination indicators were fitted only to Nos. 312, 323 and 324. The others displayed the Departmental monogram at the end indicator position with the exception of No. 319 which had the monogram in the usual place on the upper deck side panelling, and consequently had plain ends.

At the time these cars were inspected in Newcastle in August 1941 other possible second-hand cars were viewed at Hampstead Depot in London. These were offered by the London Passenger Transport Board and are believed to have been ex East and West Ham Class E1 cars built in 1929-31 with enclosed upper decks and open platforms. They had an overall length of thirty-three feet ten inches and were mounted on maximum traction bogies with thirty-one inch diameter driving and twenty-one and three quarter inch diameter pony wheels. They were reported to be in good condition and although they were rejected by reason of having bogies, open platforms and low powered fifty h.p. BTH motors, it appears that they would have been a much

[2]See "Raiders over Sheffield" by Walton and Lamb.

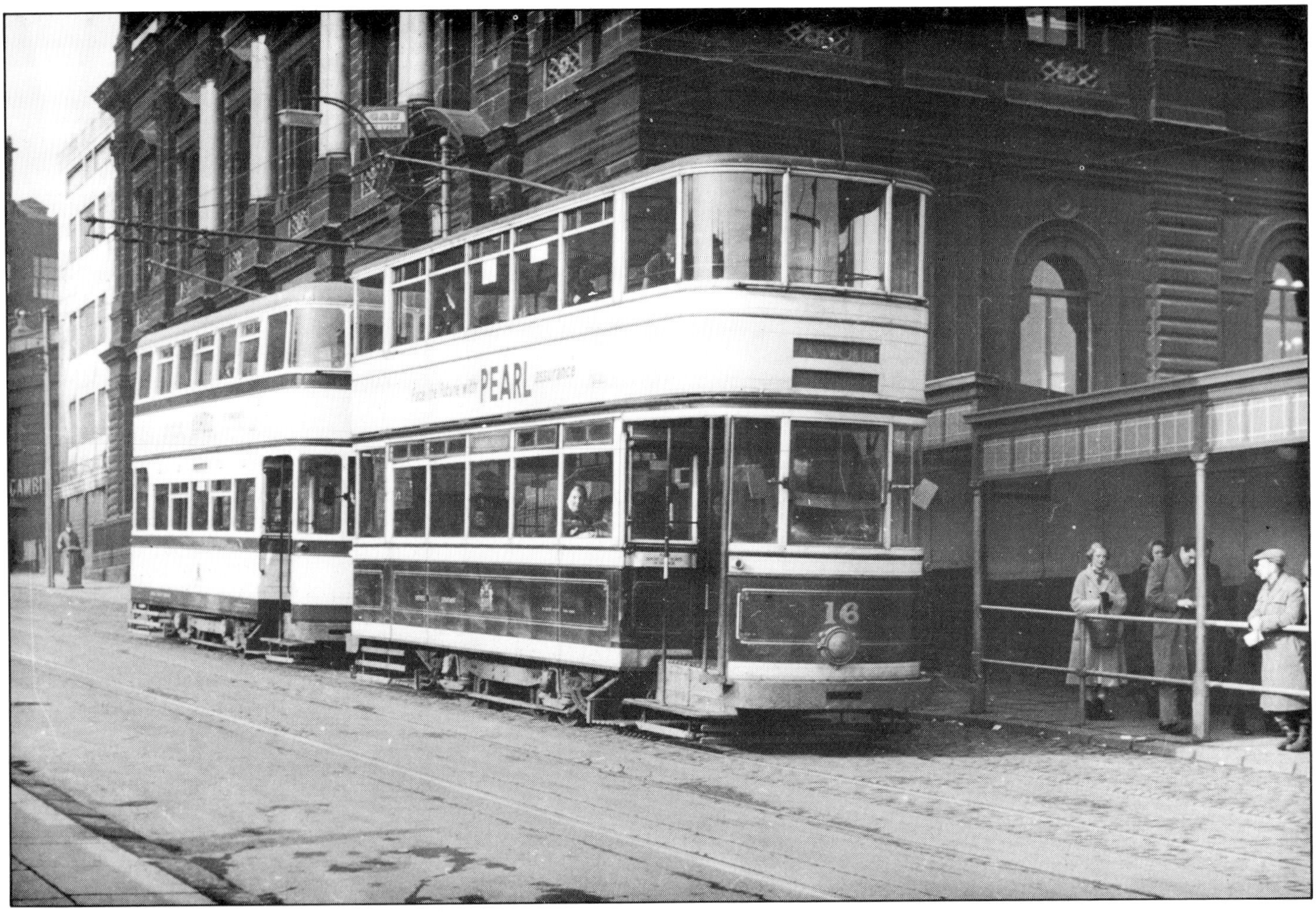

R. J. S. Wiseman.
In Commercial Street on 25th February 1956, with unusual upper deck sliding ventilator windows installed following December 1940 war damage.

better purchase for the rush hour purposes on the more evenly graded routes for which they were required than the Newcastle cars which even after rebuilding were miserable little vehicles.

The introduction of the Newcastle cars and the two replacements built at Queen's Road, Nos. 83 and 85, brought the passenger tramcar fleet to 446 at the end of 1941.

On 12th October 1941 some route rearrangements were made involving the following services:

Woodseats to Crookes via Queen's Road or Shoreham Street
City (Leopold Street) to Handsworth
City (Fitzalan Square) to Wadsley Bridge

The Woodseats cars were switched to Wadsley Bridge, travelling via Pond Street, Flat Street and Fitzalan Square instead of Sheaf Street and Commercial Street to Crookes. The Crookes service was linked with Handsworth via Commercial Street, Sheaf Street and Blonk Street. These changes had the effect of bringing the Pond Street line into regular use whereas previously it had no service.

Similarly, the short section in Sheaf Street from Broad Street junction to Exchange Street junction returned to use, both tracks having previously been used only for service cars—between January 1900 and February 1903 by the Intake service, between January and March 1904 by the "City Circular" service and between July and October 1941 by the Tinsley cars on the through route from Millhouses. An evening rush hour service, southbound, had used and continued to use the southbound track.

There was still a shortage of tramcars, so towards the end of 1942 the Corporation decided to buy ten cars from Bradford Corporation for rush hour use. They were vestibuled top covered open balcony four wheelers, priced at £175 each. Upon arrival in Sheffield their trucks had to be altered from Bradford's four foot gauge to Sheffield's four foot eight and a half inch, and all of them were converted into fully enclosed cars, with livery of plain wartime grey, white window pillars and a minimum of lining[3]. These cars were fitted with straight glass in the upper deck vestibules to match the existing Bradford platform vestibules. They belonged to a class of forty-six built by the English Electric Company of Preston between 1919 and 1921. Seating was transverse with a capacity of forty-three on the upper deck and nineteen on the lower. The original wooden seats had been replaced by upholstered ones except on the open balconies. In Sheffield the upper deck capacity was reduced to forty by the removal of the trap doors over the staircases.

[3]Along with the war damage replacement cars painted grey and the ex Bradford cars, several standard cars were repainted grey during the war; they included Nos. 26, 74, 96, 141 and 159 which received new 1935 livery after the war.

A. D. Packer.
War damage replacement car approaching Elm Tree at the head of the Prince of Wales Road reservation on 17th March 1956.

The trucks were U.E.C. 21E wide-wing type with seven foot wheelbase and mechanical track brakes, and by this time they were said to have Dick Kerr 31D motors of fifty h.p. each. The controllers were Dick Kerr DB1 form K4.

Abandonment of tramways in Bradford commenced in 1930 and proceeded at the rate of one route per year. The cars purchased by Sheffield had been offered for sale on the closure of the Stanningley route in October 1942. The first of them to arrive in Sheffield was No. 214 on 21st November 1942, having been transported by the L.M.S. Railway.

Although in Bradford they had worked successfully on steeper hills, in Sheffield they were not permitted to work on the Intake-Walkley route because they had no air-brakes. These cars, and even more so the Newcastle ones, were generally regarded in Sheffield as inferior to the Sheffield Brush cars of 1914 whose numbers they took. They were not popular with drivers, and conductors did not like their narrow gangways.

The braking equipment on the already vestibuled Bradford cars had not required the Sheffield type "banjo-glass". When converting the Newcastle cars, the platform vestibules were built out (in a rather less pronounced fashion than on the snowploughs being vestibuled at the time), to avoid the need for "banjo-glasses".

In Sheffield the ten Bradford cars became Nos. 325 to 334 as follows:

Bradford 214 became Sheffield 325
Bradford 243 became Sheffield 326
Bradford 242 became Sheffield 327
Bradford 216 became Sheffield 328
Bradford 237 became Sheffield 329
Bradford 251 became Sheffield 330
Bradford 257 became Sheffield 331
Bradford 215 became Sheffield 332
Bradford 219 became Sheffield 333
Bradford 217 became Sheffield 334.

With the acquisition of these cars and the completion of the war damage replacements, by about the end of 1944 the tramcar fleet reached its maximum strength of 468 passenger cars, fourteen snowploughs and five other works cars of which one, No. 372, was disused.

Before leaving the subject of the sale or purchase of second-hand cars, wartime rolling stock developments at Rotherham may be noted. After the "single ended" cars had gone into service in 1934 and 1935 all the older Rotherham cars had been withdrawn and scrapped excepting one which was retained for rush hour short workings to Ickles (Bessemer Bridge) or Templeborough, and for snow clearance. This car was a Rotherham rebuild numbered 12, with E.M.B. air-brakes, moquette upholstered seating for twenty in the six side window saloon and for thirty-four on the upper deck, but with wooden seats on the open balconies. It had a domed roof of Dick Kerr type. This car was unpopular with drivers who had become accustomed to the vestibules and heaters of the "single ended" cars. In consequence, in 1939 vestibuled platforms were fitted and, to allow for the rotation of the hand brake handle, two second-hand Sheffield "banjo" glasses were used, otherwise the corner windows were flat, in contrast to Sheffield's curved ones.

The pressing demand for additional cars during the war meant that No. 12 had to return to regular service, so in 1942 it was converted into a fully enclosed car by the provision of seven flat windows round each end of the upper deck, with the end indicators fitted in a position just above the upper deck floor level. The car was repainted on comparable lines to the "single ended" ones.

In 1943, to relieve the rolling stock shortage, Rotherham Corporation borrowed a double deck car from Leeds City Transport. It was one of a class of twelve built in 1908 by Leeds City Tramways, originally numbered 115-126. These cars had top covered extended canopy normal staircase bodies with platform vestibules which did not extend around the staircase side. At a later date the vestibules were continued behind the staircases and the dash side panels were filled in, and side indicator screens were fitted at the saloon ventilator position above the side windows. The cars were mounted on Brill 21E trucks with Dick Kerr 9A type motors and DB 1K controllers (later replaced by K3's).

Little use was made of them from the early 1930s and finally, with the exception of the car which went to Rotherham and two which had been rebuilt, they were all scrapped in 1945. When their numbers were required for the Leeds pivotal cars in 1926 they received the suffix letter "A"; accordingly it was No. 125A which went to Rotherham and became No. 14. Before going into service there, this car was fitted with top deck vestibules, with windows which matched those of the Leeds vestibules, and it was repainted in a livery similar to that of Rotherham No. 12. It was an ugly tramcar.

Its duties comprised peak hour specials to Ickles and Templeborough and it also made an occasional visit to Sheffield. At this period, therefore, tramcars which had originated from five different undertakings could be seen on the Sheffield-Rotherham route (i.e. Sheffield, Rotherham, Newcastle, Bradford and Leeds).

A. D. Packer.

One of the fourteen war damage replacement cars descending Crookes Road at Roslin Road on 21st April 1957.

Returning to Sheffield, in addition to the wartime programme of work at Queen's Road comprising war damage replacement and adaptation of the Newcastle and Bradford cars, eight of the fourteen snowploughs were fitted with vestibuled platforms as follows:

August 1940	No. 354
September 1940	Nos. 361 and 365
October 1940	No. 352
May 1942	No. 359
October 1942	No. 357
October 1943	No. 360
January 1944	No. 364.

In October 1943 Mr. R. C. Moore was appointed Deputy General Manager of the Transport Department. He was born in Sheffield in 1896 and educated at Ackworth School near Pontefract. In 1914 he obtained employment with Sheffield Corporation Tramways where he remained until taking up an appointment at Stockton-on-Tees in 1929. In 1932 he became Traffic Superintendent to Hull Corporation and in 1935 he was appointed to the same post with Liverpool Corporation Passenger Transport Department. Shortly before his return to Sheffield he had also been acting as Deputy General Manager at Liverpool. Upon the retirement of Mr. Harris Watson in 1945 Mr. Moore was appointed General Manager at Sheffield and remained so until his own retirement.

During the later years of the war, people were urged to spend holidays at home and advertisements appeared in the local press entitled "Use the Trams" and stating that bus travel would be difficult. Before August Bank Holiday 1942, a list of eight tram rides and rambles was advertised, suggesting travelling out by one route, walking across country and returning by another tram route. In 1943 complaints were received by the Transport Department concerning overcrowding on cars from Fulwood on Sunday evenings and the Ramblers Association asked for more cars to provide adequately for this officially encouraged traffic. This situation would not have arisen had the Corporation not in 1936 replaced the trams via Broomhill by fifty-six seater buses on a ten minute interval service which could not be augmented due to the national emergency.

Although during the war there were serious shortages of many commodities and particularly of steel, the Corporation managed to maintain its tramway track in satisfactory order, but never again attained the high standards of the inter-war years.

In addition to ordinary track relaying, contracts were entered into for the supply of replacement trackwork for the following important junctions:

Fitzalan Square[4]

[4]This junction required relaying every six years.

Wicker Arches[5]
High Street–Fargate–Church Street[6]
Fargate–Leopold Street
Brightside Lane–Upwell Street
City Road–Prince of Wales Road (Elm Tree)
Holme Lane (Hillsborough)
Sheaf Street–Pond Street
Attercliffe Road–Staniforth Road[7]
Blonk Street–Exchange Street
Abbeydale Road South (Millhouses loop)
Fitzalan Square (special crossover)
High Street–Angel Street
Savile Street–Attercliffe Road (Twelve o'Clock junction)
The Moor–Ecclesall Road–London Road
Tenter Street Depot entrance
Lady's Bridge–Wicker–Blonk Street
Lady's Bridge–Nursery Street
Hounsfield Road–Western Bank–Winter Street.

In 1942 Rotherham Corporation completely relaid the track in High Street and, because of the narrowness of the street, closure to traffic was necessary during the period of the work. Westgate became the temporary terminus for trams. At the same time the loading island in Effingham Street was lengthened to about 150 feet and a glazed metal shelter was constructed, with accommodation for 300 people.

In February 1944, to assist with trolley swinging, a slip wire was fitted above the crossover at Bessemer Bridge. This made provision for the trolley to be swung on to the wire over the car and then to trail across to the other wire as the car reversed over the crossover.

Finally in March 1945 Rotherham Corporation relaid and repositioned the curve at the junction of Sheffield Road and Canklow Road.

[5]Work was done early in 1944 on a Saturday night with the aid of special screened lights and the Water Department's crane.
[6]Work was carried out in 1943—actual replacement of the track was done in three hours.
[7]Work in progress at beginning of September 1944.

Chapter 11

The Period of Recovery 1945 to 1951

When the war in Europe ended in May 1945 the whole system as it had existed in 1939 remained intact, albeit in a somewhat rundown condition. All the cars which had existed at the outbreak of war together with the reinstated "Preston" car No. 339 were still in service with the exception of the cars which had been destroyed and replaced as listed in chapter ten. In addition there were the fourteen ex Newcastle and ten ex Bradford cars. The total number of passenger cars thereby increased from 443 in 1939 to 468 as already mentioned, the highest total at any one time. The fourteen snowploughs (Nos. 352-365) and four other works cars (Nos. 371, 373-375) were still serving.

Along with the task of restoring the system to its former quality and condition after six years of the strain of war, the Department was soon engaged in preparations for the celebration of the 50th anniversary of the Corporation's takeover of the City's urban transport system. The main feature of this was the placing in regular service on 12th August 1946 of a completely new type of tramcar numbered 501. This car had a new form of integral body construction of great strength. It differed from all previous Sheffield cars by the absence of upper deck bulkheads or screened staircases. This completely open design of upper deck saloon was made feasible by the provision of folding platform doors. Fluorescent lighting was installed, which was unique in Sheffield and perhaps in the whole country. The truck was also unique in Sheffield, being of Maley and Taunton hornless type, retaining the usual four wheels but with six inches longer wheelbase of nine feet and reduced diameter wheels of two feet three inches. It was the last car built by Sheffield Corporation at Queen's Road.

In addition to this fine new car, the breakdown car No. 375, originally horse car No. 15 which had been withdrawn from service earlier in 1946, was altered for use as a horse car in connection with the Jubilee celebrations of that year. For a week in July 1946 it travelled between Leopold Street and Moorhead drawn by two brewery horses, taking passengers for one shilling per ride. For the occasion the trolley gear and controllers were removed but the truck and electric motors were retained. Seats were installed and advertisement boards fitted at roof level and the car was renumbered 1.

There were several developments of importance on the Rotherham route between 1946 and 1949. In November 1946 both tracks were relaid by the Ickles Goit[1] and this work necessitated single line working for the period of the job. Other work of the period included track renewal over the Bow Bridge in September 1948 and the provision of a new track entrance fan at the Rotherham Depot situated in Rawmarsh Road (north of Don Bridge) on the former Swinton and Mexborough route.

After the war traffic remained heavy on the through route, and between January and April 1947 Rotherham Corporation found it necessary to hire two cars at a time from Sheffield for periods of up to five days. More than thirty different Sheffield cars were involved in these loans.

In 1948 it was decided to proceed with the long proposed rebuilding of Tinsley Bridge which spanned the ex L.N.E.R. line and the South Yorkshire Canal. Part of the widening on the south-east side had been done before the war caused suspension of the work (including the steel parapet wall from which were sprung new tramway standards).

It was agreed that during the period of reconstruction Sheffield trams would run only as far as Vulcan Road and the Rotherham cars would terminate at the Templeborough triangle. On 11th December the through service ceased and was replaced by buses which worked over the temporary bridge.

By 1947 the Rotherham "single ended" cars had become severely worn by twelve years of heavy service and maintenance was becoming an increasing problem. It was clear that if the joint service were to be maintained Rotherham Corporation would need new cars.

However, in 1949 it was decided that track would not be laid over the new bridge and the Vulcan Road to Templeborough section was consequently abandoned. Together with Petre Street in 1925, Nether Edge in 1934 and Fulwood via Broomhill in 1936, this section provided the total of Sheffield route closures before general abandonment was decided upon.

Rotherham Corporation continued operation between College Square and Templeborough but in August 1949 it was decided to discontinue the service, which finally ended at 10.42 pm on Sunday 13th November 1949 when the last tram left Templeborough triangle for Rotherham.

By this time the Leeds car (Rotherham No. 14) which had been on loan since 1943 and purchased by Rotherham in 1948 had already been withdrawn. No other tramway operators offered to purchase the other twelve cars and on inspection the trucks of the eleven "single ended" cars were found to be in poor condition and the front wheel flanges were badly worn by continuous use in one direction only. The cars were therefore scrapped, but Sheffield Corporation purchased certain items of equipment including the Bessemer crossover which was in good condition. Accordingly the Sheffield-Rotherham joint tram service ended permanently.

This closure also reduced the Sheffield rolling stock requirement, as cars were no longer required for the joint service. The following twenty-five were withdrawn from service and did not appear in the Department's fleet list dated 15th March 1950:

9 cars ex-Newcastle	Nos. 312, 314, 316, 317, 320-324
5 cars ex-Bradford	Nos. 326-329[2], 332
2 cars "Preston" type	Nos. 336, 345[3]
3 cars Brush 1924-5	Nos. 36, 37, 46
4 cars Brush 1919-20	Nos. 414, 419[3], 425, 427
2 cars Cravens 1926-7	Nos. 460, 493[3]

The last nine of these were the first post 1918 Sheffield cars to be withdrawn.

[1]Flowed just east of the Midland main line Chesterfield–Rotherham, and under the road 167 yards east of the railway over-bridge.

[2]No. 326 was the first ex Bradford car to be withdrawn, in December 1949.

[3]These cars were withdrawn following damage in accidents. In addition No. 438 was damaged beyond repair in the Derbyshire Lane accident on 17th July 1950.

A. D. Packer.

The 1946 "Jubilee" car reversing at Meadowhead terminus.

Lens of Sutton.

No. 501 at Market Side at night. The only car with fluorescent lighting.

H. B. Priestley.

The water car in grey livery (previously numbered 211) in Sheffield Road, Tinsley on 30th March 1951. The bridge widening works can be seen in the distance.

A. D. Packer.

Approaching Vulcan Road terminus. Ahead is the widened Tinsley Bridge over the railway and canal, the rebuilding of which led to the closure of the Rotherham joint service.

Chapter 12

Rolling Stock Developments 1950 to 1953

Early in 1948 Sheffield Corporation obtained permission from the Ministry of Transport to raise a loan of over £200,000 for the purchase of thirty-five new cars costing about £6,850 each. Some delay was experienced in obtaining supplies of materials, a common feature of the years following the Second World War. Delivery from the builders, Charles Roberts and Co. Ltd. of Horbury, Wakefield, commenced in 1950.

The first car, No. 502, went into service on 15th May and by mid December 1950 a further eight cars numbered up to 510 were in service. They were being used normally on Middlewood–Ecclesall, Intake–Walkley and Prince of Wales Road routes.

These cars, which were similar in design to No. 501, differed mainly in that they had an all-metal body structure. They did not constitute any substantial departure from established British tramway practice but they were the last and best stage "in a long and successful history of well-tried arrangement and sound workmanship, retaining those elements which, though old, had been found best, yet incorporating also new ideas insofar as they were reconcilable with the general design."[1]

Because these efficient and elegant tramcars were the last double deck cars to be built in Britain, it is appropriate that they be described in detail, as shown in Appendix A.

The last of these cars, No. 536, entered service on 11th April 1952. It was the highest numbered car ever to run in Sheffield, and was the 876th and last electric passenger car to be brought into service by Sheffield Corporation.

The introduction of these cars in 1950-52 was probably the only really good thing which happened in Sheffield urban transport after 1939! It was reported in 1950 that Motorman Bert Youle, who drove No. 502 on the occasion of the official trials, and who had had thirty-one years driving experience and eighteen years test-driver service, said "I wish I had nothing else to drive; it is a lovely tram to handle". It is doubtful whether there had ever been a more comfortable public service vehicle on a highway anywhere in Britain.

Before the war, the water car No. 372 was standing disused in Brightside Yard at Tinsley Depot, and in 1946, as already mentioned, the breakdown car No. 375 had been withdrawn. Also mentioned earlier was the vestibuling of eight of the snowploughs during the war and the renumbering of several cars in 1937. Otherwise the fleet of snowploughs and other works cars had remained almost unchanged from 1933 and by 1950 most of the fleet was becoming worn out and some cars were in urgent need of replacement.

Lower saloon interior of Roberts car No. 518. *The late D. Tate.*

[1] "The Modern Tramway", July 1950

When the Newcastle cars arrived in 1942, the truck and other equipment of the disused No. 372 were used for one of them, and 372's body was finally broken up in December 1950.

By this time the other water car No. 371 required a new body. Because of its strong body, ex Bradford car No. 330 was chosen for the purpose. It was withdrawn from passenger service on 11th April 1951. The top deck, stairs and truck were removed, the latter being replaced by that of No. 371 with all the mechanical and electrical equipment and the two water tanks. The platform entrances were reduced in width to minimise draughts as the car was to spend most of its time on night duty. It was fitted with a roof frame for the trolley base which made possible the use of a standard double deck trolley.

Just before this work was carried out in February 1951 the Stores car No. 373 was also withdrawn from service.

Further changes in the departmental fleet took place as follows:

The Stores car No. 374 was replaced by "Preston" car No. 349 which was withdrawn from passenger service on 22nd January 1951. Following conversion, it entered service as a Stores car on 28th March 1951. However, No. 374 appears to have been retained as it did not reach T. W. Ward's scrapyard until 14th June 1956. The remaining ex horse car snowploughs Nos. 353 and 355 were withdrawn in March 1952, and by the end of that year the departmental fleet had declined from nineteen to fourteen, the cars remaining in service being Nos. 352, 354, 356-365, 330 and 349. The two latter cars were the only ones in Sheffield to be fitted with a roof frame to carry the trolley base. In addition to the withdrawal of No. 349 for conversion to a Stores car, several other "Preston" cars were withdrawn from service and scrapped, as follows:

336 on 9th November 1950
345 damaged in 1947 and not used thereafter was scrapped in May 1951[2]
347 on 22nd July 1952
348 on 26th October 1951

leaving Nos. 339, 342, 343, 344, 346 and 350 in service after July 1952. No. 350 was withdrawn from passenger service on 19th March 1953 and converted to a snowplough. This was the last conversion into the works fleet.

None of the above mentioned rolling stock changes resulted from the abandonment decision of April 1951 and would have occurred in any case.

The withdrawal from passenger use of the six "Preston"

Upper deck interior of Roberts car No. 502. *The late D. Tate.*

[2]The undamaged platform of this car was used to repair No. 348 which received platform damage soon after the accident to No. 345.

cars referred to above was made possible mainly by the gradual introduction of the new "Roberts" cars, which also facilitated the removal from service of the remainder of the ex Newcastle and Bradford cars. In addition the following post 1918 cars of standard Sheffield designs were removed from the fleet list on 1st July 1951:

11 S.C.T. Standard 1928-1935	Nos. 9, 22, 80, 88, 90-93, 101, 106, 120
4 Hills Standard 1929-1930	Nos. 137, 138, 139, 142
4 Brush	Nos. 432, 439, 443, 444
3 Cravens	Nos. 459, 461, 496

The "Preston" car No. 347 (originally numbered 269) was the last Sheffield car in service with upper deck sliding door bulkheads.

During the years 1948 to 1950, major body overhauls were undertaken on fifteen cars and medium overhauls on a further five. The first group comprised Nos. 61, 71, 76, 131, 134, 135, 143, 145, 155, 218, 416, 436, 441, 447 and 497. The second group was Nos. 109, 278, 367, 413 and 469.

At this time five cars had received the post 1927 type smaller diameter hand brake controls which eliminated the need for the "banjo-shaped" end glasses which were consequently removed. As altered, these cars numbered 367, 413, 441, 447 and 469 assumed a "Preston" type end appearance rather than that of 1913-1927 Sheffield cars. In the case of No. 413, this car was listed as scrapped on 17th November 1951 but No. 465, which was in the works for minor repair, was instead sent for scrapping in error. In consequence, the body of No. 413 was placed on the truck of No. 465 and received that number.

In April 1954 both ends of car No. 55 were rebuilt so that the upper deck side panelling had the appearance of the 1919-1922 Brush cars.

During the ensuing two years it appears that an additional six cars underwent major rebuilding, Nos. 62, 74, 77, 149, 153 and 154. In the case of No. 153 some alterations had already been made by the spring of 1948 including side lights moved to the dash and simplified lining-out and gilt Gill Sans numerals on the old style livery.

A programme of rebuilding of the lower saloons of Standard cars built between 1929 and 1934 commenced in 1952, and when this work came to an end in 1956 the following twenty-three cars had been so treated:

Nos. 25, 27, 68, 69, 72, 73, 75, 87, 89, 97, 98, 102, 115, 122, 128, 151, 161, 167, 170, 173, 174, 183 and 191, the last of these being No. 183 in 1956 as a result of collision damage, and this was probably the last car to be changed from old to new livery. With the exception of No. 87, the first car to be dealt with, the rebuilt lower saloons were similar in appearance to those of the Improved Standard cars.

Between 1951 and 1954 six other cars had overhauls, three described as "medium" and three as "major", the former being Nos. 121, 203 and 209[3] and the latter Nos. 123, 150 and 219. The last was No. 123 in 1954, again as a result of collision damage. No alteration in the appearance of the lower saloon was made in these cases.

Of the Standard cars which had been painted in the old livery and referred to in the six foregoing paragraphs, only four failed to re-emerge in "new" livery after overhaul. These were Nos. 71 and 145 (although No. 71 had a simplified lining-out), and Nos. 150 and 219 which were among the cars experimentally painted green, though these two latter cars received the new livery at a later date.

Science Museum.
One of the first group of Standard cars to be withdrawn from service in 1951 when most of the earlier post-1918 cars were still in use.

J. H. Meredith.
Brush car of 1920 in High Street on 15th June 1952 after removal of "banjo end".

[3]Following collision damage at the foot of Meadowhead.

R. J. S. Wiseman.

Standard car with rebuilt lower saloon in snow on Abbeydale Road South reservation approaching Beauchief on Boxing Day 1956. Millhouses Park is on the right and Ecclesall Woods on the left.

R. B. Parr.

Cars at Midland Station junctions on 15th February 1958. No. 128 had rebuilt lower saloon but retained original dash which was not usual with these rebuilds.

J. H. Meredith.

No. 213 the first Standard car to be built with the headlamp in the raised position, seen in Fargate on 15th June 1952 in two tone green livery.

No. 285 at Market Side in the short-lived green livery of 1952-3.

A. D. Packer.

In the period between March and July 1952 an experimental green livery was applied to twenty-three cars, fourteen of which were Standard and nine Improved Standard. The following twelve were in two shades of green: Nos. 33, 76, 150, 211, 212, 213, 215, 219, 253, 254, 284 and 290, whereas the remainder were in one shade only: Nos. 32, 35, 83, 202, 216, 221, 252, 256, 285, 286 and 287. All the green cars had gilt numerals. In the case of the Hills car No. 150 which had no "lower beading", the green was not relieved by a second shade at the foot of the dashes and side panels.

The experiment (which was also tried on fifty-eight buses) received widespread disapproval from the public, and in consequence, between July and December 1953, all the trams were repainted in 1935 livery. Had the Corporation paid as much heed to public opinion in 1951 concerning tramway abandonment as they did in 1953 on a far more trivial matter, the City would doubtless have retained a superior transport system.

The following cars had before the experiment been in the old colour scheme: Nos. 32, 33, 35, 76 and 150. In addition to these and the twenty-three rebuilds, other cars were also repainted from old to new livery; No. 26 received this treatment as early as 1949. Also another twenty of the original total of 176 old livery Standard cars were repainted in the new scheme, as follows: Nos. 28, 61, 62, 74, 77, 96[4], 109, 121, 123, 127, 131, 134, 135, 141[4], 143, 149, 153, 154, 155, 157[5] and 159[4], some already referred to in this chapter.

In consequence of these events a total of fifty Standard cars numbered up to 201 received new livery, in addition to nine war damage replacement cars which fell within this number range.

Rising costs in the post-war years had made necessary a search for economies and as the cheaper green livery had been rejected by the public, the Corporation adopted advertising as an additional source of revenue. In 1952 after an interval of thirty-six years they decided to display advertisements on the outsides of trams and buses. On the trams the lining-out of the upper deck side panelling was adjusted to provide an advertisement panel on either side of the cars, which necessitated the removal of the S.T.D. monogram. Advertisements were not displayed on pre-1928 cars, with the sole exception of Brush car No. 60.

[4]Early in the war period these three cars were repainted in grey livery but when repainted again in 1945 they received the 1935 new livery.

[5]Following accident damage in October 1955 this car was returned to service with only the lower deck repainted in the new livery. Repainted in full new livery in April 1957.

Chapter 13

The Closure Report and Proceedings

Private and commercial motor interests had for many years campaigned for the removal of the tramways in Sheffield as well as in other towns. The extensive war damage in the centre of the City in December 1940 had provided a golden opportunity for extensive highway improvements, but town planners never seemed to assimilate the European experience that tramways could be conveniently integrated into an urban traffic system. The continually increasing volume of road traffic caused the General Manager of the Transport Department to express apprehension about the danger to passengers boarding and alighting from tramcars in the centre of the carriageway. In addition rising costs of tramway operation were becoming a problem.

In consequence of these trends the Transport Committee submitted a report for consideration by the City Council on 4th April 1951 recommending a programme of replacement of trams by omnibuses. Whilst this report failed to produce an unassailable case for closure of the tramway system it did include a number of interesting statistics, under the following headings:

1. *Present Position* (at that time)
   Trams 452 including nineteen out of service pending disposal
   Buses 372 including sixty-nine over-age, but excluding buses for services running outside the City in conjunction with British Railways.

2. *Daily Use*

	Morning Peak	11 am	2.30 pm	Evening Peak	8.30 pm
Trams	349	155	209	370	141
Buses	271	94	148	309	99

3. *Routes and Mileage*
   Trams served seventeen routes and the circular routes to Abbey Lane and Prince of Wales Road, a mileage of forty-eight all of which was double track except for less than one mile which was single. In addition four and a half miles of single track was in depots and approaches. Buses operated on 120 miles of road within the City providing full services on twenty-six routes daily, with thirteen routes operated during part of the day, mainly for workmen.
   Trams carried 175,000,000 passengers per annum—64%.
   Buses carried 100,000,000 passengers per annum—36%.
   The corresponding figures four years earlier were 201,700,000—71% and 83,415,000—29%.

4. *Age of Trams*

Post war construction. New cars	36		
War damage replacements	14	50	
Under 15 years old		64	114
15 to 20 years old	125		
20 to 25 years old	120		245
25 to 30 years old	48		
30 to 33 years old	26		74
			433

On the basis of thirty years life, the following replacement programme was necessary if trams were to be retained.
(a) 26 over-age trams to be scrapped
(b) 1951-56 48 over-age trams to be renewed @ £7,000 — £336,000
(c) 1956-61 120 over-age trams to be renewed @ £7,000 — £840,000
(d) 1961-66 125 over-age trams to be renewed @ £7,000 — £875,000
Total cost in next 15 years £2,051,000

5. *Tram Depots*

Depot	Total Allocated		Number at Works	Number Allocated		Estimated Bus Accommodation		Remarks
	Service Cars	Others		Inside Depot	Not Under Cover	Echelon Parking	Straight Lines	
Shoreham Street	128	3	10	108	13	44	60	Alterations to make entrance from Leadmill Road.
Tinsley	100	8	8	88	12	37	65	Alterations to make exit in Weedon Street.
Crookes	67	2	8	52	9	19	25	Pillars
Hillsborough	65	—	8	55	2	—	—	Pillars, bad site
Tenter Street	92	5	8	86	3	—	—	Pillars and struts
Queen's Road Works	—	—	42	42	—	—	—	
Total	452	18	—	431	39	100	150	

The Report stated that the total bus fleet including Joint Committee buses was 532 and that 410 additional buses would be required to replace trams. In the matter of garaging accommodation, 125 spaces at Shoreham Street and Tinsley tram depots were taken into account.

6. *Number of trams required for each route (Mondays to Fridays)*

	Morning Peak	Off Peak 11 am	Evening Peak
Millhouses–Tinsley	18	8	13
Abbey Lane (Millhouses)–Vulcan Road	16	10	22
Millhouses–City	4	—	6
Tinsley–City	—	—	1
Abbey Lane (Woodseats)–Firth Park	24	10	17
Woodseats–City (via Moor)	4	—	3
Sheffield Lane Top–City (via Barnsley Road)	6	—	5
Meadowhead–Sheffield Lane Top	19	17	17
Meadowhead–City	4	—	10
Sheffield Lane Top–City (via Attercliffe)	15	6	21
Wadsley Bridge–Woodseats	20	15	24
Wadsley Bridge–City	11	—	3
Woodseats–City (via Queen's Road, or Shoreham Street)	—	—	3
Crookes–Handsworth	25	20	26
Crookes–City	6	—	14
Handsworth–City	11	—	15
Ecclesall–Middlewood	32	21	28
Ecclesall–City	7	—	5
Middlewood–City	11	—	5
Fulwood–Malin Bridge	18	17	18
Fulwood–City	—	—	2
Malin Bridge–City	7	—	9
Prince of Wales Road	30	12	50
Walkley–Intake	28	10	15
Walkley–Midland Station	5	5	4
Walkley–City	1	—	8
Intake–City	8	—	13
Brightside (via Savile Street)	6	4	4
Sheffield Lane Top (via Savile Street)	13	—	9
Totals	349	155	370

7. *Replacement Scheme Order of Route Abandonment*

	Trams Withdrawn		
	In Service	Incl. those under Maintenance	Route Miles Abandoned
1 Malin Bridge–Fulwood	13	15	1.9
2 Prince of Wales Road	50	56	2.1
3 Walkley–Intake	40	45	4.5
4 Crookes–Handsworth	55	61	5.7
5 Meadowhead +			
Woodseats via Queen's Road			
Woodseats via Shoreham Street	15	17	0.7
6 Sheffield Lane Top via Upwell Street, Brightside	53	58	3.3
7 Vulcan Road–Abbey Lane–Firth Park, Tinsley–Millhouses	57	62	7.5
8 Sheffield Lane Top–Woodseats	26	29	8.3
9 Ecclesall–Middlewood	46·	50	7.1
10 Wadsley Bridge	15	17	7.0*

+Included lines to depots and works

*Consequent on Greenhill housing development

The programme was to spread over a period of fifteen years so that an average interval of eighteen months between each stage was indicated. Assuming an operative date of January 1952 for stage one, final closure would have occurred around July 1965.

The City Council gave its approval to the replacement scheme despite the knowledge that tramway passengers were in general well satisfied with their tramway system and were opposed to the proposed replacement. Unfortunately the matter became a party political issue and voting was along party lines.

An organisation called The Sheffield Tramways Development Association was formed for the purpose of contesting the Council's decision and to campaign for tramway development and expansion. With the Labour Party so firmly entrenched in office, as it had been almost continuously from 1926, there was virtually no chance of the Association's aims being realised and after a few years it went out of existence.

Councillor R. W. Allott resigned from the Labour Group of the City Council on the tramway scrapping issue. The attitudes of the two main political parties had become reversed since the inter-war period.

Chapter 14

Contraction

The first closure under the abandonment programme was Fulwood to Malin Bridge, as proposed in the Report of 1951. This closure occurred on 5th January 1952 and involved the withdrawal of tram services between Rustlings Road junction and Fulwood and between Holme Lane Depot and Malin Bridge, a route mileage of one mile six furlongs and thirty-nine yards double track and 173 yards single.

H. B. Priestley.
1934 Standard car in Rustlings Road, Hunters Bar just beyond the turning circle on 5th September 1951.

No. 65 was the last car at Fulwood and then at Malin Bridge, returning to Holme Lane Depot.

In the first instance the replacing buses did not provide a through service over the former tram route. The Fulwood buses operated from a city terminus in Eyre Street (near the Central Library) via Bramall Lane, Boston Street, Cemetery Road, Sharrow Vale Road to Hunters Bar and thence via the tram route, but extended at Fulwood to Brooklands Crescent. Malin Bridge was served by an augmented Wisewood bus service diverted from Bridge Street to Campo Lane, and by the extension of the Stannington and Bradfield bus services from Malin Bridge into the centre of the City, also at Campo Lane. This central terminus was less convenient for tram connections for East End workers, as was Eyre Street for shoppers from Fulwood.

The tram service between Hunters Bar and Hillsborough (Holme Lane) was not reduced and so formed a short working of the still existing Ecclesall–Middlewood tram service. At Holme Lane cars entered the depot to reverse, gaining access by one of the only two facing crossovers in the City.

Public protests about the changeover were greatly increased by the nature of the changes described above. Requests for reinstatement of the whole tram route were considered by the City Council on 5th March 1952, whose first resolution required the restoration of the tramway but this was later modified to restoration of a through service. Despite this, five months elapsed before, on 10th August, that demand was met and the two sections of the former tram route were linked by a bus service following the whole course of the former route.

P. Lazenby.
No. 492 leaving Crookes Depot on 24th April 1952. This Cravens car was withdrawn from service on 1st September of that year.

No tramcars were withdrawn from service immediately after this first abandonment, and the last few Roberts cars Nos. 532, 535 and 536 were still to be delivered. In addition, as already mentioned, the rebuilding of the lower saloons of twenty-three Standard cars was to follow in the period from 1952 to 1956, as were minor improvements to a few other cars.

Following the Fulwood–Malin Bridge closure the sequence proposed in the Abandonment Report was not followed and there were no more closures for over two years until the Ecclesall–Middlewood replacement on 27th March 1954. In this case a petition by about 11,500 signatories seeking retention of this service, one of the most profitable in the system, was presented to the Transport Authority, but without success. The last car at Ecclesall was No. 234 and the last one at Middlewood was No. 513.

This closure resulted in the withdrawal of twenty-eight Brush and Cravens tramcars built between 1918 and 1927, the abandonment of track from the bottom of Ecclesall Road to Ecclesall terminus including Rustlings Road turning loop, and from Penistone Road junction (Hoyle Street) to Middlewood, a total route mileage of four miles seven furlongs and 150 yards double track and 131 yards single track, along with Holme Lane Depot which was closed on 23rd April after the last car had left. In addition the through southbound line in Pinstone Street became redundant but remained operational until the closure of the system. It was used on special occasions including the last evening.

The number of passenger cars on the fleet list at 31st March 1954 had fallen to 369.

Another two years were to elapse before any more route closures took place, but in this period several track alterations were made. In 1955 the track was singled in Angel Street on a central paved reservation, and although the line was normally used only in the downhill direction for access to Tenter Street Depot the overhead wires for both directions were retained. This work was carried out between 15th and 18th July and the line was brought into use immediately. In the same year the direct line from Tinsley Depot into Weedon Street together with the adjacent crossover and the disused spare track at the terminus were removed. In addition the points and crossings of the double track curve from Pinstone Street to Furnival Street (Moorhead) were also removed.

A. D. Packer.
On the interlaced track, later doubled, over the railway at Staniforth Road.

In 1956 the bridge over the railway in Staniforth Road was widened and this facilitated the provision of double tramway track which replaced the previous interlaced track. In the early months of 1954 the nearby canal bridge had been raised to give greater clearance for canal vessels. In neither case was tramway traffic interrupted, a single track being used first at one side of the bridges, which after partial rebuilding was slewed to the opposite side until the works were completed.

The number of tramcars withdrawn from service in the year to 31st March 1955 was only twelve (Nos. 58, 59, 60, 132, 136, 344, 387, 400, 470, 473, 486 and 490) and in the following year a further nineteen withdrawals reduced the fleet to 338. The cars withdrawn in the year were: Nos. 53, 343, 346, 377, 378, 383, 394, 433, 436, 463, 467, 469, 474, 475, 488, 489, 494, 495 and 499.

The next route closure took place on 7th April 1956 and was Walkley–Intake, which included the service between the Midland Station and Walkley, and the Fitzalan Square to Elm Tree via City Road portion of the Prince of Wales Road circular route. The resultant track abandonment was Winter Street junction to Walkley and Broad Street junction to Elm Tree. Commercial Street remained in use by late night cars from Beauchief to the Midland Station. The last car at Walkley was No. 55 and the last from Intake via City Road was No. 505. The last car to complete the Prince of Wales Road circle from Fitzalan Square via City Road to Elm Tree and Darnall was No. 65 and in the reverse direction No. 94.

The only rocker panel type cars remaining in service after this closure were Nos. 42, 52, 456 and 497.

The service between Intake (Birley Vale) and the East End via Elm Tree, Prince of Wales Road and Darnall remained in operation for a further six months until 6th October 1956, and during this period a new part day service operated between Fitzalan Square and Intake (Birley Vale) via Darnall and Elm Tree. The last car from Intake to Tinsley was No. 176. The last car of all from Intake terminus was No. 117 to the City via Darnall.

The result of these closures was that by 31st March 1957 the tramcar fleet had declined to 265 passenger cars. Withdrawals in the year to this date included the last two "Preston" cars Nos. 339 and 342. The latter car was withdrawn as from 8th April 1956 and was retained for preservation. (See chapter fifteen.)

Track mileage following the 1954 closures had been as follows:

Double track–40 miles 1 furlong 214 yards
Single track—6 furlongs 67 yards
Depots and approaches 3 miles 7 furlongs 141 yards.

After the Annual Report for the year to 31st March 1955 the Transport Department ceased to quote mileages in the above form, and adopted the less informative method of stating mileage in single line terms. It was therefore no longer practicable to refer to reductions in route mileage in precise figures. The quoted reduction in respect of the 1956 closure was nine miles and eighty-two yards.

In 1957 the pace of tramway abandonments quickened, and there were two closures per annum from that year until the final closure in 1960.

The first and largest closure of 1957 was Crookes–Handsworth including Crookes Depot on 4th May. This involved the abandonment of track between West Street junction and Crookes terminus and between Prince of Wales Road junction, Darnall and Handsworth terminus, a total length in single line terms of eight miles, six furlongs and 188 yards. This closure also included the peak hour services from Crookes and Handsworth to Brightside and Vulcan Road. The last car at Crookes was No. 194 at 1.30 on

R. B. Parr.

A leafy scene at Fulwood terminus as No. 246 leaves on 13th August 1950.

H. B. Priestley.

Malin Bridge terminus on 16th September 1951 showing unconnected track.

H. B. Priestley.

No. 249 returning to the City, at Banner Cross on 21st March 1954, a week before closure of the route. Compare with the illustration (page 56) showing the original No. 177.

R. Brook.

No. 242 on the interlaced track over the Staniforth Road railway bridge during widening operations in 1956. The temporary single line was not then completed.

The temporary track over Staniforth Road railway bridge in use on 28th March 1956. *R. B. Parr.*

Sunday morning, 5th May, and it returned directly to Tenter Street Depot; the last car from Handsworth was No. 33. Crookes Depot was later taken over by the Parks Department of the Corporation.

On 26th October the second closure of the year was the service between Exchange Street and Sheffield Lane Top via Attercliffe. The only track which went out of use as a result was Exchange Street.

The next line to be abandoned was that from the Midland Station junctions to the Moorhead via Furnival Street on 4th January 1958; the last cars being Nos. 219 and 249. In the following months the tracks were lifted for most of the way from the Midland Station but the upper section in Furnival Street from where the track doubled between Eyre Street and Union Lane was retained, together with the lines and junctions into The Moor. This layout was used once again when, on 17th May 1958, the Queen Mother visited the City, and trams from the southern suburbs were turned there.

This may be a convenient point to refer to the tramway tours which became a feature of the post Second World War period in Sheffield and elsewhere, as the Furnival Street line seemed to hold a fascination for tramway enthusiasts probably unparalleled by any other feature on the Sheffield system. This may have been due to its unique characteristics: a single line with passing loops routed through back streets close to the centre of the City and normally used in the southbound direction, for certain evening rush hour services on Mondays to Fridays and midday on Saturdays, from the East End to the southern suburbs. For many years prior to the Second World War, the line had also been used in the morning rush hour in the opposite direction by cars from the East End or Firth Park carrying a destination board in the lower saloon showing "City, Fargate". After discharging passengers these cars would traverse Pinstone Street (using the centre track after 11th September 1933) and Furnival Street. Those returning to Shoreham Street Depot usually reversed at the crossover at the Flat Street end of Pond Street but those returning to Tinsley Depot continued via Fitzalan Square. Cars engaged on these movements would still convey passengers.

The first Sheffield tour was by the Light Railway Transport League on 23rd September 1945[1] with car No. 301. There followed a tour by No. 501 on 22nd September 1946[1] when the car was parked at Temple Street siding whilst a visit to Rotherham was made using Rotherham car No. 4. Notable among those which followed were:

13th June 1948	Sheffield and Rotherham tramway works visit.
22nd May 1949	No. 501. Parked at Vulcan Road during inspection of Tinsley bridges.

[1]Furnival Street was not used on these occasions.

On the Furnival Street single line on 29th April 1956. *R. J. S. Wiseman.*

28th August 1949	No. 501. Southern Counties Touring Society tour via Furnival Street.
13th August 1950	No. 503. The first Roberts car tour.
13th May 1951	No. 522. L.R.T.L. tour during their Annual convention held in Sheffield.
23rd September 1951	No. 300. Last tour to include Malin Bridge and Fulwood (via Furnival Street).
13th July 1952	No. 370. The Experimental Car tour.
1st May 1955	No. 346. The "Preston" car tour of five hours duration.
29th April 1956	No. 1. Tour including Crookes, Wadsley Bridge, Chippinghouse Road, and Furnival Street and Angel Street single tracks.
28th April 1957	Nos. 42, 52 and 497. The last rocker panel type cars. Tour commenced at Angel Street at 1.30 pm and ended at Tinsley Depot where the cars were finally withdrawn from service[2].
30th March 1958	No. 189. A fifty mile tour which commenced at Angel Street and ended at Tenter Street Depot where the car returned to service for a few days ending on 3rd April prior to going into preservation.
22nd February 1959	No. 536. Farewell tour of Abbey Lane and Upwell Street.
27th March 1960	No. 222. Tour which included Meadowhead, Queen's Road, Leopold Street, Church Street and Angel Street.

The last tour of all was provided by cars Nos. 510, 513 and 501 on 2nd October 1960.

The Prince of Wales Road service to and from Fitzalan Square, which for two years had operated only via Darnall, came to an end on 12th April 1958. Car No. 300 was the last at Elm Tree and No. 210 was the last at Darnall Main Road siding. The track which went out of use with this closure was Staniforth Road junction (Attercliffe) to Darnall Main Road and Elm Tree, a single track mileage of six miles five furlongs and 154 yards.

The second closure of 1958 took place on 6th December with the withdrawal of services between Fitzalan Square and Brightside via Savile Street (last car No. 210) and between Brightside and Sheffield Lane Top (last car No. 191). The resulting track abandonment was Hawke Street junction to Brightside terminus, a single line distance of six furlongs, 216 yards. The replacing service of buses over the

[2]These cars had spent their last year of normal service on the Brightside route and peak hour specials.

P. N. Williams.

No. 275 on Intake service at Walkley terminus on 24th July 1950.

J. H. Meredith.

At South Road terminus, Walkley, looking towards the City on 15th June 1952. No. 77 waits behind No. 109 which is on the Midland (LMS) Station service.

H. B. Priestley.

On Wadsley Bridge to Woodseats service, at Parkside Road junction, Owlerton, on 22nd February 1954. This car remained in service until 1957 and was the next to the last of the 1926-7 Cravens cars to be withdrawn.

Saturday midday rush-hour extras in Brown Street on 3rd October 1953.

R. J. S. Wiseman.

R. J. S. Wiseman.

Cars at Moorhead leaving and entering the Furnival Street line during the visit of the Queen Mother to the Town Hall on 17th May 1958.

Brightside tramway was accomplished by increasing the frequency of the Midland Station–Brightside–Wincobank–Firth Park route which already traversed the same roads.

The next closures followed very soon afterwards, when on 28th February 1959 the Abbey Lane route between Beauchief and Woodseats (Camping Lane) was closed as well as Fitzalan Square to Sheffield Lane Top via Savile Street. The latter brought the end of services reversing in Fitzalan Square or Flat Street. The last car to leave Beauchief for Woodseats was No. 199 which was the last car in service in the old livery; it was withdrawn after the closure of the Abbey Lane section. The last car in the opposite direction was the war damage replacement No. 274. They made their stop side by side at Beauchief. The last car on the Sheffield Lane Top via Savile Street route was No. 233.

In addition to Abbey Lane, tracks abandoned at this time were Twelve o'Clock junction–Upwell Street–Page Hall Road and Newhall Road, which had not been in regular use since the Sheffield Lane Top via Attercliffe service was discontinued sixteen months earlier. Shoreham Street Depot closed on the same day and was subsequently converted for use by buses.

Following the above mentioned route closures the tramcar fleet diminished to 200 at 31st March 1958 and to 130 at March 1959.

On 3rd October 1959 the service between Wadsley Bridge and Woodseats via Queen's Road and via Shoreham Street was withdrawn. From the same date the workmen's service, Meadowhead–Vulcan Road via Shoreham Street along with the late night journeys to and from Meadowhead were provided by buses. The Wadsley Bridge–Woodseats closure resulted in the abandonment of tracks from Nursery Street junction to Wadsley Bridge, West Bar Green to Hillfoot Bridge and Parkside Road which was used for football specials to Sheffield Wednesday's ground, also Shoreham Street and Cherry Street siding used for football specials to Sheffield United's ground. The tracks in Blonk Street, Sheaf Street, Leadmill Road, Suffolk Road and Queen's Road to Heeley junction, along with Wolseley Road, were retained for access to Queen's Road Works and for other departmental purposes.

Tinsley ceased to be an operational depot as from the Wadsley Bridge–Woodseats closure and from then until the end of 1960 it was used for storing withdrawn tramcars awaiting scrapping (see chapter fifteen) as well as a few cars which were to be preserved. This depot had in the past served the Rotherham, Brightside, Firth Park via Attercliffe or Savile Street, Firth Park via Pitsmoor, Abbey Lane, Meadowhead and Tinsley routes, also early and late cars to Handsworth.

The last car from Woodseats to Wadsley Bridge was No.

A. D. Packer.

Football special cars parked in Parkside Road during a match at Sheffield Wednesday's ground on 20th March 1954.

210 which had also been the last at Darnall Main Road siding and at Brightside.

A gradual withdrawal of redundant cars occurred during 1959 so that immediately after the Woodseats–Wadsley Bridge closure the fleet total had fallen to exactly 100 cars which were as follows:

Standard cars	Nos. 121, 150, 206, 208, 210, 219, 220, 221, 222, 230, 244, 248.	12
Rebuilt Standard cars	Nos. 25, 68, 69, 72, 73, 75, 87, 89, 97, 98, 102, 115, 122, 151, 161, 167, 170, 173, 174, 183.	20
Improved Standard cars	Nos. 231, 233, 234, 251, 252, 254, 256, 258, 259, 264, 265, 267, 269, 270, 272, 279, 281, 286, 287, 291, 293, 296, 298.	23
Improved Standard cars (war damage replacements)	Nos. 83, 85, 100, 112, 192, 201, 227, 430, 483.	9
Jubilee car	No. 501.	1
Roberts cars	Nos. 502-536.	35
		100

All these cars were housed at Tenter Street which was the sole remaining operational depot for the last year of the system's existence. The snowploughs which were also stationed there were last used on 17th February 1960.

The service between Meadowhead and Firth Park and Sheffield Lane Top via Pitsmoor ended on Saturday night 2nd April 1960. The last car at Meadowhead was No. 121 and the last at Sheffield Lane Top was No. 100.

Following this closure there remained only the through route between Beauchief, Millhouses, The Moor and Tinsley (Weedon Street and Vulcan Road). In the centre of the City, Church Street and Leopold Street remained operational for passenger carrying cars whereas West Bar was used for access to and from Tenter Street Depot, entering via Angel Street and Snig Hill and departing via Bridge Street. In addition the lines from Blonk Street to Heeley and Wolseley Road inclusive via Midland Station and Queen's Road, already mentioned, were retained.

This pattern of track use remained unchanged throughout the final months of tramway operation in Sheffield, except that in March 1960 the track had been singled from the Midland Station crossover to Leadmill Road to facilitate the construction of a traffic roundabout opposite the foot of Howard Street. Additionally from 29th August the Millhouses turning loop was closed to trams so that conversion works could be carried out to adapt it for use by

R. B. Parr.

"Preston" cars Nos. 339, 342 and 346 and Cravens car No. 474 at Tinsley Depot on the occasion of the "Preston" tour of 1st May 1955.

A. D. Packer.

The last tramcar tour in Wolseley Road on 2nd October 1960. The 'To City' line in this street was used until October 1959 for parking trams during football and cricket matches at Bramall Lane. Reversal of these cars took place at Chippinghouse Road crossover.

A. D. Packer.

The last car to enter service in Sheffield on 11th April 1952. Seen on the Abbey Lane reservation on 22nd February 1959 between Folds Lane and Dalewood Road a few days before the closure of the route.

R. J. S. Wiseman.

Entering the double track in Neepsend Lane on the approach to Rutland Road on 1st June 1957.

R. J. S. Wiseman.

1924 Brush car in final condition at Corn Exchange on a football special to Bramall Lane on 18th April 1953.

buses in an anti-clockwise direction (the opposite direction from tram use). From that time until final closure Millhouses cars used the crossover opposite "The Waggon and Horses" as they had done when the route was first extended to that point in 1926 and beyond in 1927. On 1st September 1960 a trolley reverser was installed and the overhead wiring round the loop was dismantled.

The Meadowhead–Sheffield Lane Top closure in April brought about the withdrawal of a further forty tramcars as follows:

Standard cars	Nos. 121, 206, 208, 210, 219, 220, 230, 244, 248.
Rebuilt Standard cars	Nos. 25, 69, 73, 75, 87, 89, 98, 151, 161, 170, 173, 174.
Improved Standard cars	Nos. 233, 234, 251, 254, 259, 265, 267, 269, 270, 272, 279, 291, 293.
War damage replacements	Nos. 83, 85, 192, 201, 227.
Roberts car	No. 520.

In consequence of these withdrawals, there remained in service sixty passenger cars, namely: Nos. 68, 72, 97, 100, 102, 112, 115, 122, 150, 167, 183, 221, 222, 231, 252, 256, 258, 264, 281, 286, 287, 296, 298, 430, 483, 501 and all the Roberts cars excepting No. 520.

In mid-June 1960 the Stores car No. 349 was sent to Queen's Road Works to be converted into an illuminated car for touring the system during the last week. During the year the snowplough No. 354 was at Tinsley Depot being reconverted by members of the Tramway Museum Society to a single deck passenger car with its original number 46.

As from 10th August another fifteen cars which were no longer required were withdrawn from service and sent to Tinsley Depot on 12th and 13th to await scrapping. These were Nos. 68, 72, 100, 150, 252, 256, 286, 287, 298, 430, 483 and Roberts cars 511, 512, 525 and 533 which required new tyres. From 10th August therefore, there remained in service eight Standard cars of 1928-1935 (97, 102, 115, 122, 167, 183, 221 and 222) all of which had received rebuilt lower saloons excepting Nos. 221 and 222; five Improved Standard cars of 1936-1939 (Nos. 231, 258, 264, 281 and 296), one war damage replacement (Improved Standard type) No. 112; the Jubilee car of 1946 No. 501 and thirty of the Roberts cars numbered between 502 and 536 inclusive, a total of forty five.

As in the case of No. 349 which went in June, by 16th August Nos. 510 and 513 were at Queen's Road for repainting in commemorative style for service during the Last Week, 2nd to 8th October.

By the end of September Nos. 221, 505, 531 and 532 had been withdrawn, being in need of replacements or repairs, and the snowplough No. 361 arrived at Tinsley by 28th

C. C. Thornburn.

The last car of the ordinary service from Beauchief and Millhouses entering Tinsley Depot on 8th October 1960.

September as it was no longer required. Nos. 508 and 524 followed on the afternoon of 7th October, having developed motor and gear faults respectively. The Water Car No. 330 and the snowplough No. 350 were also sent to Tinsley on the same day.

Accordingly on the last day, 8th October 1960, there were thirty-nine cars in service. These cars were engaged on one or other of two different duties. Twelve of the Roberts cars were reserved for the ceremonial tramcar procession in the evening including No. 521 which along with the remaining twenty-seven cars (Nos. 97, 102, 112, 115, 122, 167, 183, 222, 231, 258, 264, 281, 296, 501, 502, 506, 509, 514, 515, 516, 517, 519, 522, 526, 528, 535 and 536) maintained the normal service until it was gradually replaced by buses during the mid-afternoon, the trams terminating their last duties at Tinsley Depot, excepting No. 264 which was due for preservation and accordingly went to Queen's Road Works.

No. 502 was the last rostered normal service car to Beauchief and No. 222 was the last from Vulcan Road to Millhouses and back to Tinsley Depot. In the event, by a last minute decision, No. 222 ran on from Millhouses, where it loaded to capacity, to Beauchief. As no-one alighted there, none of the large crowd at Beauchief could be accommodated.

No. 517 was the last at Vulcan Road at about 4.10 pm. No. 536 was the last ordinary service car to leave Tenter Street Depot and No. 521 was the last to arrive there, for use in the evening following normal service earlier in the day. The last car of all to arrive at Tinsley was No. 504 at 8.19 pm., whilst the official last car No. 510 went to Queen's Road.

There were fifteen cars in use for the final processional journey and each carried a numbered label signifying its order of travel. The capacity number of passengers boarded the cars in Tenter Street Depot where music was provided by the Transport Department Band.

At 6.03 pm the cars began to move out of the depot for the last time, to the tune "Bless 'em all", and into the very wet night. The cars in their correct order were as follows:

1. No. 349 — The Illuminated Stores Car (originally "Preston" type passenger car No. 271 of 1907).
2. No. 46 — The restored single decker of 1899, which was a snowplough from 1920 and latterly numbered 354, carrying Tramway Museum Society members.
3. No. 189 — The Standard car of 1934 presented to the Tramway Museum Society by Sheffield Corporation and carrying Society members.

A. D. Packer.
Improved Standard car No. 290 in two-tone green livery and Brush cars in Fitzalan Square in August 1953. No. 405 is a football special to Bramall Lane. The war damage site beyond the tram shelter may be compared with the illustration at the end of chapter nine.

P. N. Williams.
The top of the climb of Meadowhead on 6th August 1951. This car was next to the last in the pre-war building programme. It was withdrawn from service on 4th August 1959.

A. D. Packer.

Standard car at Millhouses "Waggon and Horses" on 14th August 1955.

H. B. Priestley.

No. 501 returning from Vulcan Road on the morning of the Last Day before the rain started. The tracks into Weedon Street and into Tinsley Depot yard are in the foreground.

4.	No. 503	Roberts cars of 1950 carrying members of the City Council and Corporation officials and guests.
5.	No. 504	
6.	No. 507	Roberts cars of 1950-52 carrying members of the public who had reserved accommodation in advance.
7.	No. 518	
8.	No. 521	
9.	No. 523	
10.	No. 527	
11.	No. 529	
12.	No. 530	
13.	No. 534	
14.	No. 513	Roberts car of 1950 repainted and suitably inscribed for the "Last Tram Week". Carrying official passengers as cars Nos. 503 and 504.
15.	No. 510	Roberts car of 1950 repainted and suitably inscribed. The official "LAST CAR". Also carrying official passengers.

The procession was routed via West Bar, Bridge Street, Waingate, Haymarket, High Street, Fargate, Pinstone Street (through line), The Moor, London Road, Abbeydale Road to Millhouses and Beauchief. Despite the heavy rain large crowds of people lined the route.

A telling feature was the delay caused to the tramcars especially on the outward journey by other traffic, but when the trams escaped on to their reserved tracks at Millhouses they left behind a traffic jam of cars and buses as they proceeded without interruption to Beauchief.

On the return journey after Pinstone Street, the fifteen cars took up different routes and destinations: Nos. 349, 503 and 504 travelled via Fargate to Tinsley, Nos. 503 and 504 taking on members of the public in Fargate for the remainder of the journey, whilst Nos. 46, 189, 513 and 510 travelled via Fargate, Blonk Street and Sheaf Street to Queen's Road Works, these being cars destined for preservation. All the cars routed via Fargate stopped at the Town Hall so that passengers who were to attend the official ceremony there could alight. The other eight cars travelled via Leopold Street and Church Street to Tinsley, there to join, along with Nos. 503 and 504 which followed them, the cars which went out of service earlier in the day and some of the cars previously withdrawn from service.

Chapter 15

The Winding up of the System

During the period of route closures it had been the practice to remove the overhead wiring very soon after the closures as they took place, but in most cases the roadside poles remained in position as many of them carried the brackets for street lights. In due course the streets were resurfaced with tarmacadam covering over the tramway tracks. On the Wadsley Bridge route, Nursery Street was treated in this way on 12th and 13th March 1960 almost six months after closure.

Following the final closure a much greater quantity of dismantling remained to be done, but the work proceeded expeditiously. The removal of all overhead wiring had been completed in about four weeks. Whilst nearly all track was still visible, many points and track at pedestrian crossings had been filled with tarmacadam. By mid-November the section of streets from Commercial Street to Corn Exchange inclusive had been resurfaced covering over the tracks.

Barnsley Road was resurfaced during the third week of October 1960. The bracket arms on the Millhouses–Beauchief section had been removed by the end of November.

The depot at Tenter Street which was vacated on the last day, was eventually sold about 1968 after the bus garage above had also been vacated. The site was eventually redeveloped with the construction of "The Pennine Centre" completed in 1977.

During the Autumn of 1960 most of the tramcars which had been in use up to or just before the last day were at Tinsley Depot until, at the rate of about four per week they were pushed by a diesel tractor the short distance across Attercliffe Common to Ward's Yard for dismantling. Those in use on the last days were despatched in this way during the last three months of 1960 as follows:

October 3	511	October 31	535	November 28	504
October 4	221	November 1	524*	November 29	503
October 5	532	November 2	508*	November 30	534
October 6	505	November 3	522	December 1	530
October 7	—	November 4	—	December 2	—
October 10	531*	November 7	509	December 5	529
October 11	231	November 8	506	December 6	527
October 12	115	November 9	519	December 7	523
October 13	183	November 10	501	December 8	—
October 14	—	November 11	—	December 9	—
October 17	97	November 14	528	December 12	521
October 18	167	November 15	516	December 13	222
October 19	258	November 16	515	December 14	296
October 20	122	November 17	518	December 15	350◁
October 21	—	November 18	—	December 16	‡
October 24	281	November 21	507	December 19	—
October 25	112	November 22	517	December 20	361◁
October 26	102	November 23	526	December 21	536
October 27	514	November 24	502		
October 28	—	November 25	—		

*Car sent to Wards after 8th October but withdrawn from service before that date.
‡No. 330 taken to Wards for loading for despatch to Crich.
◁Snowploughs.

As shown in the foregoing table, Sheffield's newest and highest numbered car was the last to go to Wards—on board were the General Manager of the Transport Department, the Chairman of the Transport Committee and Mr. Frank Simpkin, age ninety-five, who eighty-seven years earlier had helped to push the first horse car out of Tinsley Depot into the forecourt so that the horses could be hitched up.

So on 21st December 1960 the sad procession to the scrapyard of Sheffield's fine tramcars came to an end. Not only was this a gross waste of superb rolling stock but the City has not again seen such comfortable, efficient and reliable all weather public service vehicles.

Preserved tramcars

During most of the last quarter of 1960 the departmental cars 330, 349, 350 and 361 were also at Tinsley but finally Nos. 330 and 349 joined in preservation those which since the closure of the system had been stored at Queen's Road, namely, the restored single decker No. 46, the Standard car No. 189, the Improved Standard car No. 264 and the Roberts cars Nos. 510 and 513.

(1) The first car to go into preservation had been the "Preston" type car No. 342, built in 1907 and originally numbered 264. As already mentioned this car left Queen's Road Works on Friday 8th June 1956 for London Transport Board's Charlton Works where it joined Chesterfield, Douglas and West Ham cars awaiting their place in the British Transport Commission's Collection at Clapham. Unfortunately, for most of its time at Clapham No. 342 was not on show to the public, and eventually it was disposed of by the Museum of British Transport. It left Clapham on 13th June 1967 and arrived at Consett, County Durham

three days later, where it was placed in store. Following the opening of the tramway at the Northern Open Air Museum at Beamish in 1974 No. 342 has become operational again, but because of its condition the upper deck has been removed. The car has been repainted in the livery of Gateshead.

(2) Following the restoration of the 1874 horse car No. 15 for the Jubilee celebrations of Sheffield Corporation Tramways in 1946 the car was stored at Tinsley Depot until it was sent to the Tramway Museum Society at Crich where it arrived on 21st November 1959. It was fitted with an ex Glasgow truck and was restored and repainted by Sheffield Corporation in 1961. It was first operated by the Society during the summer of 1963. These two cars were the only ones to leave Sheffield before the final closure of the system, but afterwards and until mid December 1960 a further seven were to depart for preservation (Nos. 46, 189, 264, 330, 349, 510 and 513), all from Queen's Road except Nos. 330 and 349 which left from Tinsley.

(3) After withdrawal from service in April 1958 the Standard car No. 189, built at Queen's Road in 1934, was presented to the Tramway Museum Society. This car was stored at Tinsley Depot for over two years until September 1960 when it was moved to Queen's Road to be prepared for running in the Last Tram Procession on 8th October, followed by despatch to Crich, where it arrived on 28th October 1960.

(4) Early in 1960, the snowplough No. 354, which until 1920 had been a single deck passenger car, one of the original twelve single deckers of 1899, was purchased by the Tramway Museum Society. It was stored at Tinsley Depot after withdrawal from departmental service, and whilst there it was converted back to a passenger car using seats and other fittings from the lower saloon of the original short ended open top double decker No. 133, built in 1903 and withdrawn in 1928 and later used as a tea-room at Calver Sough. The work was done by Society members, who gave the car its original number 46. As in the case of No. 189, Society members travelled in this car in the final procession on 8th October. Along with No. 189, No. 46 reached Crich on 28th October 1960.

(5) The next departure was "Sheffield's Last Tram", the 1950 Roberts car No. 510 which arrived at Crich on 29th October 1960.

(6) The Stores car No. 349 converted from "Preston" type of 1907 and originally numbered 271, which was further converted to an illuminated car for the Last Tram Week celebrations, was a late acquisition by the Tramway Museum Society, who purchased it. It was moved from Tinsley Depot to Ward's Yard on 9th December for loading for its journey to Crich. Before transit it had been repainted bearing an advertisement of Cockaynes, the Sheffield department store. At Crich it was repainted again, in a brown and cream livery and went into use as a mobile electrical generating unit. It has since been broken up.

(7) On 3rd December 1960, No. 513 left Queen's Road for the Middleton Railway at Leeds. This car, unlike the seven which went to Crich, has had a nomadic existence. It is believed that it was never used at Middleton and in 1963 it went into storage for seven years in the railway goods shed at Cullingworth near Keighley.

In 1970-71 it was stored in the open air at Oxenhope on the Keighley and Worth Valley Railway. The next "port of call" was the Castle Museum Store at Fulford, York where it was observed in December 1973. Early in 1977 it arrived at Beamish in a neglected condition, and there joined No. 342. It has since been restored and is on loan to Blackpool Corporation at the time of writing (1985).

(8) & (9) The final departures from Sheffield were for Crich. No. 264, the Improved Standard car built in 1937, was despatched from Queen's Road Works, the last tram to leave there and the only car to be preserved which remained in normal service right up to the last day. No. 330, the Corrugation Car, the only second-hand car to be converted in Sheffield for departmental use, went to Ward's Yard at Tinsley on the afternoon of 16th December 1960 for loading. Both cars arrived at Crich on the 17th.

By this time, as noted earlier, there remained only the snowplough No. 361 and the newest car No. 536 at Tinsley Depot, and when they went to the scrapyard early in the following week, there were no trams left in Sheffield for the first time for over eighty-seven years[1].

The horse car No. 15 was however lent to the Transport Department on two later occasions—as part of the pre-Christmas celebrations in 1961 when it ran on the still existing track along The Moor[2], and secondly for display at the Open Day at Queen's Road Works on 13th July 1975.

It follows from the foregoing that there are eight Sheffield trams in preservation: six at Crich and two at Beamish.

In addition to the tramcars, which went to Crich in 1959 and 1960, a number of items of equipment including the Beauchief crossover followed in due course.

So ended what had been the finest urban public transport service Sheffield has ever known, and probably the best in the United Kingdom.

[1]Tinsley Depot was not converted to a bus garage as earlier proposed, and was disposed of by the Department after 1960.

[2]After such use on 17th December it was placed on a plinth as a static exhibit at the junction of High Street and Change Alley (below Walsh's) where it remained until the illuminations ceased about the end of the year.

Chapter 16

Services

Part 1—The Early Years

During the earlier years of horse tram operation it was usual for manual workers to live within walking distance of their place of work and this state of affairs was reflected in the horse car services of the period. It will be noted that by later standards the service commenced at a late hour of the morning and finished fairly early at night.

There were no through routes, partly because of the narrowness of the streets in the centre of the City, but the inner termini at Snig Hill, Lady's Bridge and Moorhead were partially linked by the horse bus service between Moorhead and Fitzalan Square.

The services advertised in 1876 were as follows:

Horse Trams:

Lady's Bridge—Attercliffe and Carbrook

Horse Buses:

*Market Hall—Brightside
Market Hall—Pitsmoor
Market Hall—Botanical Gardens
Market Hall—Broomhill
Market Hall—Ranmoor
Market Hall—Steel Bank, Upperthorpe and Walkley
*Market Hall—Hillsborough
Market Hall—Grenoside
Market Hall—Cherrytree
*Post Office[1]—Heeley
*Post Office—Nether Edge

The routes marked with an asterisk were discontinued as further horse tram routes superseded them, though by 1885 additional horse bus services ran to Broomhall Park from Market Hall and to Heeley via The Moor, Hereford Street and Shoreham Street from the Post Office.

The horse tram services of 1880 were as follows:

Lady's Bridge—Attercliffe and Carbrook, every five minutes daily

Carbrook depart 8.00 am to 10.30 pm (11.00 pm on Saturday) Sunday 1.00—10.00 pm

Attercliffe depart 8.15 am to 10.45 pm (11.15 pm on Saturday) Sunday 1.10—10.20 pm

Sheffield depart 8.40 am to 11.15 pm (11.45 pm on Saturday) Sunday 1.40—10.45 pm

Workmen's cars:	Carbrook depart	5.50 am	5.05 pm
	Attercliffe depart	6.00 am	5.15 pm
	Sheffield depart	6.25 am	5.40 pm

Lady's Bridge—Brightside (Wellington), every thirteen to fourteen minutes 8.30 am (1.00 pm on Sunday) to 10.00 pm

Lens of Sutton.

Brush single deck car No. 92 returning to the City from Walkley, at the point where short workings to Spring Vale reversed in Commonside.

[1]Between 1872 and 1909 the Post Office was located at the corner of Commercial Street and Haymarket.

Open topped "short ended" car at Chantrey Road terminus showing then undeveloped land beyond. This car remained in service until 1960 as snowplough No. 360.

Return 9.00 am (1.30 pm on Sunday) to 10.30 pm
Later cars ran on Saturday nights and special ones were added when occasion required.

Hillsborough—Snig Hill, every eight minutes
Hillsborough depart 8.00 am to 10.45 pm
Snig Hill depart 8.30 am to 11.15 pm

Heeley—Crimean Monument, every eight minutes
Heeley depart 8.00 am to 11.00 pm (11.15 pm on Saturday)
City depart 8.20 am to 11.15 pm (11.30 pm on Saturday)
On Sundays, Heeley depart 9.30 am and every thirty minutes to 1.00 pm then 1.20 pm and every few minutes to 10.30 pm. Corresponding services from City.

Nether Edge—Crimean Monument, every fifteen minutes
Nether Edge depart 8.00 am to 10.30 pm (11.10 pm on Saturday)
City depart 8.23 am to 11.00 pm (11.30 p.m. on Saturday)
No Sunday service.

An omnibus ran every few minutes between Post Office and Crimean Monument to meet Heeley and Nether Edge cars.

The normal service interval of the horse bus services at this time was hourly, and only Broomhill and Ranmoor appear to have had an operating period exceeding twelve hours per day.

The population of Sheffield grew rapidly during the horse car era and the residential suburbs expanded accordingly so that by the time the Corporation took over the system in 1896 there were insufficient cars to meet the increasing traffic demands. Despite the early intention of the Corporation to electrify the system it proved necessary to place in service additional horse cars as described in chapter three. The service was accordingly improved and earlier morning journeys were provided.

One of the earliest actions of the Corporation after taking over the undertaking was the fixing of prescribed stopping places on each route. Particulars are shown in chapter three.

Part 2—Corporation Services

Before describing the services operated it should be noted that during the early years route letters were used along with destination descriptions which in some cases were not consistent with the geographical locations concerned. In the following particulars the appropriate geographical destinations have been used.

The destination descriptions referred to were:

Nether Green:	Via Broomhill known as Fulwood
	Via Hunters Bar known as Nether Green

Hunters Bar[2]:	Known as Ecclesall
Banner Cross:	Known as Ecclesall until extension to Millhouses Lane opened
Hangingwater Road:	Known as Ecclesall until extension to Nether Green opened
Woodbank Crescent:	Known as Heeley (until about 1930)
Chantrey Road:	Known as Norton Woodseats or Norton during the early years after the extension to this point
Hillsborough (top of Parkside Road):	Via Neepsend known as Owlerton Via Langsett Road known as Hillsborough
Page Hall Road (junction):	Via Barnsley Road known as Pitsmoor Via Upwell Street known as Firth Park
Carbrook (Weedon Street):	Known as Tinsley (until about 1950).

The route letters in use during the period 1900-1905 were:

A	Abbeydale, also Attercliffe	M	Millhouses
B	Brightside	N	Norton Woodseats
C	Crookes	NE	Nether Edge
D	Darnall	NG	Nether Green
E	Ecclesall	O	Owlerton
F	Fulwood	P	Pitsmoor and Osgathorpe
FP	Firth Park	SV	Spring Vale
H	Hillsborough, also Heeley	T	Tinsley
I	Intake	W	Walkley

In addition to the five horse car routes taken over from the Company, the Corporation introduced the following services during the period from July 1896 to early February 1901:

7th November 1898	Church Street–Harcourt Road (Horse cars).
5th September 1899	High Street–Nether Edge, and Haymarket–Tinsley[3] (first electric services. Operated as two separate sections after opening day).
18th September 1899	Church Street–Walkley.

City Museum.

1900 car standing in Nether Green Road at the Hangingwater Road terminus, known at the time as Ecclesall.

[2]The terminus appears to have been at what was to become Rustlings Road junction.

City Museum.

No. 112 standing in Batley Street siding, Osgathorpe. The siding led out of the 'From City' line and required a crossover on the through lines for return working. The point lever can be seen beside the far standard. The street lamp bears the legend "Tram Station".

27th September 1899	Haymarket–Pitsmoor (via Barnsley Road).
30th September 1899	Haymarket–Osgathorpe.
1st October 1899	High Street–Hunters Bar (horse cars until 12th April 1900).
10th January 1900	Broad Street--Norfolk Park (from Fitzalan Square via Blonk Street from 14th April 1900).
6th May 1900	High Street–Abbeydale (horse cars until 27th July 1900).
1st November 1900	High Street–Albert Road (horse cars withdrawn 5th May 1900).
26th November 1900	Fitzalan Square–Brightside via Savile Street[3] (electric service).
26th January 1901	Nursery Street–Owlerton Bridge.
9th February 1901	Nursery Street–Owlerton (Parkside Road top).

The services reversing around High Street and Fitzalan Square caused traffic congestion in the central area, so it was decided to operate a series of through routes to improve traffic conditions. Through services commenced operation on 14th February 1901 but they were withdrawn after two days because of trouble with the track for cars turning out of Haymarket into High Street. During the period of interrupted through running, the separated services reverted to their previous central termini except that, following the construction of a crossover in Haymarket, from 2nd April cars which had previously turned in Fitzalan Square commenced turning at Haymarket. The southern and western routes terminated at High Street or Church Street.

The period of interruption of through running lasted over nine months and during that time, in 1901, further routes came into use as follows:

24th March	Church Street–Broomhill (and Ranmoor from 1st August).
1st April	Church Street–Lydgate Lane (Crookes).
11th April	Haymarket–Darnall.
and 1st March	extension of Abbeydale route from Woodseats Road to Bannerdale Road.
28th October	extension of Hunters Bar route to Hangingwater Road.

[3]Following the introduction of electric traction on the Tinsley route the horse car service to Brightside was cut back to commence at Twelve o'Clock junction, the horse cars connecting there with the Tinsley electric cars. On 24th July 1900 the Tramways Committee resolved to provide two double deck electric cars to run between Fitzalan Square and Twelve o'Clock junction to connect with the horse cars. The arrangement lasted until electrification of the Brightside route.

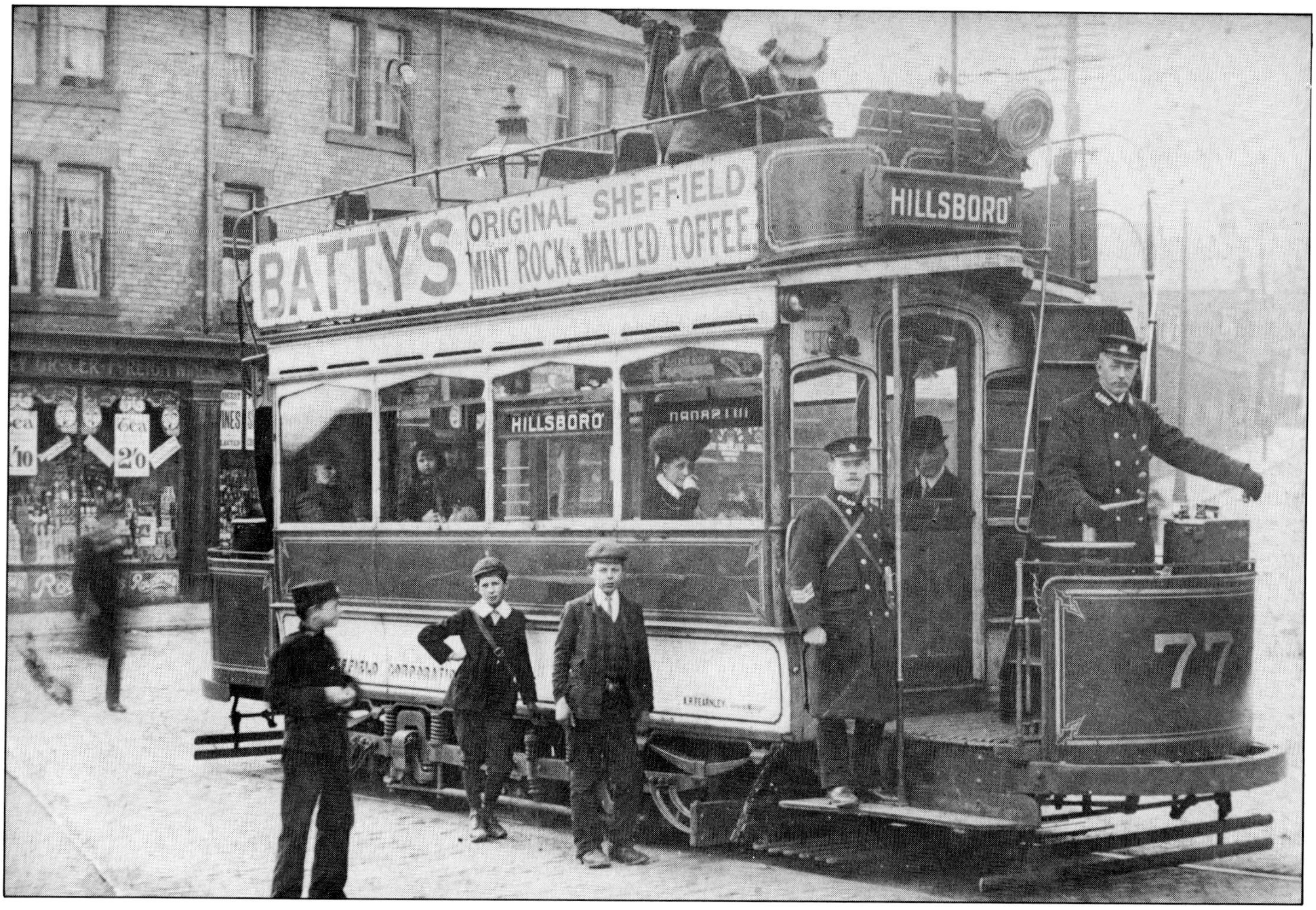

Open top car No. 77 built in 1900, at Nether Edge terminus. The original depot and workshops are hidden by the car.

The third layout at the Fitzalan Square junctions was completed in October 1901 and this enabled the northern services which had been turning in Haymarket to resume using Fitzalan Square. At the same time the Ranmoor cars (extended to Nether Green on 12th October) and the Crookes cars were extended from Church Street to the Commercial Street siding. During the same month the Nether Edge cars which had been reversing in High Street commenced using the newly completed Market Place siding. This obviated delay to through running which recommenced on 25th November 1901 involved the following services:

Tinsley–Abbeydale (Bannerdale Road), Millhouses Lane from 17th April 1902.

Tinsley–Heeley (Albert Road), Woodbank Crescent from 1st November 1902 and Chantrey Road from 6th April 1903.

Owlerton (Parkside Road top) via Neepsend Lane–Hangingwater Road

followed by Walkley–Pitsmoor via Barnsley Road (single deck cars) and Harcourt Road–Osgathorpe (double deck cars) on 20th April 1902.

There were a number of developments and alterations to services in 1902. On 17th April the Intake route from Fitzalan Square was extended from Manor Lane to Woodhouse Road, whilst on 28th of that month the Commercial Street–Crookes route was extended from Lydgate Lane to School Road. Later in the year on 25th November the Crookes and Intake routes were linked (via Blonk Street) but this arrangement lasted only until 12th December when double deck cars were introduced for the Crookes service starting at Commercial Street once more and the Intake service was again from Fitzalan Square.

On 19th May 1902 peak hour services were introduced from Millhouses and Hunters Bar to and from the Moorhead siding. The Millhouses peak hour service was short lived, being withdrawn completely on 12th January 1903 whereas the Hunters Bar peak cars were extended through to Osgathorpe.

On 1st August 1902 the short working on the Walkley–Pitsmoor route operated by double deck cars between Harcourt Road and Osgathorpe was replaced by a service between Hangingwater Road and Osgathorpe; the Harcourt Road cars terminating in the City at Church Street, but a fortnight later the Hangingwater Road–Osgathorpe service was reduced to peak times only and the regular service from Hangingwater Road was diverted to Darnall.

The "Upwell Street line" came into partial use on 9th August between Pitsmoor and the Reform Chapel traversing Page Hall Road and Owler Lane. The track in Upwell Street between Brightside Lane and the Reform Chapel came into use on 20th October. Two services were then instituted

A. D. Packer.

Penistone Road on the section between Hoyle Street junction and Hillfoot Bridge used normally only for football specials to and from Owlerton. On 27th September 1959 just before closure of the line.

running at infrequent intervals alternately via Brightside Lane and via Pitsmoor, where an awkward reversal at Page Hall Road top was required. A curve to avoid this was eventually authorised under an Act of 1928 but was never built. The two services had a common terminus at the Reform Chapel and, strangely, do not seem to have operated as a circular route. This arrangement seems to have lasted just over a year, until on 26th October 1903 an early timetable shows a service to Firth Park (Bolsover Road) via Upwell Street. Originally it had been intended to provide a service between Pitsmoor and Tinsley via Upwell Street and the projected Weedon Street line, with no service to and from the City centre via Upwell Street.

In 1905 this service was linked with Walkley as stated later. All these services were operated by single deck cars.

In September 1902 the short working on the Walkley–Pitsmoor route between Harcourt Road and Church Street (prior to 1st August 1902 to Osgathorpe) was withdrawn. The whole service between Pitsmoor via Barnsley Road and Walkley was then provided by single deck cars terminating alternately at Springvale and South Road (Walkley).

In connection with the electrification of the horse car route from Snig Hill to Hillsborough Bridge, track relaying commenced in West Bar in August 1902 and the service was progressively cut back to Corporation Street early in September and to Hoyle Street "New Inn" by 29th of the month. A temporary horse car service was introduced in October 1902 from Hoyle Street to Hillfoot Bridge (instead of the service to Hillsborough Bridge via Langsett Road), where it connected with the electric cars on the Owlerton service, but on 11th November 1902 horse car operation ended completely.

For several months no trams ran between Hoyle Street and Hillsborough Bridge but even before the end of the temporary horse car service an augmented service of electric cars was provided on the Owlerton route via Neepsend as far as Owlerton Bridge.

On 12th February 1903 the section between Moorfields (Bowling Green Street) and Hillfoot Bridge via Shalesmoor and Penistone Road was electrified, the service continuing to Owlerton (Parkside Road). The augmented service via Neepsend was withdrawn at the same time.

On 14th of the month the Moorfields terminus was extended inwards to West Bar (North Church Street). On 30th May 1903 this service was brought still closer to the centre of the City at the foot of Snig Hill, and on the same day the electrified service to Hillsborough (Willis Road) commencing at North Church Street was introduced. In June the foot of Snig Hill became the central terminus for this route also.

"Short ended" car No. 78 at Millhouses Terminus (Archer Road). Open topped when built in 1900 and later fitted with top cover. T.M.S.

Further service developments took place in 1903. On 12th January the Crookes service became a through route to Darnall instead of terminating at Commercial Street. At the same time a peak hour service was introduced between Darnall and Tinsley and soon afterwards between Darnall and Heeley (Albert Road).

In addition to the Walkley–Pitsmoor service, a service from Walkley to Intake via Blonk Street commenced at the end of January, and almost immediately on 2nd February was rerouted via Commercial Street.

On 6th April a service between Newhall Road (Attercliffe) and Woodseats (Chantrey Road) was introduced.

On 21st July Rotherham Corporation opened their line to Tinsley Depot but there was no connection between the Sheffield and Rotherham tracks at that time.

A new Sheffield route to Petre Street (Canada Street) came into use on 24th September, the service commencing at Fitzalan Square. This service, and also those from Pitsmoor and Firth Park via Brightside Lane resumed entry to the City centre via Blonk Street, Sheaf Street and Commercial Street, although using Haymarket, Waingate and Lady's Bridge on the outward journey.

An innovation of 1904 was the "City Circular" service which commenced on 25th January. The route was via High Street, Fargate, Pinstone Street, Moorhead, Furnival Street, Midland Station, Sheaf Street, Victoria Station Approach, Blonk Street, Lady's Bridge, Waingate and Haymarket and in the reverse direction. The service was not a success and early in March it was altered to omit Victoria Station, Blonk Street, Lady's Bridge, Waingate and Haymarket by running directly between Sheaf Street and High Street via Commercial Street. The Victoria Station was then provided with a separate service in one direction only commencing at the Moorhead via Fargate, High Street, Commercial Street, Sheaf Street, Victoria Station Approach, returning to Moorhead via Blonk Street, Waingate, High Street and Fargate. This latter service lasted only about two weeks. Little improvement resulted from these changes and at the close of 18th May the Midland Station portion of the "City Circular" service was also withdrawn. Latterly only four cars had operated on this service as related in the next paragraph.

The following day with the opening of the Shoreham Street line, there commenced the "Shoreham Street Circular" routed via High Street, Fargate, Pinstone Street, The Moor, and London Road to Heeley (Albert Road), returning via Queen's Road, Shoreham Street, Midland Station, Sheaf Street and Commercial Street to High Street. The service was operated in both directions with the use of eight cars, four[4] of which had been used on the "City

[4]At rush hours more cars were required.

Sheffield City Libraries.

"Short ended" cars and Corporation steam wagon in Mowbray Street.

Circular" and four released by the cutting back of the Heeley to Darnall rush hour service to operate between Fitzalan Square and Darnall.

The "Shoreham Street Circular" was extended to Derbyshire Lane in September 1905 and to Woodbank Crescent in the summer of 1909. The service lasted for seven and a half years when it was replaced by the through route between Woodbank Crescent and Crookes via Shoreham Street or Queen's Road.

On 14th May 1904 Nether Green via Hunters Bar was linked to Owlerton via Nursery Street and Neepsend Lane.

On 3rd August with the completion of the Angel Street, Snig Hill track, the Nether Edge–Angel Street siding (Market Place) and West Bar–Hillsborough (Willis Road) services were linked to form another through route. At the same time Nether Green via Broomhill was linked to Owlerton via West Bar and Penistone Road.

Because of inconsistencies in records of this period, it has not been possible to establish with certainty the dates of opening of the following services:

Fitzalan Square–Brightside via Newhall Road, along with a workmen's service terminating at Hawke Street (Brightside)

Angel Street–Nether Green via Broomhill and a peak hour service between Angel Street and Hunters Bar.

There is reason to believe that they were opened in 1904 but certainly were operating by 23rd January 1905. In the case of the Newhall Road line, use of double deck cars commenced, making the first through service along that road and allowing double deck cars to reach Brightside for the first time. Until then Newhall Road had had no through service to either Pitsmoor or Brightside but it had been used as a terminus for Attercliffe cars (firstly at the Attercliffe Road end but later at the Brightside Lane end) which ran to and from Woodseats (Chantrey Road). That service was now withdrawn.

On 14th May 1905 the service between West Bar or Nether Green via Broomhill and Owlerton (Parkside Road) via Shalesmoor and Penistone Road was withdrawn. Thereafter, except for about two months after the December 1940 air raids and other short emergency periods, the section of this line between Hoyle Street junction and Hillfoot Bridge was used only for football traffic to Owlerton.

On or about 23rd January 1905 Walkley ceased to be linked with Pitsmoor via Barnsley Road. This service which had been provided by single deck cars was replaced by a service of single deckers via Brightside Lane. Pitsmoor via Barnsley Road was then connected to Crookes using double deck cars, the first to negotiate the steep hill between Osgathorpe and Firvale. Accordingly the use of Batley Street siding at Osgathorpe (for turning double deck cars) ceased permanently. The cars which had provided the Walkley–Intake service continued to do so.

R. B. Parr.

In Savile Street on the Brightside route at Sutherland Street on 24th August 1957.

Another major development of 1905 took place on 11th September when all Tinsley cars were routed to Millhouses instead of the divided service to Millhouses or to Woodseats. Woodseats was then connected to Pitsmoor via Barnsley Road. These changes established a general pattern for these routes which lasted until 1960. Through working of the joint service from Fitzalan Square to Rotherham was introduced on the same day.

Two further services introduced in 1905 were Woodseats–Petre Street (as well as the Pitsmoor service), and Hunters Bar–Darnall.

In the years which followed, reroutings were few compared with the numerous changes of the first six years of electrification. Most of the service changes during the years of expansion from 1906 to 1935 were in the form of route extensions.

The reroutings or alterations of existing services in the period from the end of 1905 until the outbreak of war in 1914 were:

(i) On 28th January 1906 the alternate cars to Springvale on the Walkley route were withdrawn, the whole service running to and from the South Road terminus.

(ii) In February 1907 a peak times service between Darnall and Brightside was introduced.

(iii) With the opening of the Hunters Bar to Banner Cross line on 1st August 1908 a service was provided to and from Hillsborough.

(iv) A more extensive programme of alterations took effect on 31st August 1908:

(a) The Malin Bridge service which opened on 19th May and had run to and from West Bar was extended to Nether Green via Hunters Bar.

(b) Nether Edge cars ceased to run to Hillsborough, and instead provided a service to Leopold Street with alternate cars continuing to Nether Green via Broomhill. The cars terminating at Leopold Street were soon diverted via Fargate to Petre Street, though some Petre Street cars continued to reverse at Fitzalan Square.

(c) The Hillsborough service was worked (along with the Malin Bridge service) to Nether Green via Hunters Bar or to Banner Cross.

(d) The Owlerton via Neepsend service to Nether Green via Hunters Bar was curtailed to either Fitzalan Square or Hunters Bar.

(e) The Darnall service to Crookes and to Hunters Bar was cut back to Fitzalan Square.

(v) In November 1911, as mentioned earlier, the "Shoreham Street Circular" service was withdrawn and replaced by the extension of the service between Crookes (School Road) and the Midland Station to Woodbank Crescent via either Shoreham Street or Suffolk Road and Queen's Road. The new arrangements provided the first regular passenger

T.M.S.

No. 112 ascending the Crookes Valley Road curves between Harcourt Road and Crookesmoor Road on the Walkley route on 16th April 1955.

service along Suffolk Road and Queen's Road as far as Havelock Bridge.

The route extensions of the 1906-1914 period have been described already but are summarised here for convenience:

29th May 1909	Darnall (Main Road) to Handsworth (Finchwell Road).
25th August 1909	Pitsmoor (Bolsover Road) to Firth Park (Bellhouse Road).
8th September 1913	Hillsborough (Willis Road) to Catch Bar Lane.
26th November 1913	Catch Bar Lane to Middlewood (Langsett Avenue).
26th November 1913	Crookes (School Road) to Heavygate Road.

Holme Lane junction to Malin Bridge on 19th May 1908 and Rustlings Road to Banner Cross on 1st August 1908 were new branch routes rather than extensions of existing ones.

In 1912 a service of workmen's cars had been requested, and granted, between Nether Edge and Brightside in the mornings, and later a return service in the evenings was also granted; but they were poorly patronised and accordingly had a limited life.

The pattern of services at the outbreak of the First World War was therefore:

Tinsley–Millhouses
Firth Park–Woodseats (via Barnsley Road)
Middlewood–Nether Green (via Hunters Bar)
Middlewood–Banner Cross
Malin Bridge–Nether Green (via Hunters Bar)
Walkley–Intake
Crookes–Woodbank Crescent (or possibly Woodseats, Chantrey Road) (via Shoreham Street or Queen's Road)
Nether Edge–Nether Green (via Broomhill)
Nether Edge–Petre Street
Fitzalan Square–Handsworth
Fitzalan Square–Brightside (via Attercliffe and via Savile Street)
Fitzalan Square–Owlerton (Parkside Road top)
Fitzalan Square–Rotherham
and probably Fitzalan Square–Firth Park (via Savile Street) and Midland Station–Walkley.

In addition there were the peak hour services.

In November 1914 the work of lowering the road and track level under the railway bridge in Brightside Lane was completed and consequently the Brightside service reverted to the direct route via Savile Street and Brightside Lane using double deck cars. The Firth Park via Savile Street cars were rerouted via Attercliffe at the same time.

In December 1915 the through service between Walkley and Intake was severed when double deck cars commenced working from the City to Intake. On 27th May 1918 double

R. B. Parr.

Walkley to Intake car at the summit point after the ascent of Commonside about to descend Barber Road at Board of Trade stopping place, on 20th November 1954.

deckers were introduced on the Walkley route, in the first instance only during the morning, noon and evening rush hours. The following month a member of the public requested, through the press, resumption of the through running to avoid the long walk betwen the Intake City terminus at Commercial Street and that for Walkley at Church Street. In due course the through service was restored.

No other changes during the First World War have been traced except those occasioned by the quarrels between the Corporations of Sheffield and Rotherham in respect of the joint service. On 30th September 1914 the through working ceased, but was resumed on 17th May 1915, though in the following month Sheffield cut back the service from Fitzalan Square to Bridge Street on Saturday evenings and Bank Holidays. From the following 12th October Bridge Street became the Sheffield terminus at all times. From 27th November 1915 the joint service was augmented by one between Templeborough and Bridge Street provided by Rotherham cars.

In 1920 work commenced on the lowering of the carriageway and track under the Upwell Street railway bridge and during the period of work change of cars was necessary at either side of the bridge. Through running between Commercial Street and Firth Park via Attercliffe was resumed on 23rd April 1922 using double deck cars.

Prior to 1924 there had never been Sunday morning services apart from the "church cars" (for churchgoers) which had ceased about the turn of the century, and the munition workers' cars of the First World War. Details of the latter service are shown in Appendix H(2).

On 16th November 1924 the City Council authorised the introduction, on an experimental basis, of the fifteen minute interval service from 9 am on Sunday mornings. The arrangement was not completely successful and after three months the services to Petre Street, Wadsley Bridge, Firth Park via Attercliffe and Brightside were withdrawn, and on 15th September 1931 the City Council authorised the withdrawal of the entire ordinary Sunday service to Brightside which was already covered by the Wincobank buses. However the early morning workmen's cars between 5 and 9 am continued to run and were supplemented during the Second World War.

During the 1930s Sunday morning services were resumed on the Wadsley Bridge route, and to Firth Park via Attercliffe from 10 am and the buses to Petre Street, which had by then replaced the trams, commenced at 9.20 am.

Just as the Intake route received the benefit of double deck cars at some date earlier than Walkley, the same pattern was followed in the case of air-braked cars, although

A. D. Packer.

The ascent of Barber Road towards Walkley on 1st April 1956. The steepness of the hill is apparent from the levels of the buildings. The Board of Trade stop can be seen at the top.

only as far as Elm Tree. From the commencement of the Prince of Wales Road service on 24th February 1928 that type of car had operated along City Road and Duke Street, the curve from Sheaf Street into Broad Street having been adjusted to accommodate these cars.

On 18th November 1926 an air-braked car was tested on the Walkley route and it seems that this isolated car was still operating on the route in early June 1927. However no quick action seemed to be possible in those years of financial stringency and it was only in January 1929 that it was reported to the City Council that expenditure of approximately £2,780 would be needed to increase the clearance between the tracks on the bends of the Walkley route, to permit the safe operation of these much longer cars. It is not known how quickly this work was put in hand, but it is likely that by the end of the year the whole-day services at least would have been operated by air-braked cars. A compelling factor in the change over to this type was the run-down of the fleet of "short ended" cars which had monopolised this route. At the beginning of 1930 only twenty nine of them remained in service.

During the post war years up to 1935 inclusive, the following route extensions came into use, but route groupings were not affected:

Banner Cross to Ecclesall—14th April 1922
Chantrey Road to Woodseats (Abbey Lane)—22nd January 1923
Nether Green to Fulwood (Canterbury Avenue)—12th July 1923
Owlerton (Parkside Road) to Wadsley Bridge—7th June 1924
Millhouses (Millhouses Lane) to "Waggon and Horses"—31st July 1926
Woodseats (Abbey Lane) to Meadowhead—12th July 1928
Handsworth (Finchwell Road) to Orgreave Lane—7th September 1934
Firth Park (North Quadrant) to Sheffield Lane Top–18th November 1934
Intake (Woodhouse Road) to Hollinsend Road—8th February 1935.
Intake (Hollinsend Road) to Birley Vale—29th December 1935.

In addition, there were the two circular routes of Abbey Lane and Prince of Wales Road opened on 14th April 1927 and 24th February 1928 respectively. These routes which have been described already made no material difference to existing off-peak services (except Elm Tree to Intake referred to in part three of this chapter), though the latter brought into existence a variety of peak hour cross country journeys between Intake and Tinsley, Templeborough,

Rotherham, Brightside, Firth Park and later Sheffield Top. A peak hour service was also introduced between Sheffield Lane Top and Brightside.

Most of the other service developments of the inter-war years were occasioned by the three route closures of the period, and the opening of the Exchange Street line. On 22nd September 1924 Exchange Street became the terminus for Firth Park via Attercliffe instead of Commercial Street top and for Handsworth instead of Fitzalan Square. On 12th January 1925 the Nether Edge cars ceased to serve Fulwood via Broomhill and Petre Street and the whole service was routed to Handsworth. The Fulwood cars then terminated and reversed at Leopold Street. The Petre Street cars also terminated at Leopold Street, inward via Church Street and out via Fargate, but this service was withdrawn completely on 19th April, when the route was abandoned.

Two other changes occurred on 12th January 1925. The Rotherham service was rerouted into Exchange Street via Blonk Street and outward via Waingate instead of terminating in Bridge Street, and a new service from Exchange Street to Darnall was introduced.

On 24th March 1934 the Nether Edge route closed, and in consequence Handsworth was linked to Fulwood via Broomhill (via Fargate and Leopold Street). The Fulwood via Broomhill service was itself withdrawn on 22nd August 1936 and thereafter the Handsworth service was routed to Leopold Street via Church Street and outward via Fargate.

The rush hour services from the "East End" to the southern suburbs routed via Furnival Street (by way of Blonk Street and Sheaf Street) are referred to in chapter thirteen.

The City centre routing of the Prince of Wales Road service was altered in December 1939 to reduce congestion and to ease difficulties caused by the war-time "black-out" at the busy junctions at the east end of Fitzalan Square. During the weekday evening peak period between 4.30 and 6.45 pm, on Saturdays after 12 noon, and on Sundays after 6 pm cars proceeding via City Road and Elm Tree to Prince of Wales Road no longer reversed in Flat Street but continued from there, along Pond Street to the Midland Station junctions and thence along Sheaf Street to rejoin their normal route at the foot of Commercial Street. By this method, no trams needed to make a right hand turn from Fitzalan Square during busy periods. Cars arriving from Elm Tree via City Road continued to ascend Commercial Street and enter Fitzalan Square. A result of this procedure was that trams were being driven from one end only throughout the period of the operation, as they did not reverse in the City centre. Cars to and from Prince of Wales Road via Darnall were not affected and used Haymarket in both directions, their City terminus continuing to be in Fitzalan Square. What had started as a wartime measure continued to the end of the service on this route.

There was only one further major rerouting during the tramway era and this occurred on 12th October 1941 when the following previously existing services:

Crookes–Woodseats via Shoreham Street or Queen's Road
Fitzalan Square–Wadsley Bridge, and
Leopold Street–Handsworth

were altered to:

Crookes–Handsworth (via Church Street)
Woodseats via Shoreham Street or Queen's Road—Wadsley Bridge as described in chapter ten.

On 15th July 1941 it was decided to reroute Tinsley cars at busy times, via Commercial Street and Blonk Street instead of via Haymarket and Waingate, with the City terminus moved from High Street (Market Side) to the lower end of Commercial Street. This was to apply during the Monday to Friday evening rush hour and on Saturdays from midday to reduce traffic congestion at the foot of High Street, but when the above mentioned route alterations took place on 12th October the arrangement was discontinued. During the period of this part time diversion via Commercial Street, Sheaf Street and Blonk Street to the Wicker, cars returning from Tinsley had continued to operate via Waingate and Haymarket.

A. D. Packer.
No. 268 on the Crookes service at Handsworth terminus in Retford Road on 2nd February 1957.

There were no more alterations to through route destinations and even during the period of general closure of the system between 1952 and 1960 through routes were closed as a whole with the exception of the circular routes. Elm Tree via Prince of Wales Road was for a final period worked only via Darnall, whilst with the Abbey Lane closure Beauchief was served as an extension of the Millhouses service.

Valuable adjuncts to the tram services in general were the late evening postal cars which operated from October 1902 until the outbreak of the Second World War in 1939. In the early years there were two collections nightly by tram and in 1915 these were timed as follows:

(i) Leaving suburban termini between 9.30 and 9.50 pm for the 10 pm collection at the G.P.O. for the general night mail for London and the South.
(ii) Leaving suburban termini between 10.30 and 10.50 pm for the 11 pm collection at the G.P.O. for the supplementary night mail for London and for the general night mail to the North.

The services at 9.30 and 10.30 pm were from Handsworth. The indicator blinds at each end showed "Postal Car" in red capital letters, and the post boxes were fitted to a bracket on the inside of the dash near the steps to the platform, so that the box could be reached without boarding the car.

D. A. Thompson.

In Commercial Street on 6th August 1939, on the Crookes–Woodseats service.

In later years there was a single service on most routes but the Saturday night postal service was withdrawn after 2nd April 1927 as the mail did not leave the City on Saturday nights.

In 1939 the departure times of the postal cars on Mondays to Fridays (Bank Holidays excepted) were as shown in Appendix H(4).

Part 3—Frequency and Duration of Services

Information on these matters concerning the earlier years is limited as no regular timetables for public use were published until free issue commenced in 1924. Two early issues which have survived were for the years 1904 and 1905; an extract from the latter is shown in Appendix H(1). During all the years which followed, the timetable books were far from explicit in a number of ways. Instances of this are the lack of information concerning rush hour extra services, the service to and from the Midland Station, the absence of fare tables and the omission of any form of route map in the last twenty-five years of tramway operation.

From the commencement of electric operation it soon became clear that services were inadequate for the demand and as more rolling stock and power generating equipment became available they were augmented where necessary.

The opening electric service intervals in 1899 for Tinsley and Nether Edge do not appear to have been recorded. For Walkley the interval was twelve minutes (commencing at 7 am from Church Gates, and 7.30 from South Road), and for Pitsmoor via Barnsley Road it was twelve minutes. An earlier start of service on the Tinsley route was introduced for workers in 1900, at 4.17 am from Tinsley and 4.45 am from the City. A twenty minute interval was prescribed for Broad Street–Manor Lane (Intake route).

The press reported in December 1900 that the following intervals were in operation:

Hunters Bar, Nether Edge, Heeley, Newhall Road, Tinsley	6 minutes
Abbeydale, Walkley	7 minutes
Harcourt Road, Pitsmoor, Brightside	10 minutes
Intake	12 minutes
Osgathorpe	15 minutes

In 1901 the Darnall service was at fifteen minute intervals and Crookes (Lydgate Lane) was at twenty minutes.

When through running commenced on a permanent basis on 25th November 1901 the weekday service was as follows:

Tinsley to Abbeydale 4.15 am and every six minutes to 11.09 pm

Abbeydale to Tinsley 5.15 am and every six minutes to 11.09 pm

Heeley to Newhall Road 5.30 am and every six minutes to 11.00 pm

P. N. Williams.

Standard car in pre-1935 livery at Woodseats terminus on 19th March 1950, with substituted corner windows to platform.

Walkley to Pitsmoor 6.00 am and every seven minutes to 10.55 pm
Harcourt Road to Osgathorpe 7.15 am and every twelve minutes to 11.15 pm
Owlerton to Hunters Bar 5.00 am and every seven minutes to 11.05 pm
The latter four times were the same in the reverse direction.

The last car from Walkley was to Tinsley at 11.51 pm and the last from Hunters Bar was to Queen's Road Depot via Heeley.

When the Upwell Street line was opened the service commenced at Fitzalan Square at 7.00 am to the Reform Chapel via Brightside Lane, and at 7.30 am via Barnsley Road and then hourly by each route throughout the day.

In 1903 the peak hour service between Darnall and Tinsley was every ten minutes; the Hillsborough service was every five minutes commencing at Willis Road at 5.00 am and at West Bar at 5.27 am. The Petre Street service from its opening was every twelve minutes.

The "Stations Circular" of 1904 ran every five minutes in each direction, the frequency being increased for a short period to two and a half minutes.

In January 1905 the Pitsmoor service via Barnsley Road, which previously had comprised a ten minute service of double deck cars to Osgathorpe and ten minutes to Page Hall Road by single deckers, was replaced by a five minute service of double deck cars for the whole journey.

When the Crookes (School Road) service was switched from Pitsmoor to the Midland Station in July 1906 the frequency was improved from ten to seven minutes.

With the rerouting of Nether Green cars to Hillsborough and Malin Bridge instead of Darnall in 1908 the interval became five minutes instead of six, and Hunters Bar to Hillsborough instead of Darnall became two and a half instead of three minutes.

In 1909 with the linking of Nether Edge to Nether Green via Broomhill alternate cars from Nether Edge terminated at Leopold Street, providing a five minute interval to that point and ten minutes beyond to Nether Green. Soon after when the Nether Edge to Leopold Street cars were diverted and extended to Petre Street the same interval of ten minutes applied.

In the years following the 1905 timetable (see Appendix H(1)) the general trend was towards improvement and this remained the case until the post Second World War period. There were, however, setbacks resulting mainly from the two World Wars.

In November 1915 a decision was made that last cars from the City centre should run at 11.10 pm and there was a further cut back as from 30th October 1916 when the last journeys were made at 10.40 pm.

On 1st July 1918 a number of request stops were

H. B. Priestley.

Cars at the Midland Station junctions on 1st May 1955.

eliminated to save fuel and some of these were never reinstated.

Immediately after the Armistice the early morning cars for munition workers were withdrawn on Sundays from 17th November 1918, these being services on certain routes which the General Manager had been authorised to operate after 31st August 1915. An application to the City Council on 26th November 1918 for suspension of tramway services on Christmas Day was acceded to in view of the cessation of hostilities, without making it a precedent. As from 3rd March 1919 the time of the last cars again became 11.10 pm.

At some time after the opening of the Prince of Wales Road route in February 1928 it was decided that a four minute service to Intake was no longer needed as the new route covered most of the Intake route. The service on the latter was consequently reduced to an interval of eight minutes.

The services to Nether Green and Fulwood were altered in the 1920s. In the middle of that decade the service via Hunters Bar was at five minute intervals to Nether Green and that via Broomhill at ten minute intervals. By 1928 the latter service had been increased to a five minute interval also. The through service beyond Nether Green to Fulwood (Canterbury Avenue) was one of twenty minutes by both routes, a combined interval of ten minutes. On the closure of the Broomhill route in 1936, the service via Hunters Bar to Fulwood was doubled to a frequency of ten minutes, thus preserving the previous interval between Nether Green and Fulwood of the former combined routes.

Part 4—1939 Services

By 1939, with a modern fleet of tramcars and a high standard of reliability, the system had reached its zenith of operating efficiency; a standard of service which deserves description in some detail.

The weekday service commenced at 3 am with the early morning cars as follows:

3.00 Church Gates to Woodseats via Queen's Road
dep. Woodseats 3.30 to Tinsley via The Moor (Market Side 3.50)

3.10 Fitzalan Square to Handsworth
dep. Handsworth 3.40 to Fitzalan Square

3.10 Tinsley to Sheffield Lane Top via Newhall Road
dep. Sheffield Lane Top 3.38 to Fitzalan Square via Newhall Road

3.20 Tinsley to Nether Green (High Street 3.40)
dep. Nether Green 4.00 to Tinsley (Market Side 4.23)

3.20 Shoreham Street Depot to Beaumont Road via Elm Tree
dep. Beaumont Road 3.40 to Depot via Elm Tree

3.30 Pinstone Street to Millhouses and Woodseats
continuing 4.00 to City via Queen's Road

R. B. Parr.
Nos. 253 and 245 at the Wicker Arches on 16th April 1955. LNER (ex-GC) J.11 goods engine is standing on the viaduct. The Wicker served seven northern routes as well as most of the rush hours extras; it was one of the busiest tramway thoroughfares in Sheffield.

3.35 Holme Lane Depot to Angel Street dep. 3.50 to Holme Lane Depot
dep. Holme Lane Depot 4.05 to Angel Street dep. 4.20 to Holme Lane Depot
3.45 Crookes Depot to Church Gates dep. 4.00 to Crookes
dep. Crookes 4.25 to Church Gates
4.05 Shoreham Street Depot to Firth Park via Savile Street
dep. Firth Park 4.30 to Fitzalan Square via Newhall Road
4.12 Pinstone Street to Meadowhead
dep. Meadowhead 4.36 to Market Side via The Moor
4.30 Tinsley to Firth Park via Newhall Road
dep. Firth Park 4.50 to Fitzalan Square via Savile Street
4.40 Fitzalan Square to Darnall
continuing 4.55 to Fitzalan Square via Elm Tree
5.23 Woodseats to Brightside via Shoreham Street.

These journeys were followed by the ordinary off peak weekday services with which in some cases they merged. Until about 6.45 am service intervals were normally fifteen to twenty minutes. Thereafter off-peak intervals were as shown in Appendix H(3). These services were lavishly augmented during morning and evening rush hour periods on Mondays to Fridays and morning and midday on Saturdays. At these times the centre of the City was "full of tramcars"!

Some additional through journeys from East End termini were routed to southern and western destinations different from those of the normal service and similarly in the opposite direction on weekday mornings. There were a number of short workings.

During Monday to Friday evenings and Saturday midday rush hours a number of cars to southern suburbs were routed via Furnival Street to avoid traffic congestion in central streets as referred to in chapter thirteen.

None of the augmented rush hour journeys serving the City centre were advertised in the timetables issued to the public. In contrast the "cross country" services to and from the East End via Prince of Wales Road were shown. They are referred to later.

After the close of the ordinary service there were the late night cars which served most routes.

On Monday to Friday nights the following services operated from the City:

at 12.10 am to Brightside (S); Beauchief; Ecclesall; Intake; Meadowhead via Shoreham Street (S); Beaumont Road via Elm Tree (S); Sheffield Lane Top (S); and Tinsley.
at 12.17 am to Holme Lane Depot.
at 12.30 am to Hillsborough; Darnall via Elm Tree; and Sheffield Lane Top via Savile Street.

A. D. Packer.

Reversing to return to the City at Dane Street crossover in Brightside Lane on 2nd February 1957. One of the numerous short workings at rush hours.

at 12.35 am to Crookes Depot (S); Handsworth; and Tinsley.
at 12.40 am to Intake via Darnall (S).
at 12.45 am to Intake; and Sheffield Lane Top.
at 12.50 am to Holme Lane Depot.
at 1.00 am to Crookes Depot.
at 1.05 am to Sheffield Lane Top.
at 1.25 am to Beauchief; Intake; Holme Lane Depot; Meadowhead via Queen's Road; Nether Green; and Sheffield Lane Top.

There were return journey as follows:
at 12.15 am from Sheffield Lane Top to Fitzalan Square via Attercliffe; and Tinsley to Fitzalan Square.
at 12.29 am from Intake to Shoreham Street Depot.
at 12.30 am from Ecclesall to Angel Street (and Holme Lane Depot); and Beaumont Road to Shoreham Street Depot via Elm Tree (S).
at 12.33 am from Beauchief to Angel Street.
at 12.35 am from Meadowhead to Shoreham Street Depot via Shoreham Street (S).
at 12.37 am from Firth Park to Fitzalan Square (S).
at 12.45 am from Darnall to Fitzalan Square via Elm Tree.
at 12.55 am from Sheffield Lane Top to Fitzalan Square; and Holme Lane Depot to Angel Street.
at 1.05 am from Crookes Depot to Church Gates (S); and Tinsley to City (and Beauchief).
at 1.10 am from Intake to Shoreham Street Depot (S); and Sheffield Lane Top to Fitzalan Square.
at 1.45 am from Intake to Shoreham Street Depot; and Nether Green to Market Side.
at 1.46 am from Beauchief to Shoreham Street Depot via Queen's Road.
at 1.47 am from Sheffield Lane Top to Fitzalan Square.
at 1.48 am from Meadowhead to Shoreham Street Depot via Shoreham Street.

(S) indicates services also operated on Saturdays.

On Saturday nights following the close of the ordinary service late night cars left the City on nearly all routes at thirty minute intervals until 1.30 am, departing from suburban termini thirty minutes later. In addition there were the journeys marked (S) in the foregoing lists, as well as, at 1.20 am, cars from Market Side to Firth Park (returning at 1.43), Angel Street to Holme Lane Depot, Commercial Street to Intake (returning at 1.40), and Fitzalan Square to Meadowhead via Queen's Road (returning at 1.45 to Shoreham Street Depot via Shoreham Street).

By the time the last of the late night cars were back at their depots, there was an interval of less than one hour until the departure on weekdays of the first early morning cars of the next day. Thus apart from a period of about two

R. B. Parr.

Reversing at Pitsmoor on short working to Woodbank Crescent on 19th July 1958. Page Hall Road lines can be seen entering from the right.

and a half hours early on Sunday mornings, only during this short interval each day were there no trams in passenger service.

In addition to the services terminating or passing through the City centre there were the "cross country" peak time services connecting the housing estates of the northern and eastern suburbs with the industrial area of the East End. These services worked on the Sheffield Lane Top–Upwell Street–Attercliffe–Darnall–Intake axis, branching to Brightside at Hawke Street junction, and to Tinsley, Templeborough, Bessemer Gates[5] or Rotherham at Newhall Road junction, Attercliffe. This axis was completed in 1928 with the opening of the Prince of Wales Road line, which enabled Intake cars to travel direct via Darnall instead of via the City centre.

Whereas cars between Firth Park and Brightside worked via the Hawke Street triangular junction, those between Firth Park and Tinsley and beyond had to reverse at Attercliffe. In view of the number of cars to and from Tinsley Depot via Newhall Road, it is surprising that a triangular junction was never installed at the Attercliffe end of that road.

[5]Bessemer Gates were situated at Sheffield Road, Rotherham between Temple Street and Ickles, at the entrance to the Bessemer furnaces of Steel Peech and Tozer Ltd.

The advertised Monday to Friday service via Prince of Wales Road is summarised as follows:

Between 5.00 and 8.26 am there were thirty-three departures:

From Intake 13, Woodhouse Road 6, Elm Tree 12, Beaumont Road 2.

To Tinsley 1, Vulcan Road 14, Templeborough 9, Brightside 6, Firth Park 3.

From Intake or Elm Tree there were 3 journeys between 1.10 and 1.20 pm, 17 between 4.12 and 6.46 pm, and finally 8 between 7.30 and 10.40 pm, but none of these served Brightside.

There were corresponding services in the opposite direction:

28 departing between 4.50 am and 7.51 am, 3 between 12.50 and 2.06 pm, one at 3.44 pm, 29 between 4.40 and 7.11 pm and lastly at 10.06 pm from both Bessemer Gates and Vulcan Road to Intake.

The Saturday morning service was as on Mondays to Fridays, but after midday the only advertised services were: eleven journeys between 12.02 and 12.31 pm from Brightside, Templeborough, Vulcan Road or Tinsley to Elm Tree or Intake, and in the evening 4.40 Vulcan Road to Intake, 5.04 Tinsley to Elm Tree and 5.06 Vulcan Road to Elm Tree.

Before the commencement of the Sunday morning

A. D. Packer.
Rush hour cars on the Prince of Wales Road central reservation, providing "cross country" and circular route services.

fifteen-minute interval service at 9.00 am there were almost one hundred departures from central terminal points, intended primarily for workmen. The first fourteen cars left between 4.38 and 6.00 am as follows:

4.38 Shoreham Street Depot to Woodseats via Shoreham Street
4.45 Fitzalan Square to Wadsley Bridge
4.55 Fitzalan Square to Firth Park via Savile Street
5.00 Shoreham Street Depot to Woodseats via Shoreham Street
5.05 Fitzalan Square to Sheffield Lane Top via Savile Street
5.20 Fitzalan Square to Handsworth
5.25 Fitzalan Square to Brightside via Savile Street
5.25 Fitzalan Square to Rotherham
5.30 Bridge Street to Middlewood
5.35 Fitzalan Square to Firth Park via Savile Street
5.40 Fitzalan Square to Brightside via Savile Street
5.45 Fitzalan Square to Wadsley Bridge
5.45 Fitzalan Square to Templeborough
5.55 Fitzalan Square to Firth Park via Savile Street

There were corresponding return workings, the first of which was at 5.00 am from Woodseats and from Tinsley. No through journeys were advertised before 9.00 am but by that time nearly every route had been served.

From midday until the end of the ordinary service, which was about thirty minutes earlier than on weekdays, service intervals varied only slightly from those of the weekday ordinary service and in no case by more than two minutes, except Rotherham which was at an eight minute interval instead of five.

The late night cars ran at half hourly intervals until 1.30 am from the City as on Saturday nights, along with four additional journeys between 12.10 and 12.53 am.

In summary, from about 7.00 am on weekdays and from noon on Sundays until the close of the ordinary service, the interval between cars in no case exceeded ten minutes! Weekday frequencies were as little as two minutes to Hunters Bar, and three minutes to Tinsley and to Firth Park via Pitsmoor. Five minutes was the maximum interval on nearly all routes even on Sundays (after midday).

Sunday facilities also included "cross country" services for workmen to and from the East End. There were nine such services between 5.12 and 7.28 from Intake, Elm Tree or Handsworth to Tinsley, Vulcan Road, Templeborough or Brightside, and at 12.15 pm and 9.15 pm from Elm Tree to Templeborough. There were four services in the opposite direction at 4.47 and 5.17 am Tinsley to Handsworth, and 6.10 and 7.35 am Templeborough to Intake and Darnall respectively. There were cars to Intake at 1.06 pm from Bessemer Gates and at 5.06 pm from Vulcan Road. Of particular interest was the inclusion of Handsworth in these services on Sundays only.

Part 5—1939 to 1960

During the Second World War services were maintained as near to normal as possible except for staff shortages causing some midday services to be temporarily reduced. The 1.00 am and 1.30 am weekend late night cars (see later) were withdrawn on 23rd October 1939. Even as late as 19th November 1940[6] the City Council was assured that following consultations with the Trade Unions, and subject to certain safeguards, services would continue to operate during air raid alerts until an air attack seemed imminent.

Following the restoration of routes after air raid damage as described in chapter ten, a restricted service was provided on Christmas Day 1940 between 10.00 am and 6.20 pm and from 30th December a modified evening service was introduced from 7.15 pm. Trams then ran at half hourly intervals on all routes until 10.45 pm ex-City centre (10.15 pm on Sundays) and where two services were run over the same route for part of the distance, to Hunters Bar for Ecclesall or Fulwood for instance, the running times were staggered to give a quarter hourly service over the combined section.

By 1942 the last cars on Sundays were at 10.45 pm as on weekdays. It was the first time in the Department's history that last cars departed at the same times on all seven days of the week and this remained the case until the end of tramway operation.

On 13th August 1945 last cars from the City centre (in the ordinary service) reverted to the pre Second World War time of 11.30 pm.

During the difficult years following the Second World War reliability of service fell below that of the inter-war years but in general it was good until the end.

As a result of the Suez Crisis in the Autumn of 1956, late bus services were curtailed because of the threat of fuel oil scarcity, and in order to conform, albeit illogically, with bus practice, from 30th December 1956 the last cars of the ordinary service left the City centre at 11.15 instead of 11.30 pm and that later timing was never restored. Had this action not been taken for the thirteen tram services still operating, it would have highlighted the superiority of the trams and their non-dependence on imported fuel. However, late night journeys from midnight continued to operate.

After the closure of the Abbey Lane route at the end of February 1959 the off-peak service to Beauchief was at a fifteen minute interval and during the final months of operation it was altered to thirty minutes.

During the summer of 1960 and until the final closure of the system only nine cars were required to work the ordinary evening service on the remaining Tinsley–City–Millhouses–Beauchief route.

A. D. Packer.

War damage replacement car No. 100 and No. 231, the first of the improved standard cars, near Staniforth Road Junction, Attercliffe, on 28th April 1957. The curve towards the cars was used by 'cross country' services to and from Intake.

[6]The air raid which brought about the premature end of the Coventry tramway system occurred on 14th November 1940.

Part 6—Daily Work Periods of Individual Trams

Some duties occupied only a few hours, but the same cars might be required for a second or third spell of duty on the same day. There were, however, many whole day duties on which the only respite was a few minutes "lay over" at termini or depots. In some cases cars which were twenty or thirty years old were in continuous operation for an entire day, a tribute to both the builders and to the Department's standards of maintenance. Cars which had performed a long programme of duty would not normally be expected to undertake similar duties on the following day.

Examples of typical duties are shown in Appendix H(5).

Appendix A(1)

The principal types of electric passenger cars 1899-1960

During the sixty-one years of electric operation there were 876 different passenger cars and of this total the Corporation built 341 in their own workshops, forty-four at Nether Edge and 297 at Queen's Road. The whole fleet was mounted on four wheel trucks and current collection was by trolley and wheel (excepting one short-lived experiment with a bow collector) from overhead wires. There were sixty-nine single deck cars built between 1899 and 1904, the last of which was withdrawn from passenger service in 1921; otherwise the whole fleet was double deck. The track gauge was four feet eight and a half inches.

All sixteen foot saloons had four side windows except Nos. 244 and 245 which had five, and the ex-L.C.C. "B" class which had three. All the twenty foot saloons had five side windows except Nos. 501-536 which had four.

From 1918, 483 new cars were placed in service, 272 of which were built at Queen's Road. All cars built from 1927 had upholstered seats from new and most of the 154 of 1918-1927 were so equipped in the 1930s or later.

Rebuilding and improving formed an almost continuous programme from 1903-1955, and embraced nearly the whole of the original fleet by 1927.

With the exception of Nos. 130 and 212 which were purpose-built, the departmental fleet comprised converted horse cars and single and double deck passenger cars of the original electric fleet.

The Corporation's type classification was not particularly descriptive in respect of the double deck passenger cars; for example all cars built and almost all rebuilt after 1918 were VV, indicating vestibuled balconies and platforms. Other classifications used were SE "short ended"; SD single deck; OO open balconies and platforms; OV open balconies and vestibuled platforms; and VO vestibuled balconies and open platforms. The classification of departmental cars was: S/P snowplough; W/C water car (corrugation car); SC stores car; BW breakdown wagon or car. These classifications are shown in parentheses in the following tramcar type pages.

Second-hand transactions: forty-six cars were sold (1918-1923) and fifty-two were purchased (1917-20, 1926 and 1941-42). Two of the purchased cars were never used in service and were scrapped. There were numerous transactions in trucks and electrical equipment.

TYPE Open top double deck (SE)

The conductor in the above picture was the grandfather of Mr. G. Whitehouse, who generously supplied the photograph.

BUILT IN 1899-1904 **BY**

Milnes	Nos. 1-38, 131-155
E.R. & T.C. Co.	Nos. 59-88
Brush	Nos. 104-123, 219-243
Cravens	Nos. 167-186
Sheffield Corporation	Nos. 193-198, 213-218
Sheffield Corporation	Nos. 244 and 245 rebuilt Milnes horse cars.

NO. OF CARS 172

LENGTH: LOWER SALOON 16′ 0″

TRUCK Brill 21 E (See notes below)* **WHEELBASE** 6′ 0″

MOTORS G.E.52, G.E.58 from No. 131

CONTROLLERS B.T.H. B.13

NUMBER OF SEATS: LOWER SALOON 22 **UPPER DECK** 29 **TOTAL** 51

TYPE Wooden longitudinal in saloon, 11 double and 1 single reversible transverse and 3 fixed transverse at each end on upper deck.

NOTES All cars from No. 167 had improved type ventilator top windows to lower saloon.

*Other types of trucks: Nos. 1-38 Peckham Cantilever, Nos. 193-198, 213-218 Milnes Girder, Nos. 219-245 Brush.

All converted to top covered cars between 1903 and 1913:

126 with short upper deck covers

43 rebuilt as open balcony and platform cars (OO)

3 rebuilt as open balcony and vestibuled platform cars (OV).

WITHDRAWN FROM SERVICE None in original form.

TYPE Single deck (SD)

BUILT IN 1899-1904 **BY** Milnes — Nos. 39-50, 51 and 52, 187-192

FLEET NUMBERS

E.R. & T.C. Co. — Nos. 53-58

Brush — Nos. 89-103

Sheffield Corporation — Nos. 124-129, 200-211

Cravens — Nos. 156-165

NO. OF CARS 69

LENGTH: LOWER SALOON 20′ 0″ **OVERALL** 28′ 6″ to 29′ 6″ originally*

WIDTH: **OVERALL** 6′ 9″

HEIGHT over trolley plank 10′ $1\frac{3}{4}$″, Brush cars 10′ $2\frac{1}{2}$″

TRUCK Brill 21 E (except Nos. 39-52 Peckham Cantilever 10A) **WHEELBASE** 6′ 0″ (originally 5′ 6″)

MOTORS 2 B.T.H. G.E.52 25 h.p.† (except Nos. 53-58 G.E.58 35 h.p.)

CONTROLLERS B.T.H. B.13

NUMBER OF SEATS: LOWER SALOON 28 **UPPER DECK** — **TOTAL** 28

TYPE Wooden longitudinal in saloon (except Nos. 51 and 52 longitudinal seats for 16 in saloon and 6 in each smoking compartment to either end of centre saloon). No. 56 was refitted with transverse seats in 1904.

NOTES All cars were built to Sheffield standards except Nos. 53-58 which were those of the Preston Works. Magrini-type drop windows were fitted to No. 56 in 1904. All cars were fitted with trolley standards except those used on the low bridge routes.

* Most cars later received extended platforms making overall length 30′ 4″ or 32′ 4″.

† G.E.58 motors eventually became standard.

9 cars received vestibuled extended platforms between August 1913 and September 1914.

21 cars were rebuilt as double deckers in 1906-7 and between 1915 and 1918.

35 cars were sold between 1918 and 1920.

9 cars were converted to snowploughs in 1913 and between 1919 and 1921.

WITHDRAWN FROM SERVICE 1921 (Nos. 50, 53, 57, 92).

TYPE Short canopy double deck (SE)

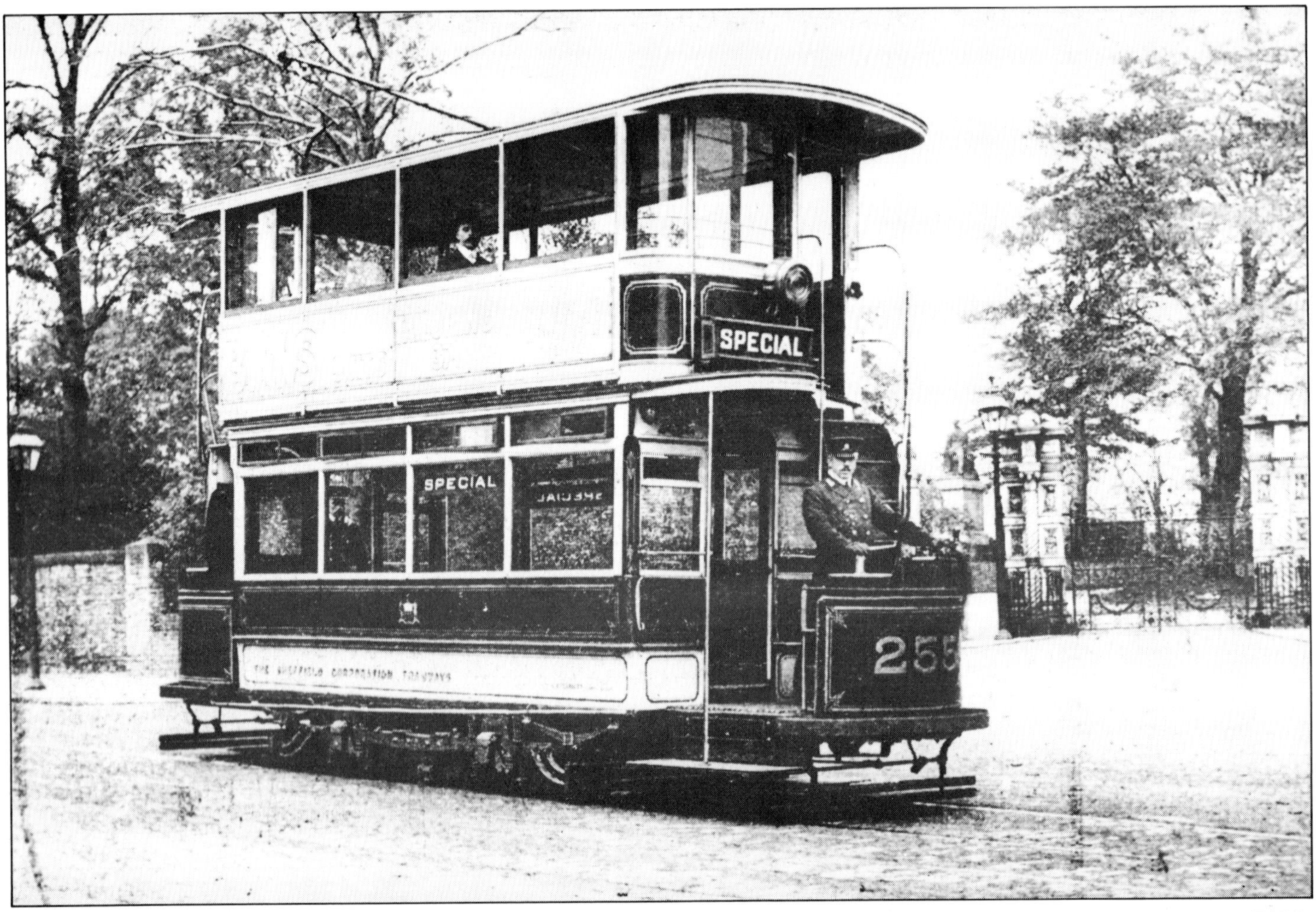

T.M.S.

BUILT IN 1905 **BY** Sheffield Corporation

FLEET NUMBERS 246-257

NO. OF CARS 12, and 126 cars originally open top, converted between 1903 and 1910

LENGTH: LOWER SALOON 16′ 0″

TRUCK Brill 21 E, Peckham Cantilever or Milnes Girder **WHEELBASE** 6′ 0″

MOTORS 2 B.T.H. G.E.52 (G.E. 58 No. 131 upwards)

CONTROLLERS B.T.H. B.13

NUMBER OF SEATS: LOWER SALOON 22 **UPPER DECK** 30 **TOTAL** 52

TYPE Wooden longitudinal in saloon, 12 double transverse and 3 fixed transverse at each end on upper deck.

NOTES

(1) All cars from No. 167 had improved type ventilator top windows to lower saloon.

(2) The following 27 cars were further rebuilt as shown below:
Open balcony, vestibuled platform (OV) 1913-19 Nos. 59, 60, 88, 107, 120, 167, 171, 173, 174, 181, 198, 225, 238
Fully enclosed (VV) 1919-25 Nos. 177, 179, 194, 197, 214, 220, 224, 228*, 229, 230, 234, 236, 237, 239

(3) The following 11 cars were sold:
In December 1922 to Gateshead Nos. 16, 35, 37, 38, 74, 176, 182, 186
In August 1923 to Musselburgh Nos. 141, 170, 252.

(4) The following 6 cars were converted between 1923 and 1929 for Departmental use:
Nos. 77, 111, 172, 185 and 226 became snowploughs and No. 142 a Water car.

WITHDRAWN FROM SERVICE 1922-1931.

*Improved type and not until 1927. The last of the original fleet of electric cars to be rebuilt.

TYPE Single deck rebuilt as large double-deck open balcony (OV)

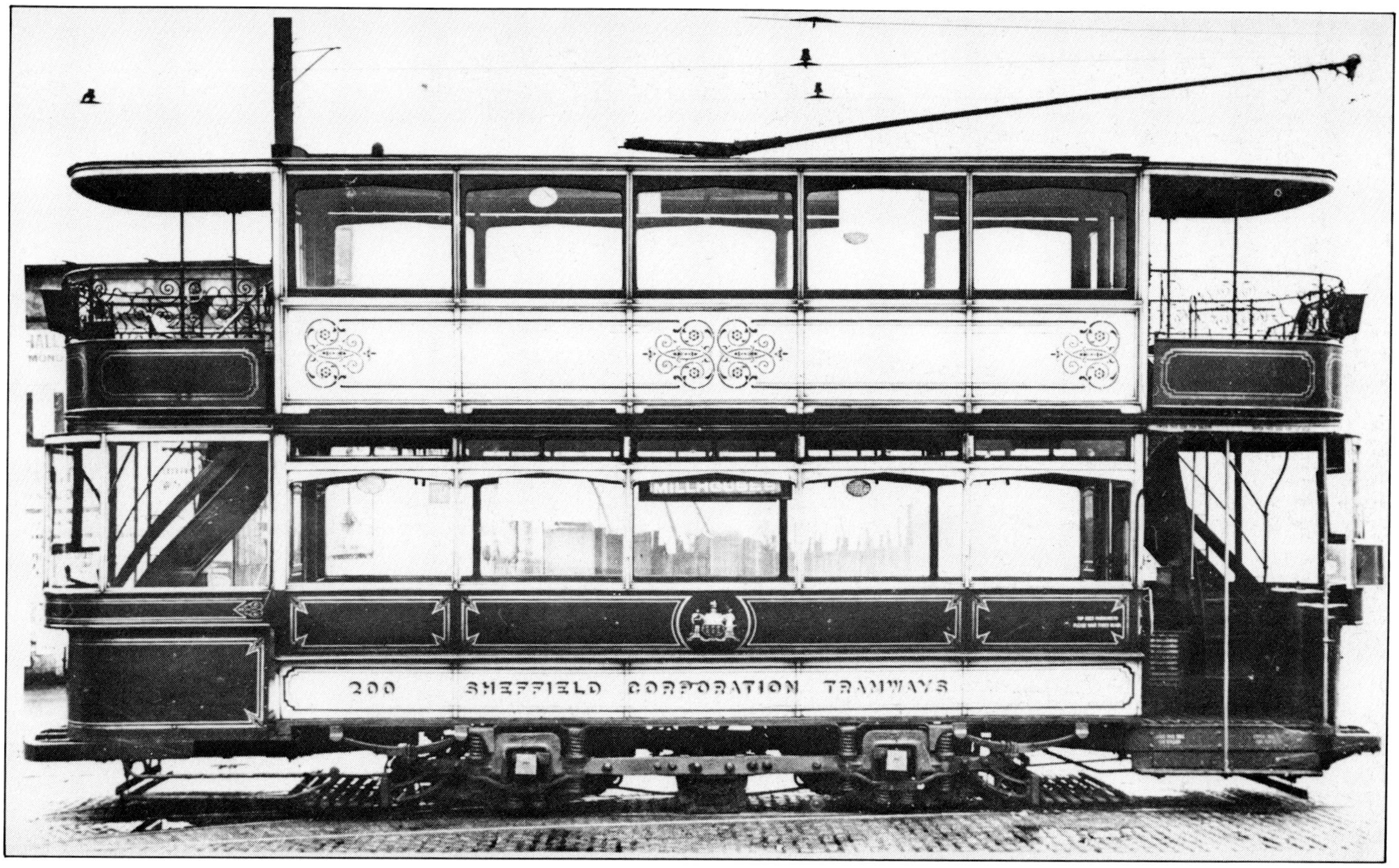

T.M.S.

REBUILT IN 1906-1907 and 1915-1918 **BY** Sheffield Corporation
FLEET NUMBERS 48, 124, 127, 156-165, 189-192, 200, 201, 205, 208
NO. OF CARS 21
LENGTH: LOWER SALOON 20′ 0″ OVERALL 33′ 0″
TRUCK Peckham P22* **WHEELBASE** 8′ 6″
MOTORS 2 B.T.H. G.E.58
CONTROLLERS B.T.H. B.13
NUMBER OF SEATS: LOWER SALOON 28 **UPPER DECK** 44 **TOTAL** 72
TYPE Wooden longitudinal in saloon, 18 double reversible transverse on upper deck and 2 double transverse seats (one reversible) on each open balcony.

NOTES The nine cars rebuilt in 1915-1918 received vestibuled platforms (Nos. 163-165, 189-192, 201 and 205). The original twelve had open platforms which were vestibuled between 1914 and 1916.
Cars rebuilt in 1906 were the first in Sheffield to have headlamps on the dashes.
*Prior to 1915 Brush Conaty radial trucks were utilised.

WITHDRAWN FROM SERVICE 1933-1935.

TYPE U.E.C. or "Preston" (OV)

T.M.S.

BUILT IN 1907 **BY** United Electric Car Co.
FLEET NUMBERS 258-272
NO. OF CARS 15
LENGTH: LOWER SALOON 16′ 0″ **OVERALL** 28′ 4″ (5′ 6″ platforms)
WIDTH: **OVERALL** 7′ 1″
HEIGHT over trolley plank 15′ 9$\frac{1}{8}$″
TRUCK Mountain and Gibson Radial* **WHEELBASE** 8′ 6″*
MOTORS B.T.H. G.E.58, replaced by 1926 with B.T.H. R.G.E. 20 (excepting Nos. 260 and 268, M.V.102, No. 272 B.T.H.503)
CONTROLLERS B.T.H. B.13, replaced by B.T.H. B.510
NUMBER OF SEATS: LOWER SALOON 22 **UPPER DECK** 36 **TOTAL** 58
TYPE Wooden longitudinal in saloon, 14 double reversible on upper deck and 2 double transverse (one being reversible) on each open balcony.

NOTES
*Replaced by Peckham P.22 8′ 0″ wheelbase trucks in 1918-1920.
No. 259 experimentally rebuilt in 1911. Fully enclosed, 60 seats.

WITHDRAWN FROM SERVICE See Rebuilt "Preston" type.

TYPE U.E.C. or "Preston" Rebuilt Fully enclosed (VV)

H. B. Priestley

REBUILT IN 1924-27 **BY** Sheffield Corporation

FLEET NUMBERS 258-272. Renumbered consecutively 336-350 in 1937

NO. OF CARS 15

LENGTH: LOWER SALOON 16′ 0″ **OVERALL** 28′ 4″ (5′ 6″ platforms)

WIDTH: **OVERALL** 7′ 1″

HEIGHT over trolley plank 15′ 9⅛″

TRUCK Peckham P.22 **WHEELBASE** 8′ 0″

MOTORS B.T.H. R.G.E.20 (excepting Nos. 260 and 268 M.V.102, No. 272 B.T.H.503)

CONTROLLERS B.T.H. B.510

NUMBER OF SEATS: LOWER SALOON 22 **UPPER DECK** 40 **TOTAL** 62

TYPE Wooden longitudinal in saloon, 12 double reversible on upper deck and 2 4-seat longitudinal in each end bay.

NOTES Nos. 263 and 269 fitted with vestibuled balconies in 1925 and 1924 respectively. Longitudinal seats for 4 and 2 in each balcony. All others along with No. 259 rebuilt with fully enclosed upper decks and quarter turn screened staircases in 1925-1927.

WITHDRAWN FROM SERVICE
Nos. 337, 338, 340 and 341 (ex. No. 263) 1938-1939
Others 1947-1954
No. 346 driver training car 1955-1957
No. 349 Stores car 1951-1960
No. 350 Snowplough 1953-1960.

TYPE Open balcony and platform (OO)

Sheffield City Libraries

BUILT IN 1912 **BY** Sheffield Corporation
FLEET NUMBERS 281-295
NO. OF CARS 15, and 44 rebuilt into this type as shown below.
LENGTH: LOWER SALOON 16′ 0″
TRUCK Brill 21 E
MOTORS B.T.H. G.E.203 40 h.p.
CONTROLLERS B.T.H. B.18
NUMBER OF SEATS: LOWER SALOON 22 **UPPER DECK** 36 **TOTAL** 58
TYPE Wooden longitudinal in saloon, 14 double reversible transverse on upper deck and 2 double transverse seats (one being reversible) on each open balcony.

NOTES

No. 290 was rebuilt as a fully enclosed car following an accident in 1919.
The following 44 short open top cars were rebuilt in this form between 1911 and 1913:
Nos. 2, 3, 5, 6*, 7-12, 14, 15, 17-19, 24-32, 64, 65, 70, 73, 75, 104, 105, 108, 112-119, 222, 235‡ and 243‡.
*No. 6 was first rebuilt with vestibuled platforms in 1913 and was again altered to this type in 1920 by the removal of the vestibuling.
Because of events concerning this car and No. 290 there were never more than 58 cars of this type at any one time.
‡Nos. 235 and 243 were again rebuilt as fully enclosed cars in 1925 and 1924 respectively.

WITHDRAWN FROM SERVICE 1923-1933.

TYPE Open balcony, vestibuled platform (OV)

Sheffield City Libraries

BUILT IN 1913-15 **BY** Brush Electrical Engineering Co. Ltd. Nos. 296-345
Sheffield Corporation Nos. 346-355

NO. OF CARS 60, and 16 rebuilds as shown below.

LENGTH: LOWER SALOON 16′ 0″

TRUCK Brill 21 E

MOTORS B.T.H. R.G.E.20 or B.T.H. G.E.203 40 h.p.

CONTROLLERS B.T.H. B.18

NUMBER OF SEATS: LOWER SALOON 22 **UPPER DECK** 36 **TOTAL** 58

TYPE Wooden longitudinal in saloon, 14 double reversible transverse on upper deck and 2 double transverse seats (one being reversible) on each open balcony.

NOTES

The following 16 short open top cars, 13 of which had received top covers between 1903 and 1910 were rebuilt in this form between 1913 and 1919:

Nos. 6*, 22*, 33*, 59, 60, 88, 107, 120, 167, 171, 173, 174, 181, 198, 225 and 238.

*Rebuilt direct from short open top cars in 1913. No. 6 ceased to have vestibuled platforms in 1920.

No. 179 which had received a short top cover by 1910 and had been rebuilt as a fully enclosed car in 1919 was again rebuilt in 1928 with open balconies, so becoming a car of this type.

Nos. 296-349, 351, 354 and 355 were rebuilt as fully enclosed cars between 1919 and 1922 and consequently after 1922 there remained only 18 cars of this type in service.

WITHDRAWN FROM SERVICE 1929-1935.

TYPE Ex-L.C.C. B class. Enclosed upper deck open platform (VO)‡

T.M.S.

BUILT IN 1903 **BY** Electric Railway and Tramway Carriage Works

FLEET NUMBERS 356-365
56, 94, 125, 129, 187, 188, 203, 207, 209, 210

NO. OF CARS 20

LENGTH: LOWER SALOON 16′ 0″ **OVERALL** 28′ 9″

WIDTH: **OVERALL** 7′ 1″

HEIGHT over trolley plank 16′ 4″

TRUCK Brill 21E* or Peckham P.22 **WHEELBASE** 6′ 6″* or 7′ 0″

MOTORS Dick Kerr 25A* or B.T.H. G.E.58 or 203

CONTROLLERS Dick Kerr D.B.1. Form D* or B.T.H.

NUMBER OF SEATS: LOWER SALOON 22 **UPPER DECK** 34 **TOTAL** 56

TYPE Plywood longitudinal in saloon. Double reversible transverse on upper deck.

NOTES

Purchased from L.C.C. 1917 and 1918.
*L.C.C. equipment replaced by S.C.T. on some cars.
No. 56 renumbered 128 in 1924, No. 94 renumbered 90 in 1925.
‡Rotherham cars purchased from L.C.C. in 1917 and converted to open balcony cars in 1922, transferred to Sheffield in 1926 and numbered 91-96. All withdrawn in 1931.

WITHDRAWN FROM SERVICE 13 cars 1926-1928, 7 cars 1931.

– TYPE Fully enclosed rebuilds, retaining sliding door – bulkheads on upper deck and half turn staircases (VV)

M. J. O'Connor

REBUILT IN 1919-1925 **BY** Sheffield Corporation

FLEET NUMBERS 296-349, 351, 354, 355
177, 179, 194, 197, 214, 220, 224, 229, 230, 234, 235, 236, 237, 239, 243, 290

NO. OF CARS 73 (and 2 others Nos. 263 and 269)

LENGTH: LOWER SALOON 16′ 0″

TRUCK Brill 21 E*

MOTORS B.T.H. G.E.203 40 h.p.

CONTROLLERS B.T.H. B.18

NUMBER OF SEATS: LOWER SALOON 22 **UPPER DECK** 40 **TOTAL** 62

TYPE Wooden longitudinal in saloon, 14 double reversible transverse on upper deck and 6 longitudinal seats in each end bay.

NOTES

No. 179 rebuilt for third time in 1928 and became open balcony car with vestibuled platforms (i.e. similar to 1913-15 cars).

*No. 349 had Peckham P.22 8′ 0″ wheelbase trucks.

No. 355 had Brill Radiax 9′ 0″ wheelbase trucks.

"Preston" cars No. 263 and 269 rebuilt in 1925 and 1924 respectively, in this style. No. 228 (short canopied car) rebuilt in 1927 in the same form as the other 13 rebuilt "Prestons" with enclosed quarter turn staircases. It was the last car of the original electric fleet of cars to be rebuilt and the only one to be rebuilt to the general pattern which was standard for all cars built between 1918 and 1944.

WITHDRAWN FROM SERVICE

1933-1939. The "Preston" car No. 269 (later 347) was not withdrawn until 1952 and was the last car in service in Sheffield with upper deck sliding door bulkheads.

— TYPE Standard fully enclosed 1919-1927 (VV) —

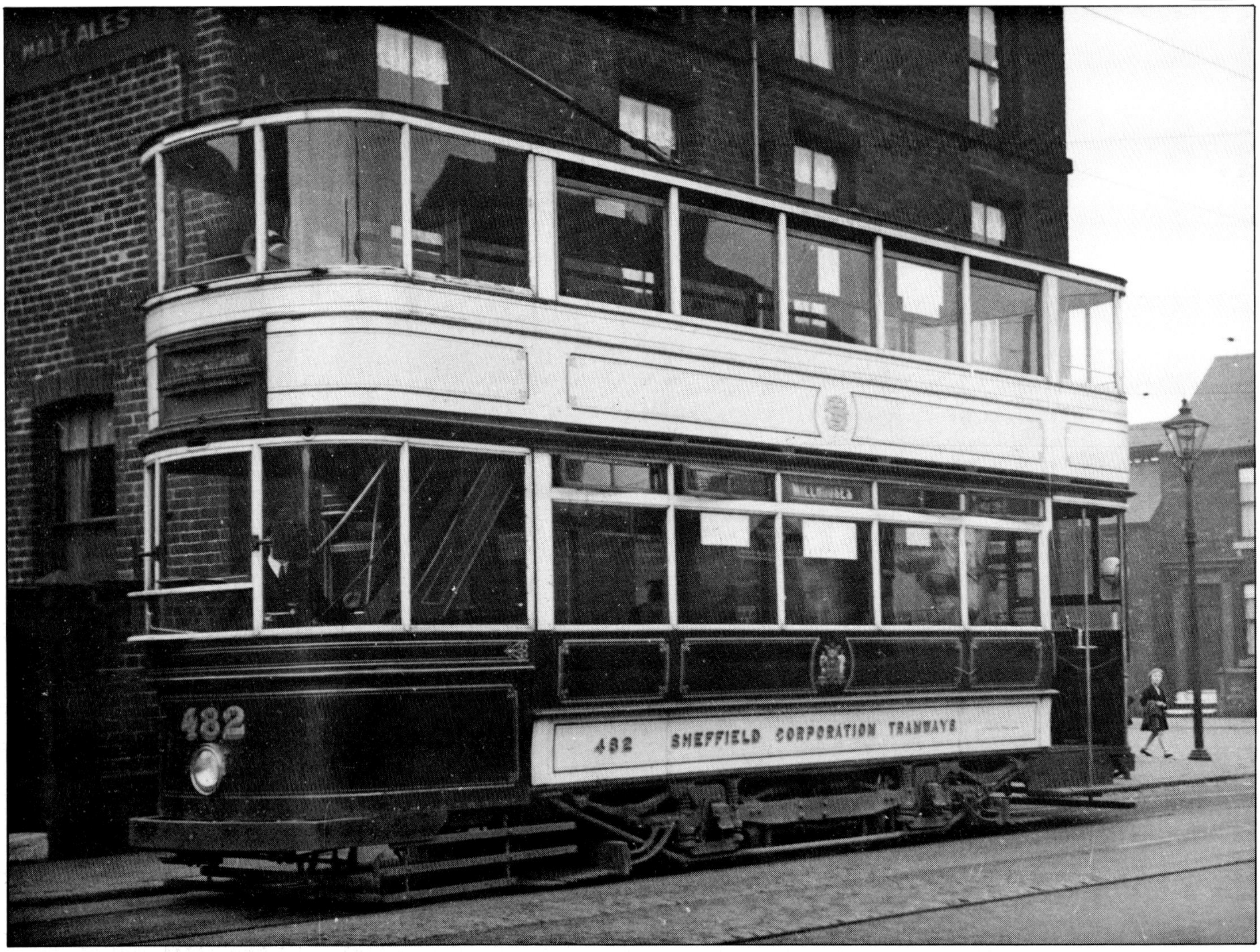

D. A. Thompson

BUILT BY Brush Electrical Engineering Co. Ltd. in 1919-1922 Nos. 376-450
Brush Electrical Engineering Co. Ltd. in 1924-1925 Nos. 36-60
Cravens Railway Carriage & Wagon Co. Ltd. in 1926-1927 Nos. 451-500

NO. OF CARS 150 also Nos. 366-369 built experimentally between 1918 and 1921 by Sheffield Corporation.

LENGTH: LOWER SALOON 20′ 0″ **OVERALL** 32′ 6″

WIDTH: **OVERALL** 7′ 3″

HEIGHT over trolley plank 16′ $2\frac{1}{2}$″

TRUCK Peckham P.22 **WHEELBASE** 8′ 6″

MOTORS 2 B.T.H. G.E.203 40 h.p. except Nos. 36-60 B.T.H. B.503 and Nos. 451-500 M.V. 102D 50 h.p.

CONTROLLERS B.T.H.

NUMBER OF SEATS: LOWER SALOON 28 **UPPER DECK** 48 **TOTAL** 76 (Nos. 366-369, 376-450)
LOWER SALOON 28 **UPPER DECK** 40 **TOTAL** 68 (Nos. 36-60, 451-500)

TYPE Originally wooden throughout. Longitudinal in saloon, 8 double reversible transverse seats on each side and 8 longitudinal in each bay on upper deck. The later cars had 8 double and 8 single transverse seats and 8 longitudinal in each bay on upper deck.

NOTES Most of these cars were re-equipped with upholstered seats as described in chapter nine.
A number of improvements were made to these cars including the provision of air brakes to Nos. 366-369 and 376-450. The later cars were fitted from new.

WITHDRAWN FROM SERVICE
1950-1957 except No. 493 in 1946. Nos. 430 and 483 were destroyed by enemy action on 12th December 1940.

TYPE Standard fully enclosed 1928-1935 (VV)

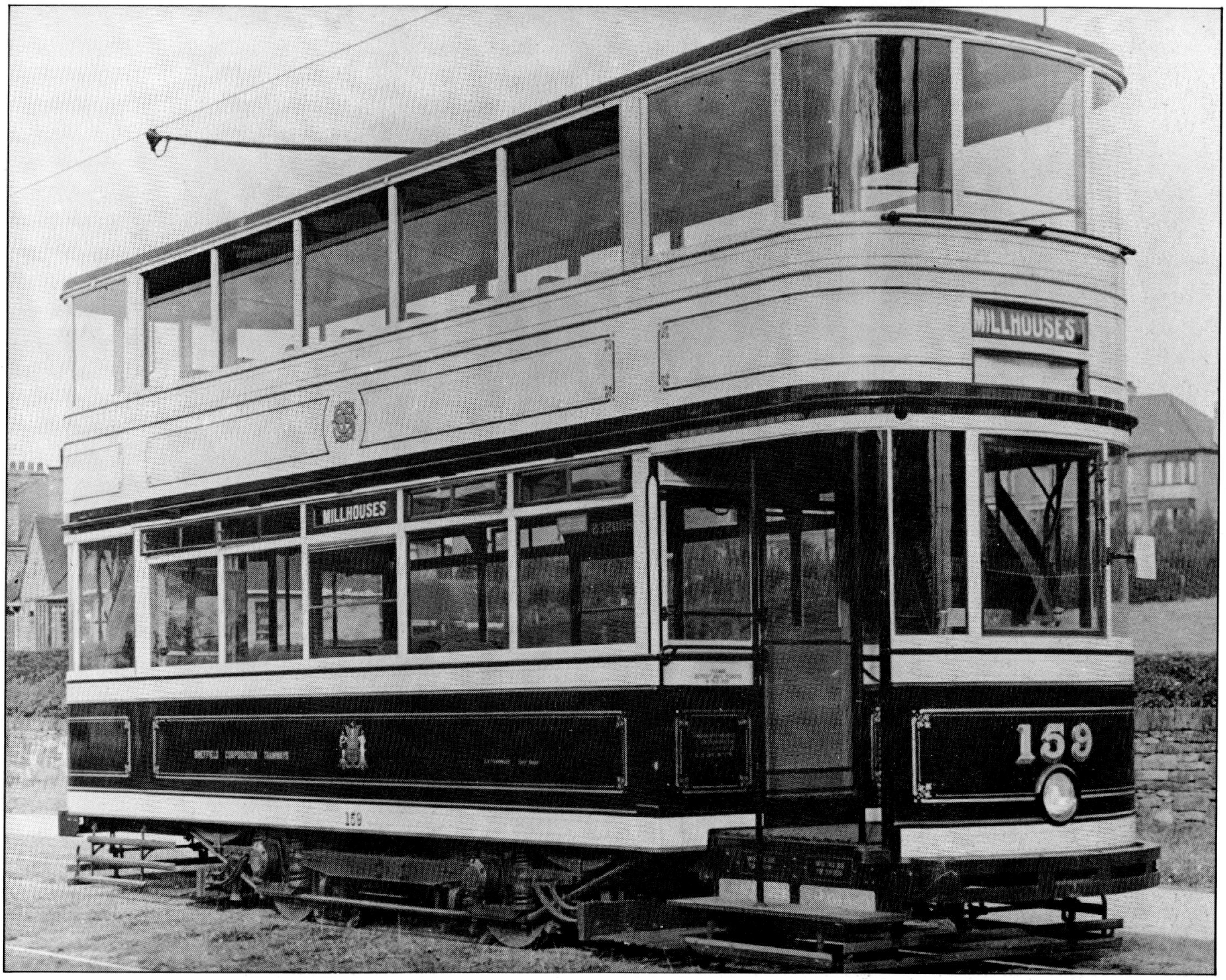

Sheffield Transport Department

BUILT IN 1928-36 **BY** Sheffield Corporation Nos. 2-35, 61-130, 156-230, 243-248
W. & E. Hill Ltd. Nos. 131-155

NO. OF CARS 210 also Nos. 1 and 370 (see notes below)

LENGTH: LOWER SALOON 20′ 0″ **OVERALL** 32′ 7″

WIDTH: **OVERALL** 7′ 3″

HEIGHT over trolley plank 16′ 2½″

TRUCK Peckham P.22 (33″ diameter wheels) **WHEELBASE** 8′ 6″

MOTORS 2 M.V. 102D.R. 50 h.p.

CONTROLLERS B.T.H. B.510

NUMBER OF SEATS: LOWER SALOON 24 **UPPER DECK** 37 **TOTAL** 61

TYPE Upholstered throughout.
Saloon: 4 double and 4 single reversible transverse, and longitudinal for 3 in each corner.
Upper deck: 7 double and 7 single reversible transverse and 2 4-seater longitudinal in each end bay.

NOTES No. 1 was an experimental car built in 1927 by Cravens Railway Carriage and Wagon Co. which formed the basis of all the Standard cars which were generally similar in design and equipment.
No. 370 was an experimental car built in 1931 by Sheffield Corporation. It was generally similar to the Standard cars but was of aluminium construction of lighter weight, utilising M.V. 116Z 40 h.p. motors.

WITHDRAWN FROM SERVICE
1951-1960. Nos. 83, 85, 100, 112, 119, 129, 133, 192, 201 and 227 were destroyed by enemy action on 12th December 1940.

TYPE Improved Standard fully enclosed

Sheffield Transport Department

BUILT IN 1936-39 **BY** Sheffield Corporation

FLEET NUMBERS 231-242, 249-303

NO. OF CARS 67

LENGTH: LOWER SALOON 20′ 0″ **OVERALL** 32′ 7″

WIDTH: **OVERALL** 7′ 3″

HEIGHT over trolley plank 16′ 2½″

TRUCK Peckham P.22 **WHEELBASE** 8′ 6″

MOTORS M.V. 102D.R. 50 h.p.

CONTROLLERS B.T.H. B.510

NUMBER OF SEATS: LOWER SALOON 24 **UPPER DECK** 37 **TOTAL** 61

TYPE Upholstered throughout.
Saloon: 4 double and 4 single reversible transverse, and longitudinal for 3 in each corner.
Upper deck: 7 double and 7 single reversible transverse and 2 4-seater longitudinal in each end bay.

NOTES Nos. 261 and 274 destroyed in air raid on 12th December 1940 and replaced by similar type cars in 1943.
12 other war damage replacement cars built by Corporation between 1941 and 1944 were of this type with minor modifications, numbered 83, 85, 100, 112, 119, 129, 133, 192, 201, 227, 430 and 483.

WITHDRAWN FROM SERVICE 1957-1960.

— TYPE Ex Newcastle open balconies and platforms — rebuilt as fully enclosed

M. J. O'Connor

BUILT IN 1901 **BY** Hurst Nelson & Co., rebuilt in 1941-42 by Sheffield Corporation

FLEET NUMBERS 311-324

NO. OF CARS 14

LENGTH: LOWER SALOON 16′ 6″ **OVERALL** 29′ 0″

TRUCK Brill 21 E **WHEELBASE** 6′ 6″*

MOTORS G.E.58 35 h.p.

CONTROLLERS B.T.H. B.3 or B.18

NUMBER OF SEATS: LOWER SALOON 24 **UPPER DECK** 36 **TOTAL** 60

TYPE Wooden longitudinal on lower deck.
Wooden garden type on upper deck.

NOTES *Nos. 311 and 313 received 7′ 0″ wheelbase trucks in Sheffield.
When rebuilt only Nos. 312, 323 and 324 were fitted with end destination indicators.
Rebuilding included new brakes, sanding gear, motors and resistances, and some required extended platforms to facilitate vestibuling. (Originally 5′ 6″ platforms and 9″ fenders.)

WITHDRAWN FROM SERVICE 1948-1952.

TYPE Ex Bradford open balcony rebuilt as fully enclosed

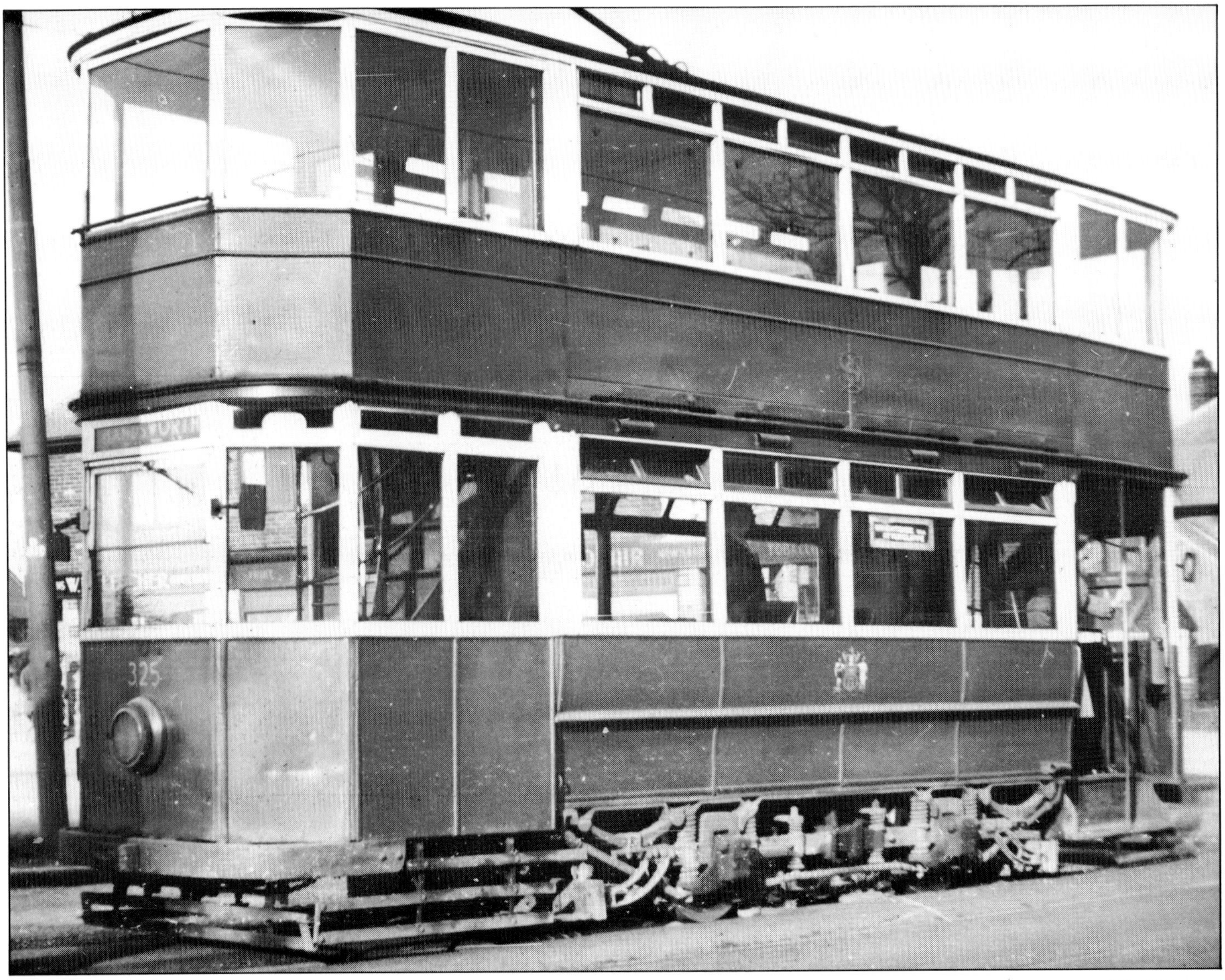

M. J. O'Connor

BUILT IN 1920-21 **BY** English Electric Co. Rebuilt in 1943 by Sheffield Corporation

FLEET NUMBERS 325-334

NO. OF CARS 10

LENGTH: LOWER SALOON 16′ 0″ **OVERALL** 29′ 0″

TRUCK Brill 21 E **WHEELBASE** 7′ 0″

MOTORS Dick Kerr 31D

CONTROLLERS Dick Kerr D.B.1 Form K.4

NUMBER OF SEATS: LOWER SALOON 19 **UPPER DECK** 40 **TOTAL** 59*

TYPE Leather upholstery except in upper deck balconies.

NOTES *In Bradford upper deck accommodation 43 (except Bradford No. 216 33 seats—2 one side, 1 on other) including 15 balcony seats, 3 of which were located over staircase trap doors. These seats and trap doors were removed in Sheffield.

Livery in Sheffield grey relieved in white around windows (No. 325 grey only). Maximum speed over 35 m.p.h..

WITHDRAWN FROM SERVICE 1950-1951.

TYPE "Roberts" fully enclosed with folding platform doors (VV)

J. H. Meredith

BUILT IN 1950-52 **BY** Charles Roberts & Co. Ltd.
FLEET NUMBERS 502-536
NO. OF CARS 35
LENGTH: LOWER SALOON 20′ 0″ **OVERALL** 32′ 7″
WIDTH: **OVERALL** 6′ 11½″
HEIGHT over trolley plank 15′ 9″
TRUCK Maley & Taunton hornless type 588 **WHEELBASE** 9′ 0″
MOTORS 2-65 h.p. M.V.101 D.R.3
CONTROLLERS B.T.H. N.510
NUMBER OF SEATS: LOWER SALOON 26 **UPPER DECK** 36 **TOTAL** 62
TYPE Upholstered throughout.
Saloon: 4 double and 4 single reversible transverse and longitudinal for 3 and 4 in diagonally opposite corners.
Upper deck: 8 double and 8 single reversible transverse and 2 and 4 seater longitudinal in each end bay.

NOTES See following extract from Manufacturer's Specification.
The only Sheffield cars with neither bulkheads nor fully screened staircases on the upper deck, the latter made unnecessary by platform external doors.
No. 501 the "Jubilee" car built in 1946 by Sheffield Corporation was similar in design but differed in constructional materials used. It had fluorescent lighting.

WITHDRAWN FROM SERVICE 1960

Specification of Roberts cars Nos. 502-536

As published in 1950 (Courtesy Charles Roberts & Co. Ltd.).

Double-deck tramcar to seat 62 passengers with Charles Roberts & Co. Ltd. metal framed body and underframe mounted on Maley & Taunton Ltd. two-axle truck with Metropolitan Vickers Electrical Co. Ltd. motors and British Thomson Houston Co. Ltd. controllers and switches.

Body construction

Underframing. Of hot rolled mild steel channels and angles arranged to accommodate the Maley & Taunton Ltd. two-axle truck.

Platforms. Floorbearers of hot rolled mild steel angles forming an integral part of the underframing and so arranged as to support the front and rear fenders. Two strips of polished stainless steel have been placed around the fenders to enhance the appearance.

Body shell framing. All main pillars are of hot rolled high tensile steel of Roberts special section arranged to receive timber packings for ease in affixing glazing and exterior panels. The fence rails are a specially formed mild steel cold rolled section extending the full length of the body sides and reinforced at pillar joints with brackets.

The whole structure is connected together with other rails and stout truss panels and diagonal bracing to make a perfectly rigid shell. The quarters at each end of the saloon are of double pillars trussed from crib rail to cant rail to provide the necessary triangulation to withstand stresses incurred from upper saloon loads in braking and acceleration.

The roof members are of "Welsh hat" section mild steel with timber packings fitted for securing the exterior roof and interior ceiling panels. All main body units are constructed separately in jigs and each individual part manufactured to template to ensure interchangeability.

Full measure is taken to prevent corrosion of all parts by the use of protective and priming paints, and all timber used is treated with "Permasan" solution as a preventative against rot and decay.

Panelling

All exterior panels are of aluminium. 16 swg. being used in the lower saloon and 18 swg. in the upper saloon, these being secured by means of brass wood screws to the timber packings of the framing members.

Windows and glazing

All flat windows are fitted into steel pans of the "Duflex" type for interior glazing and four windows on each side of each saloon are fitted with Rawlings Manufacturing Co. Ltd. Vita-Vent "G" type sliding ventilating windows in chromium plated frames and adapted for travel in either direction. The windscreens are of the Percy Lane Ltd. two-panel type hinged for opening at the top. The roof covings above the side windows of the upper saloon are of curved safety glass surrounded on the inside by chromium-plated frames.

All glass throughout the car is of Triplex Safety Quality.

Floors

The floors of both saloons are of tongued and grooved softwood and the platforms of hardwood, all covered with terra-cotta coloured linoleum, suitable trap doors being arranged for access to the motor units.

Staircases

The staircases provided at each end of the car are of the half-circular type with hardwood treads covered with "Ferodo" wearing strips and nosings. All handrailing and commodes are of mild steel tubing covered with "Doverite" insulation and fitted into stainless steel brackets manufactured by John Vessey and Sons, Ltd.

Doors

Double folding doors totally enclosing each vestibule are provided, being flush with the outside of the body when closed. These doors operate on Beckett, Laycock & Watkinson Ltd. sliding door gear, having top ball race runners, swivel hanger brackets and bottom spring roller guides.

Sliding doors are fitted at each entrance to the lower saloon, incorporating Laycocks sliding gear and Joseph Kaye's mortice locks.

Ventilation

Six "Airvac" Ventilators are provided for the upper saloon and six "Colt" ventilators to the side panels above the lower saloon main windows, all having chromium plated interior grills.

Rawlings Manufacturing Co. Ltd. "Lu-vent" continuous glazed louvres are fitted above the sliding windows in each saloon.

Destination indicators

The Corporation standard destination signs are arranged at the front and rear and each side with access to the interior of the illuminated boxes from the interior of the body.

Interior finish

The interior ceiling panels are finished in non-yellowing white cellulose and all polish work is prepared in mahogany polished with rubbing varnish to show the natural grain. The interior lining panels are covered with leathercloth, green being used in the lower saloon and red in the upper saloon.

Seats

All seating is of Siddall & Hilton Ltd. manufacture the transverse seats having "swing over" squabs for travel in either direction. A central gangway is used with two-passenger seats on one side and single-passenger seats on the other to give ample passage room for passengers and conductor. The upholstery has been tastefully selected being of Listers green moquette with Connolly's leather borders in the lower saloon, and Connolly's red leather throughout in the upper saloon. All cushions are of Dunlopillo rubber.

A removable pedestal type seat is provided for the driver.

Lighting

Adequate lighting is provided in both saloons, the fittings being of the Lewis Dixon enclosed type with perspex shades 2 ft. long in chromium plated frames and adapted to take the traction type of lamp 110 volt 40 watt mounted in pairs of which there are 8 in the lower saloon and 10 in the upper saloon.

An improved type of properly focused headlamp had been provided at each end.

Truck construction

The truck is of the Maley & Taunton hornless design, type 588, and possesses a number of improvements over the Peckham pendulum truck which has been operated in Sheffield for many years. There is a stronger main frame and the improved springing ensures easier riding qualities. The absence of hornway and guides eliminates noise, wear and tear between axle boxes and frames. Rubber mountings are provided in place of steel springs between axle mountings and frames, thereby insulating road impact noises from truck and body. Improved roller bearing axle boxes ensure long life with a minimum of attention. There is also an improved arrangement of brake rigging, track and wheel brake cylinders with constant pull off tension on wheel brake shoes.

The trucks have been built by W. A. Baker & Co. Ltd., Newport, by arrangement with Maley & Taunton Ltd. Wheels and axles have been manufactured by John Baker & Bessemer Ltd.

The wheelbase is 9 ft., i.e. 6 in. longer than any previous truck operated, and the wheel diameter has been reduced to 27 in. with a consequent result that access to the platform from the roadway is eased.

Braking

Braking is similar to that of the standard car, i.e. Maley & Taunton air operated wheel and track brake with the addition of the magnetic brake. There are also hand operated wheel and track brakes for parking purposes and an emergency air brake valve at each end which can be operated by the conductor.

Electrical equipment

Two motors, Metropolitan Vickers type M.V.101. D.R.3, having a rated horse power of 65 h.p. on the one hour rating, are incorporated, and the drive is obtained through resilient gear wheels with forged special steel rim and centre, the rim being oil hardened and mounted on the centre by means of Silentbloc fittings. The resilient gear adds to the quietness of the drive.

Controllers are of the British Thomson Houston Co. Ltd., type No. N.510 drum controllers, incorporating the air brake operating valve chamber.

All electrical installation has been carried out by the Corporation staff during the manufacture of the bodies, and completed after delivery of the vehicles to Queen's Road Works.

Painting

Final exterior painting has been carried out in Corporation colours of cream and azure blue with trucks in maroon, materials supplied by Latham Brown & Co. Ltd., and the work done at Queen's Road Works.

Miscellaneous

The vehicle is complete with lifeguards, sanding gear, Brecknell Willis & Co. Ltd. trolley base, electric signal bells and foot gongs. Additionally, such items as waste ticket boxes at each end of both saloons, platform chain-guards, conductor's and driver's mirrors and lockers, plate-glass saloon mirrors, match strikers, etc., are all provided which ensure efficient service conditions and show consideration for the travelling public.

Appendix A(2)

Departmental Cars 1899-1960

Original Fleet No.	Original Type	Date Built	Later type as Electric Passenger Car	Date Converted	Departmental Use
39	SD El.	9.1899		10.1921	Snowplough
42	SD El.	9.1899		8.1920	Snowplough
46	SD El.	9.1899		10.1921	Snowplough
51	SD El.	10.1900		5.1913	Snowplough
52	SD El.	10.1900		5.1913	Snowplough
54	SD El.	1.1900		9.1919	Snowplough
55	SD El.	1.1900		5.1913	Snowplough
73	DD OT El.	1.1901	DD OO	9.1926	Snowplough
77	DD OT El.	11.1900	DD SE	8.1929	Snowplough
98	SD El.	9.1900		5.1913	Snowplough
99	SD El.	9.1900		11.1921	Snowplough
111	DD OT El.	10.1900	DD SE	7.1924	Snowplough
113	DD OT El.	10.1900	DD OO	11.1929	Snowplough
130	NEW	1901			Water Car
142	DD OT El.	9.1901	DD SE	11.1923	Water Car
166	Horse 15	1874		1902	Breakdown
172	DD OT El.	12.1902	DD SE	11.1927	Snowplough
185	DD OT El.	12.1902	DD SE	11.1923	Snowplough
199	Horse	1877		6.1903	Stores Car
212	NEW	5.1904			Water Car
225	DD OT El.	2.1904	DD OV	8.1933	Snowplough
226	DD OT El.	2.1904	DD SE	11.1927	Snowplough
273	DD Horse	1897		1906-7	Snowplough
274	DD Horse	1897		1906-7	Snowplough
275	DD Horse	1897		1906-7	Snowplough
276	DD Horse	1897		1906-7	Snowplough
277	DD Horse	1897		1906-7	Snowplough
278	DD Horse	1897		1906-7	Snowplough
279	DD Horse	1897		1906-7	Salt Car
280	SD Horse	1877		1906-7	Salt Car
Ex-Bradford	DD El.	1920	DD VV	1951	Water Car
271	UEC DD OV El.	1907	DD VV	1.1951	Stores Car
272	UEC DD OV El.	1907	DD VV	3.1953	Snowplough

* Second car bearing this number

** Third car bearing this number

X Acquired by T.M.S. in 1960.

\+ Had been converted from OT (Open topped) to SE, OO, or OV prior to second conversion to Works cars; No. 225 became SE and later OV before third conversion to snowplough.

z The truck of this car was sent to Bradford Corporation for the restoration of their car No. 104 as a museum exhibit at Thornbury Works.

Intermediate Re-Numberings	Final Fleet No. and Date Received		Date Withdrawn	Notes
95(1924), 102(1926)	362	1929	5.1956	
96(1924), 103(1926)	363	1929	4.1957	
97(1924), 275*(1926)	354	1937	1960	Purchased by T.M.S. Restored to passenger car
			2.1924	
			11.1923	
100(1924)			1926	
101(1924)			8.1929	
	364	1930	4.1960	+
	365	1930	4.1960	+
277*(1926)			1931	
	361	1929	10.1960	
	359	1932	4.1960	+
	360	1932	4.1960	+
			1921	Fitted for snowclearing 1905
211(1927)	371	1935	3.1951	+
	375	1933	1946	Preserved by T.M.S.
273*(1933)	352	1937	5.1960	+
277**(1933)	356	1937	4.1957	+
			3.1922	
	372	1935	12.1950	
278*(1933)	357	1937	4.1960	Became No. 278 on conversion+
	358	1933	1.1955	+ z
			8.1926	
	353	1937	3.1952	
			2.1915	
	355	1937	2.1952	
			2.1915	
			2.1915	
	373	1937	2.1951	Became Stores Car 1919
	374	1937	1951	Became Stores Car 1919
	330		10.1960	Entered service Sheffield 1943[x]
	349	1937	10.1960	Renumbered whilst still[x] passenger cars
	350	1937	10.1960	

Appendix B(1)

Fleet list as at 31st December 1904

Car Nos.	Type	Builder	Date Built	Notes
1-33	DD OT	Milnes	1899	
34-38	DD SE	Milnes	1899	Originally OT
39-50	SD	Milnes	1899	
51 & 52	SD*	Milnes	1899	
53-58	SD	E.R. & T.C.W.	1899	
59-77	DD OT	E.R. & T.C.W.	1899-1900	
78-88	DD SE	E.R. & T.C.W.	1899-1900	Originally OT
89-103	SD	Brush	1900	
104-123	DD OT	Brush	1900	
124-129	SD	S.C.T. Nether Edge	1901	
130	SD W/C	S.C.T. Nether Edge	1901-02	
131-155	DD SE	Milnes	1901	Originally OT
156-165	SD	Cravens	1901	
166	SD B/W	S.C.T. Nether Edge	1902	Converted Horse Car 15
167-186	DD OT	Cravens	1902	Nos. 176 and 178 converted to SE
187-192	SD	Milnes	1902	
193-198	DD OT	S.C.T. Nether Edge	1903	
199	SD SC	S.C.T. Nether Edge	1903	Converted SD horse car
200-211	SD	S.C.T. Nether Edge	1903-04	
212	SD W/C	S.C.T. Nether Edge	1904	
213-218	DD OT	S.C.T. Nether Edge	1904	
219-243	DD OT	Brush	1904	
244 & 245	DD OT	S.C.T. Nether Edge	1904	

OT signifies Short Open Top
For other type abbreviations see Appendix A(1).
E.R. & T.C.W.—Electric Railway & Tramway Carriage Works Ltd.
*Experimental smoking cars

Appendix B(2)

Part 1: Fleet list as at 31st March 1927

Car No.(s)	Open or Vestibuled		Saloon Wind-ows	Notes
	Balcony	Platform		
2, 3 5-12	O	O	4	
13	—	O	4	SE
14, 17-19, 21	O	O	4	
22	O	V	4	
24-32	O	O	4	
33	O	V	4	
34, 35	—	O	4	SE
36-60	V	V	5	
61, 63	—	O	4	SE
64	O	O	4	
67-69	—	O	4	SE
70	O	O	4	
71	—	O	4	SE
73	Snowplough			
76-83, 86	—	O	4	SE
87-89	O	V	4	
91-96	O	O	3	Ex-L.C.C. B class*
99, 101-103	Snowploughs			
104, 105	O	O	4	
106	—	O	4	SE
107	O	V	4	
108	O	O	4	
109	—	O	4	SE
111	Snowplough			
112-119	O	O	4	
120	O	V	4	
122	—	O	4	SE
124	O	V	5	Rebuilt from S.D.
125	V	O	3	Ex-L.C.C. B class
126, 127	O	V	5	Rebuilt from S.D.
128, 129	V	O	3	Ex-L.C.C. B class
133, 135, 138	—	O	4	SE
142	Water car			
143, 144, 146, 148, 151, 153, 154	—	O	4	SE
156-165	O	V	5	Rebuilt from S.D.
166	Breakdown Car			
167	O	V	4	
168, 169	—	O	4	SE
171	O	V	4	
172	—	O	4	SE
173, 174	O	V	4	
175	—	O	4	SE
177	V	V	4	
178	—	O	4	SE
179	V	V	4	
180	—	O	4	SE
181	O	V	4	
183, 184	—	O	4	SE
185	Snowplough			
187, 188	V	O	3	Ex-L.C.C. B class
189-192	O	V	5	Rebuilt from S.D.
193	—	O	4	SE
194	V	V	4	
195, 196	—	O	4	SE
197	V	V	4	
198	O	V	4	
200,201	O	V	5	Rebuilt from S.D.
203	V	O	3	Ex-L.C.C. B class
205	O	V	5	Rebuilt from S.D.
207	V	O	3	Ex-L.C.C. B class
208	O	V	5	Rebuilt from S.D.
209	V	O	3	Ex-L.C.C. B class
212	Water Car			
213	—	O	4	SE
214	V	V	4	
215-219	—	O	4	SE
220	V	V	4	
221	—	O	4	SE
222	O	O	4	
223	—	O	4	SE
224	V	V	4	
225	O	V	4	
226, 228	—	O	4	SE
229, 230	V	V	4	
231-233	—	O	4	SE
234-237	V	V	4	
238	O	V	4	
239	V	V	4	
240-242	—	O	4	SE
243	V	V	4	
246-251, 253-257	—	O	4	SE
258-262	V	V	4	Screened staircase
263	V	V	4	
264	V	V	4	Screened staircase
265	O	V	4	
266	V	V	4	Screened staircase
267	O	V	4	
268	V	V	4	Screened staircase
269	V	V	4	
270, 271	O	V	4	
272	V	V	4	Screened staircase
274-277	Snowploughs			
279, 280	Stores Cars			
281-289	O	O	4	
290	V	V	4	
291-295	O	O	4	
296-349	V	V	4	
350	O	V	4	
351	V	V	4	
352, 353	O	V	4	
354, 355	V	V	4	
356, 358-360, 365	V	O	3	Ex-L.C.C. B class
366-369, 376-450	V	V	5	Screened staircase
451-500	V	V	5	Screened staircase

*From Rotherham Corporation

Part 2: Summary of types of tramcars in service at 31st March 1927

Short upper deck		69
Open balcony and open platform		52
Open balcony and vestibuled platform, 4 saloon windows		18
Open balcony and vestibuled platform, 5 saloon windows		21
Ex-L.C.C. "B" class		13
Ex-L.C.C. "B" class from Rotherham		6
Vestibuled balcony and vestibuled platform, 4 saloon windows		73
"Preston" type—open balcony, vestibuled platform		4
"Preston" type—vestibuled balcony, vestibuled platform		2
"Preston" type—rebuilt with screened staircase		9
1919-1927 standard type with screened staircase		154
TOTAL of passenger cars		421
Snowploughs	11	
Stores cars	2	
Water cars	2	
Breakdown car	1	16
TOTAL of all cars		437

Part 3: Summary of electric tramcars withdrawn by 31st March 1927

Total cars placed in service from 5th September 1899 (Nos. 1-369, 376-500, second Nos. 36-60, 91-96 and second batch of ten L.C.C. "B" class)			535
SOLD			
Short upper deck	11		
Single deck	35	46	
SCRAPPED			
Short upper deck	29		
Open balcony and open platform	3		
Ex-L.C.C. "B" class	7		
Single deck	4		
		43	
Snowploughs, water car, stores car		9	
TOTAL cars withdrawn		98	98
TOTAL of all cars in service 31/3/27			437

Appendix C

Renumbering of older passenger cars made necessary by 1928-1939 car building programme*

Type	No.	Became No.	Became Date	Later Became No.	Later Became Date
OO	2	62	1928	121	1931
OO	3	65	1928	169	1930
OO	5	68	1928	173	1930
OO	6	66	1929	170	1930
OO	7	72	1928	176	1931
OO	10	74	1928	178	1929
OO	11	75	1928	180	1930
OO	12	84	1928		
OO	17	90	1929		
OO	18	97	1929		
OO	19	98	1928		
OO	21	99	1929		
OO	24	100	1929		
OO	25	101	1929		
OO	26	110	1929		
OO	27	102	1929		
OO	28	103	1929		
OO	29	106	1929		
OO	30	116	1929		
OO	31	109	1930		
OO	32	120	1930		
OV	33	122	1929		
SE	36	35	1924		
Long OV	48	126	1924	202	1932
L.C.C. 'B'	56	128	1925		
OV	59	87	1924		
OV	60	89	1924		
OO	64	168	1930		
OO	70	175	1930		
L.C.C. 'B'	94	90	1926		
Long OV	124	203	1933		
Long OV	127	204	1933		
Long OV	156	206	1933		
Long OV	157	207	1933		
Long OV	158	209	1933		
Long OV	159	197	1933		
Long OV	160	198	1933		
Long OV	161	199	1933		
Long OV	162	201	1933		
Long OV	163	210	1933		
Long OV	164	213	1933		
Long OV	165	215	1933		

Type	No.	Became No.	Became Date	Later Became No.	Later Became Date
VV	214	281	1935		
VV	220	282	1935		
VV	224	283	1935		
VV	228	284	1935		
VV	229	285	1935		
VV	230	286	1935		
VV	234	287	1935		
VV	235	288	1935		
VV	236	291	1936	332	1938
VV	237	292	1936	333	1938
VV	239	293	1936	334	1938
VV	243	294	1935	335	1938
'Preston' VV	258	336	1937		
'Preston' VV	259	337	1937		
'Preston' VV	260	338	1937		
'Preston' VV	261	339	1937		
'Preston' VV	262	340	1937		
'Preston' VV	263	341	1937		
'Preston' VV	264	342	1937		
'Preston' VV	265	343	1937		
'Preston' VV	266	344	1937		
'Preston' VV	267	345	1937		
'Preston' VV	268	346	1937		
'Preston' VV	269	347	1937		
'Preston' VV	270	348	1937		
'Preston' VV	271	349	1937		
'Preston' VV	272	350	1937		
VV	290	331	1938		
'Long' VV	413	465	1951		

*Nos. 36-60 required in 1924-25 for new Brush cars.
No. 94 required in 1926 for ex Rotherham L.C.C. 'B' class cars, Sheffield Nos. 91-96.
No. 465 scrapped in error. Body of No. 413 fitted to truck of No. 465 and given that number.

Appendix D

Depot allocations at 1st August 1950

Type/No. Group	Tinsley	Shoreham St.	Holme Lane	Crookes	Tenter St.
1-35	—	3	—	—	1, 2, 4-35
36-60	—	36-60	—	—	—
61-130	—	61-64, 70-96, 101-129	65-69	130	97-100
131-155	152-155	—	—	131-151	—
156-230	156-184, 215-223	—	185-205	206-211	212-214, 224-230
231-242	—	238-241	232-237, 242	—	231
243-248	—	—	243-248	—	—
249-303	250-258	274-279, 288-303	249, 259-261, 280, 281	262-273	282-287
311-324*	319	313, 315	—	—	—
325-334*	—	—	333, 334	330, 331	325
336-350*	339, 342	—	349, 350	343, 344	346-348
366-369	369	—	—	—	366-368
370	—	—	—	—	370
376-450	417-422	400, 401	376-385	402-416, 423-433	386-399, 434-450
451-500†	462-500	451-459	—	—	—
501	—	—	501	—	—
502-536	—	502, 504, 506	503, 505	—	—
507-521 Delivery awaited	516-520	508, 510, 512, 514	507, 509, 511, 513, 515	—	521
TOTAL CARS IN SERVICE	100	128	62	70	94

*These classes in course of withdrawal.
†Nos. 460 and 461 were no longer allocated.

Appendix E

Single lines

The construction of single line sections of route within the electrified system was spread over the years 1899-1913, whereas their replacement by double track progressed between 1902 and (with one exception) 1927.

It was reported in 1905 that there were just over thirty miles of double track route and just over five and three quarter miles of single. By 25th March 1915 double track mileage had increased to over thirty-eight and a quarter miles resulting from the 1908 to 1913 route extensions and by doubling of single lines during the ten years from 1905. Single line mileage had declined to two and three eighths miles.

The only change in the year to 1916 was the doubling of twenty-eight yards of single line and no other track alterations were made during the next four years to 1920. The extent of single line throughout this period (excluding crossovers, sidings and junctions) was scheduled in the Sheffield Corporation Consolidation Act 1918 as follows:

	Furls.	Yds.	Doubled Year ending
Brightside Lane–Page Hall Road		142	1925
Attercliffe Road–Handsworth (Park Lane)	1	157	1926
Fitzalan Square–Intake	6	60	1923
Commercial Street–Heeley (London Road) via Queen's Road		202	1927
Paternoster Row–Moorhead	1	103	—
The Moor–Nether Edge		40	
The Moor–Banner Cross		18	
Cole's Corner–Nether Green via Broomhill		214	1925
Broomhill–Crookes		30	
Angel Street–Middlewood	2	64	1924 & 27
Holme Lane		106	—
Lady's Bridge–Parkside Road top via Neepsend Lane	1	136	50 yds. only, opened 21.7.23
2 mls.	0	172	

Most of these lines were doubled between April 1923 and March 1927. Thereafter, the only single line sections were on the Neepsend route, the Furnival Street line, near Malin Bridge terminus, over the Staniforth Road bridges, and on Rotherham lines under the railway at Ickles, and over the River Rother. Following the closure in 1931 of the Rotherham local routes, excepting Canklow, the terminal circuit of the joint Sheffield service became completely single line in 1933.

The 1937 Act authorised the doubling of one furlong in Nursery Street and the construction of a "to City" line in Harvest Lane and Burton Road, having the effect of doubling the single line in Neepsend Lane. These works would have completed the doubling of the Wadsley Bridge route, but with the exception of a short portion of the single line in Nursery Street, doubled in 1937, they were not carried out. No more doubling of single line took place in Sheffield.

The single line sections on each route as originally laid were as follows:

Tinsley
Nil

Brightside
Nil

Nether Edge
Nil

Walkley
Church Street[1] 123 yards

West Street (from Holly Street)–Glossop Road (Wilkinson Lane):
- Loop Carver Street–Rockingham Street
- Loop Charlotte Street[2]–Regent Street

Barber Road–Commonside:
- Single from beyond Crookesmoor Road
- Loop Barber Place–Springvale Road

Howard Road
- Loop Birkendale View (on bend)
- Loop Cromwell Street–Hadfield Street

South Road
- Loop Cundy Street–Hoole Street
- Double last 80 yards

Crookes (from Winter Street Junction)
Whitham Road
- Loop Tree Root Walk–Beaufort Road
- Loop Crookes Junction

Crookes Road (from Spooner Road)
- Loop Hoole Road
- Loop Roslin Road–Hadfield Dam
- Loop before Lydgate Lane–Coombe Road
- Single last 117 yards to School Road

Nether Green (from Crookes Junction)
Fulwood Road
- Loop Glossop Road Junction
- Loop Lawson Road–Ashgate Road
- Loop Ashdell Road
- Loop Shore Lane–Woodvale Road
- Loop Oakbrook Farm–Thornbury Lodge
- Loop beyond Tapton Park Road
- Loop Ranmoor Church
- Loop Graham Road
- Short siding Storth Lane–Nether Green Road

Nether Green (from bottom of The Moor)
Ecclesall Road
- Single Clarence Street–Moore Street
- Single immediately before Rustlings Road

Rustlings Road
- Double at future junction
- Loop after Peveril Road
- Loop after further 140 yards single
- Loop on bend into Oakbrook Road

[1]The Sheffield Corporation Act 1901 which authorised the doubling of this section after road widening, also authorised the construction of a siding 88 yards in length outside the Parish Church. It was never laid. The track alterations were made between February and April 1902 and through running was interrupted during this period.
[2]Charlotte Street was later renamed Mappin Street.

Oakbrook Road
  Loop on bend before Cruise Road
  Loop Hangingwater Road

Nether Green Road
  Double at top into junction with Fulwood Road tracks. (Junction incomplete in 1903)

Millhouses (from Highfield Junction)
Abbeydale Road
  Single Crowther Place–Horner Road
  Single Archer Road–beyond Troutbeck Road
  Single Marriott Road–before Springfield Road
  Double thence to Whirlowdale Road (bottom)

Woodseats[3]
Chesterfield Road
  Single from Derbyshire Lane
  Loop Meersbrook Avenue–Woodbank Crescent
  Loop Smithywood Road
  Loop Smithywood Road (S. of right curve towards City)
  Loop at S. corner of Woodside Brickworks
  Loop N. of Scarsdale Road (then Green Lane)
  Double Police Station–Chantrey Road

Intake
City Road
  Single from 50 yards before S. end of Cemetery
  Loop at Deep Pits before Windy House
  Loop on curve at Elm Tree Hill (ht. 645′)
  Loop at bridge over Woodthorpe Colliery tramway
  Double for 90 yards at terminus

Darnall
Staniforth Road
  Double except from Pinfold Bridge over Canal–Ouse Road, with loop Roundel Street–Chelmsford Street and loop at Selbourne Street
  Double track ended at Main Road corner, with trailing crossover at Irving Street

Pitsmoor
Barnsley Road
  Double nearly to Firshill Road thence
  Single with
    Loop at Norwood Road
    Loop at Osgathorpe Road (Batley Street)
    Loop at Skinnerthorpe Road–Owler Lane
  Loop Idsworth Road–beyond Bolsover Road forming double track junction with Page Hall Road lines
  Single for 47 yards at terminus

Pitsmoor (via Brightside Lane)
Upwell Street
  Single 142 yards at Upwell Lane

Owlerton
Nursery Street*
  Single Wicker Lane–near Spitalfields

Neepsend Lane*
  Single 57 yards west of Percy Street–S. of Neepsend Bridge (Rutland Road)

Penistone Road
  Single for 50 yards across Owlerton Bridge (River Loxley)
  Single midway between Burnell Road and Burrowlee Road–loop at Broughton Road
  Double Dutton Road into and along Parkside Road[4]

Malin Bridge (from Holme Lane Junction)
Holme Lane*
  Single Loxley New Road–just before Rivelin Valley Road (last 83 yards double)

Hillsborough
Infirmary Road and Langsett Road
  Double except Woollen Lane–Wood Street

Middlewood
Middlewood Road
  Single between Crofton Avenue and Withens Avenue–terminus (43 yards beyond Langsett Avenue (No loop)

*Paternoster Row, Brown Street, Furnival Street**
  Single from Howard Lane–Union Lane with
  Loop Charles Street–Brown Lane
  Loop round corner of Brown Street and Furnival Street.

All the single line sections were subsequently doubled with the exception of those marked by asterisk.

[3]Also Woodseats via Shoreham Street single along depot site, and from 47 yards before Leadmill Street–Matilda Street (147 yards), and Woodseats via Queen's Road single in Suffolk Road from Turner Street–St. Mary's Road.

[4]Single originally after loop at bottom.

Appendix F

Authorised lines not built

	From	To	Route
1897	The Moor	City Road	Ellin Street, Hereford Street, St. Mary's Road and Granville Road
1897	Glossop Road at Hounsfield Road	Broomhill	Glossop Road
1900	Glossop Road	Hunters Bar	Clarkehouse Road and Brocco Bank
1897	The Moor	West Street/Glossop Road	Fitzwilliam Street
	and Ecclesall Road	Fitzwilliam Street	Hanover Street and Broomhall Street
1900	Cemetery Road at Washington Road	Banner Cross	Cemetery Road and Psalter Lane
	and Psalter Lane	Hunters Bar	Cowlishaw Road and Junction Road
1900	Broomhill	*Crosspool* (Sandygate Road)	Manchester Road
1900	Heeley	Abbeydale	Broadfield Road
1900	Abbeydale	Nether Edge Depot	Sheldon Road
1900	Snig Hill	Waingate	Castle Street
1900	Infirmary Road	Upper St. Philips Road at Brook Hill	St. Phillips Road
	and St. Philips Road	*Upperthorpe* at Addy Street	Upperthorpe Road
1900	Bridge Street at Millsands	Penistone Road at Henry Street	Bridge Street, Alma Street and Green Lane
	and Alma Street	*Kelham Island* Power Station	Kelham Street
1900	Spital Hill	*Grimesthorpe* at Grimesthorpe Road	Carlisle Street, Carlisle Street East and Carlisle Road
1907	Brightside Terminus	*Blackburn Brook* City Boundary	Meadow Hall Road
1907	Brightside Terminus	Tinsley Terminus	Weedon Street*
1912	Infirmary Road	Crookesmoor (Crookes Valley Road)	Albert Terrace Road and Oxford Street
1912	West Bar	Leopold Street**	West Bar Green, Tenter Street and Townhead Street
	and West Bar Green	Upperthorpe Library	Scotland Street, Meadow Street and Upperthorpe Road+
1915	Sheffield Road, Tinsley	*Bawtry Road* City Boundary	Bawtry Road
1918	Sheffield Lane Top	*Ecclesfield* at Church Lane	Barnsley Road and Chapeltown Road
1918 / 1935	Meadowhead	*Low Edges* and *Dronfield*	Chesterfield Road
1919	Barnsley Road	*Moonshine Lane*	(1) Crabtree Road and Norwood Road
1919			(2) Batley Street and Piper Lane
1920 / 1928			(3) Norwood Road and Herries Road
1919 / 1935	Handsworth, Orgreave Lane	*Beaver Hill Road* and *Woodhouse Mill* (Horsewood Road)	Retford Road
1920	Attercliffe Common	Weedon Street	new road and Bright Street
1920	Darnall (Main Road at Hazel Road)	Attercliffe Common	Hazel Road, Greenland Road and Broughton Lane
1935	Sheffield Lane Top	*Shiregreen* and Firth Park	Barnsley Road[x], Hartley Brook Road, Nether Shire Lane and Sicey Avenue
1937	Neepsend Lane	Mowbray Street	Burton Road and Harvest Lane[z]

Places shown in italics represent extensions to routes built or new routes.
All other lines formed connecting links between existing routes.

* Partly built and used as terminal siding at Tinsley. Whole line never completed.
** Partly built in 1928 to form access to Tenter Street Depot.
+ Upperthorpe Road previously included in scheme of 1900.
x Same route as 1918 Ecclesfield scheme as far as Hartley Brook Road.
z Proposed rerouting of "to City" line to avoid single line section.

Appendix G

The Overhead Line Department

This Department, which had its headquarters at Leadmill Road adjoining Shoreham Street Depot, was responsible for the following equipment:

- Overhead power lines, span wires and all fittings
- Standards, bracket arms and wall rosettes
- Automatic point controllers, overhead trolley switches and control boxes
- Power supply cables and feeder boxes
- Automatic trolley reversers
- Tramway signals for single line sections and for road junctions
- Overhead contactors for switches and signals
- Maintenance and painting of all tramway and bus signs and passenger shelters.

The Department possessed five motor tower wagons, two of which were, in later years, equipped with ultra short wave radio telephones. There were no departmental electric tramcars for overhead line work.

The Department was committed to the statutory requirement that all overhead equipment should be inspected monthly but the most important sections in the City centre were examined twice a month. In addition the law required overhead power lines to be capable of isolation at half mile intervals, and power was fed in at these intervals by cables running up inside the feeder standards and emerging near the top, thence attached to span wires or bracket arms.

Power Lines. The overhead power lines were of bronze wire 0.4 of an inch in diameter. The clench ears which held them were also of bronze and were joined to the span wires or brackets. The power wires had a life varying between four and twenty years depending upon the volume of tram traffic passing under them. The clench ears had a much shorter life which might have been as little as three months. Repairs were normally carried out in the daytime, but renewal of overhead equipment (and track) was usually undertaken late on Saturday nights and early on Sunday mornings.

Standards. At the zenith of the system there were approximately 4500 standards to which span wires or bracket arms were attached. The standards were of three different weights, the heaviest being required where stresses were greatest, such as at the High Street/Haymarket corner. In a limited number of locations wall rosettes were fixed to business premises, so dispensing with the need for standards to carry span wires.

At the commencement of electric operation an elaborate colour scheme was chosen. Standards, brackets and

H. B. Priestley.

Nos. 240 and 408 at the junction of the Millhouses and Woodseats routes at Highfield on 31st May 1939. The overhead line equipment is clearly shown.

ornamental ironwork were painted in bronze green, finials and rosettes were Post Office red and ornamental bases were Midland Railway crimson lake. It is believed that repainting was undertaken by the Department at two yearly intervals. After a few years a single shade of red was adopted, and by the First World War only rosettes and bases remained red. By the end of the War only bases were painted red.

Between the two World Wars, the standards from Fitzalan Square to the Midland Station via Commercial Street were treated with aluminium paint to counter the corrosive atmosphere of the City. Similar treatment was applied in High Street after the 1940 air raids.

During the late 1920s and early 1930s almost all the decorative scroll ironwork and all the ornamental bases were removed, and then during the financial crisis of the early 1930s the spikes of the wooden ball and spike finials were sawn off as a further paint saver. In a number of cases simpler type finials were fitted, but some standards were left without finials, which exposed them to the weather. However, the Neepsend section of the Wadsley Bridge route largely escaped this treatment and the spiked finials remained long after the closure of the route.

Standards bore a route or street code letter and number to facilitate rapid location in case of emergency. About thirty-five such codes were in use on the whole system. The practice commenced with the first electrified routes: "NE" for Nether Edge, numbering from the foot of Fargate and "T" for Tinsley numbering from the top of High Street. At first small enamel plates were screwed to the standards at tram drivers' eye level, but from the 1920s the numbers were painted in white on the standards.

Point Controllers. Although the earliest known mention of point controllers was made in 1896, the first automatic point controller at facing points was installed at the Fargate/Church Street junction as the result of a decision made on 26th April 1904. The type used was Turner's Patent Point Controller and the equipment proved so successful that by 31st March 1921 there were in use thirty-one installations of this kind.

The number of automatic controllers increased to sixty-four by 31st March 1938, but during the year to March 1935 it was reported that ten of the above mentioned type had been replaced by an improved type, the Collins Automatic Point Controller supplied by the Forest City Electrical Co. Ltd. Further replacements continued slowly. The Turner system was still in use at Millhouses turning circle in the summer of 1939, and that at the eastern exit from Fitzalan Square remained until the end of tramway operation.

A. D. Packer.

No. 198 using the trolley reverser at the Ecclesall terminal siding in Millhouses Lane on 3rd August 1953.

Both systems were activated by an electrical circuit between a contactor on the power line and the track points by way of a roadside standard. The main difference between the two systems was that whereas in the Turner system the points and the overhead frog returned to their normal position electrically by the use of a second overhead contactor located beyond the frog, in the Collins system the points did not return to normal and the overhead frog was activated by contact of the trolley boom with a hanging lever, and there was no electrical control of the overhead frog. A red signal light on an adjacent standard which in the Turner system indicated that the points had been correctly set was dispensed with in the Collins system because in the latter there was no "set" or "main road".

Because of the density of tramcar traffic at this location, the turnout points and overhead frog used by cars leaving Fitzalan Square for Commercial Street were controlled by an ingenious adaptation of the Turner system.

The overhead frog was switched by the trolley boom lifting the hanging lever which dropped, so resetting the frog when the trolley had passed.

The points were set by the conductor using a normal type pull out lever with which Turner control boxes (located on the pavement) were equipped. An overhead contactor located in advance of the frog returned the points and the control box lever to normal immediately the rear wheels of the car had moved clear, whilst the conductor re-boarded the car as the rear platform passed him.

Until the closure of the Nether Edge route, the overhead frogs at the Ecclesall Road/Cemetery Road/London Road junctions were controlled by an employee who operated the overhead frogs and gave appropriate whistle signals, viz. two blasts for Ecclesall Road and one for Cemetery Road. The Turner system worked the points until the Collins system was introduced around 1935. London Road was the "set road".

Trolley Reversers. Automatic trolley reversers were installed at all terminal crossovers and at a few intermediate crossovers which were frequently used for short workings. However there remained some crossovers where trolleys had to be turned by use of the bamboo pole carried by all cars. This operation was normally performed by the conductor.

Although the trailing points on reversing tracks were not the responibility of the Overhead Line Department, it should be noted that at all terminal and important intermediate crossovers they were sprung for the reverse crossing movement.

Signals. Colour-light signals activated by overhead contactors were installed on roadside standards to control

R. J. S. Wiseman.

At Beauchief on Christmas Day 1956. The two lights of the tramway signal can be seen immediately to the left of the car which has passed the overhead contactor and is therefore waiting for the top light to replace the left-hand one to enable the car to cross into Abbey Lane.

single line sections, and also at road junctions where there were ordinary traffic signals and where tramcar movements conflicted with the flow of other traffic. At tramway junctions the tramway and traffic signals superseded the priorities previously prescribed in the Transport Department's Rule Book.

At some locations there were illuminated signs in red capital letters to warn other traffic of tramcar movements, such as "Caution—Car Turning Left" (or "Right") or "Car Crossing Ahead". These signs were activated and cancelled by overhead contactors.

At Beauchief cars leaving the Abbeydale Road reservation to turn left into Abbey Lane activated a signal in the form of a triangle of three white lights, two of which were always illuminated. Trams could enter the crossroads when the left lower light was replaced by the upper one. This signal cut into the sequence of the road signals.

During the period of police-operated semaphore signals outside the Town Hall, tramcar movements were controlled by two blue light signals. The one for northbound cars was suspended from an overhead span wire and the other for southbound cars was attached to a roadside standard. These also were operated by the policeman in the central control kiosk.

Stopping Places. Within the Overhead Line Department's painting responsibilities was the painting of white bands on certain standards to indicate stopping places: one band for a request stop, two for a normal stop, and three for a compulsory stop prescribed by the Board of Trade (later Ministry of Transport).

In addition, flag type signs were fixed to the standards, originally in white enamel lettered in red for normal stops and in blue for request stops. In the 1930s these signs were replaced by figured glass ones in varnished wooden surrounds, and later these gave way to more durable moulded metal signs.

Appendix H(1)

Length of routes and journey times in 1905

(Extracts from "Official Guide to Sheffield and Neighbourhood by the Tramway Car Routes, 1905")

Route	Distance		Journey Time (Minutes)
	Miles	Yards	
Fitzalan Square to Brightside via Newhall Road	3	305*	25
Fitzalan Square to Rotherham (College Square)	6	280*	45
Market Side to Tinsley (Weedon Street)	2	1758*	22
Market Side to Darnall	2	1177	19
Market Side to Petre Street	1	624*	12
Market Side to Pitsmoor via Brightside Lane	3	317	25
Market Side to Pitsmoor via Burngreave Road	2	838	21
Market Side to Owlerton via Nursery Street**	2	1458	21
Market Side to Walkley	2	302	19
Commercial Street to Intake (Woodhouse Road)	2	1253	25
Angel Street to Hillsborough	2	1125	22
Angel Street to Nether Edge	2	43*	18
Angel Street to Nether Green via Broomhill	3	55	25
Fargate to Nether Green via Hunters Bar	3	338	25
Fargate to Hunters Bar	2	65	17
Fargate to Millhouses (Springfield Road)	3	160	25
Fargate to Woodseats (Chantrey Road)	3	289	25
Church Street to Crookes (School Road)	2	206	18

* Route never extended.
** Parkside Road top. Alternative route from Bridge Street via Penistone Road 2 miles 1068 yards, no regular service.

Several of the locations shown above have been differently described from those shown in the Official Guide for the sake of clarity.

Extract from 1905 Time Table showing departure times from City Centre (departure points in brackets), to suburban termini.

Brightside (Fitzalan Square) via Brightside Lane
Weekdays—4.40 am, 4.50 am, 5.00 am, 5.10 am, 5.25 am, 5.30 am, 5.35 am, 5.47 am, 6.07 am, 6.25 am and 6.27 am.
via Newhall Road—5.20 am, 5.23 am, 5.26 am, 5.29 am, 5.32 am, 5.35 am, 5.45 am, 5.55 am, 6.05 am, 6.23 am, 6.33 am and every 10 minutes to 11.33 pm.
Sunday—12.33 pm and every 10 minutes to 10.33 pm.

Crookes coupled with Pitsmoor (Cutlers' Hall, Church Street/Fitzalan Square)
Weekdays—4.37 am and every 10 minutes to 11.37 pm.
Sunday—12.07 pm and every 10 minutes to 10.47 pm.

Darnall coupled with Ecclesall (Fitzalan Square/Fargate)
Weekdays—4.41 am and every 8 minutes to 11.29 pm.
Sunday—12.09 pm and every 8 minutes to 10.33 pm.

Ecclesall (Hunters Bar) coupled with Darnall (Fargate/Fitzalan Square)
Weekdays—4.40 am and every 8 minutes to 5.12 am, 5.18 am, 5.20 am, 5.25 am, 5.28 am, 5.34 am, 5.42 am and every 8 minutes to 6.38 am, then every 4 minutes to 11.34 pm.
Sunday—11.44 am and every 8 minutes to 12.16 pm, 12.22 pm, 12.24 pm, 12.30 pm, 12.32 pm, 12.38 pm and every 8 minutes to 1.50 pm, then every 4 minutes to 10.38 pm.

Firth Park via Brightside Lane coupled with Walkley (Fitzalan Square/Cutlers' Hall)
Weekdays—5.17 am, 5.36 am, 5.56 am, 6.16 am, 6.36 am and every 10 minutes to 11.36 pm.
Sunday—12.53 pm and every 10 minutes to 11.03 pm.

Fulwood (Angel Street)
Weekdays—6.34 am and every 10 minutes to 9.24 am, 9.32 am and every 10 minutes to 5.22 pm, 5.34 pm and every 10 minutes to 8.44 pm, 8.52 pm and every 10 minutes to 11.02 pm.
Sunday—12.12 pm and every 10 minutes to 10.12 pm.

Hillsborough coupled with Nether Edge (Angel Street)
Weekdays—4.38 am and every 5 minutes to 5.18 am, 5.22 am and every 5 minutes to 6.47 am, 6.50 am and every 5 minutes to 11.40 pm.
Sunday—11.35 am and every 5 minutes to 10.40 pm.

Intake coupled with Walkley (Commercial Street/Cutlers' Hall)
Weekdays—5.01 am and every 10 minutes to 11.31 pm.
Sunday—12.11 pm and every 10 minutes to 10.31 pm.

Millhouses coupled with Tinsley (Fargate/Fitzalan Square)
Weekdays—4.42 am and every 10 minutes to 6.32 am, then every 5 minutes to 11.32 pm.
Sunday—11.37 am and every 5 minutes to 10.32 pm.

Nether Edge coupled with Hillsborough (Angel Street)
Weekdays—6.52 am and every 5 minutes to 11.32 pm.
Sunday—11.42 am and every 5 minutes to 10.27 pm.

Nether Green coupled with Owlerton via Nursery Street (Fargate/Fitzalan Square)
Weekdays—5.18 am and every 8 minutes to 11.34 pm.
Sunday—12.22 pm and every 8 minutes to 10.38 pm.

Norton Woodseats coupled with Pitsmoor and Petre Street (Fargate/Fitzalan Square)
Weekdays—4.54 am and every 10 minutes to 6.14 am,

6.20 am and every 5 minutes to 11.35 pm.
Sunday—11.45 am and every 10 minutes to 12.35 pm, then every 5 minutes to 10.55 pm.

Owlerton via Nursery Street coupled with Nether Green (Fitzalan Square/Fargate)
Weekdays—4.30 am, 4.37 am and every 8 minutes to 11.33 pm.
Sunday—11.33 am and every 8 minutes to 10.37 pm.

Owlerton via Penistone Road—only used for football matches and for events at Hillsborough Park.

Petre Street coupled with Norton Woodseats (Fitzalan Square/Fargate)
Weekdays—5.27 am and every 10 minutes to 6.17 am, 6.30 am and every 10 minutes to 11.40 pm.
Sunday—12.20 pm and every 10 minutes to 10.30 pm.

Pitsmoor coupled with Crookes and Norton Woodseats (Fitzalan Square/Cutlers' Hall and Fargate)
Weekdays—4.41 am and every 10 minutes to 6.51 am, then every 5 minutes to 11.36 pm.
Sunday—11.41 am and every 10 minutes to 2.01 pm, then every 5 minutes to 11.05 pm.

*Shoreham Street** (Commercial Street)
Meersbrook Park Road to City via Shoreham Street
Weekdays—5.11 am and every 10 minutes to 11.11 pm.
Sunday—11.51 am and every 10 minutes to 2.21 pm, 2.27 pm and every 12 minutes to 10.27 pm.
Meersbrook Park Road to City via The Moor
Weekdays—6.26 am and every 10 minutes to 11.16 pm.
Sunday—1.45 pm and every 12 minutes to 10.33 pm.

Tinsley coupled with Millhouses (Fitzalan Square/Fargate)
Weekdays—4.20 am and every 10 minutes to 6.10 am, then every 3 minutes to 11.35 pm.
Sunday—11.15 am and every 5 minutes to 11.50 am, 11.53 am and every 3 minutes to 10.25 pm, then every 5 minutes to 10.50 pm.

Walkley coupled with Intake and Firth Park (Cutlers' Hall/Fitzalan Square)
Weekdays—4.36 am and every 10 minutes to 5.36 am, then every 5 minutes to 11.41 pm.
Sunday—11.41 am and every 10 minutes to 12.31 pm, then every 5 minutes to 11.11 pm.

Rotherham (Fitzalan Square)
Weekdays—5.48 am, 6.08 am and every 10 minutes to 11.00 pm, 11.28 pm.
Saturdays an additional car at 11.48 pm.
Sunday—11.58 am, 12.18 pm and every 10 minutes to 10.48 pm.

Church Street to Springvale Road—no times given but noted "Cars stop at Commonside".

The use of the location "Fitzalan Square" in this timetable does not mean that all services so shown actually entered the Square. The northbound through services usually departed from the lower part of High Street (later known as Market Side).

*Times shown for the Shoreham Street Circular service are from Meersbrook Park Road.

Appendix H(2)

Early Sunday morning cars for munition workers

Improved Service from 12th December 1915

Departure times to the East End were as follows:

From	Depart to Brightside		Depart to Tinsley
	via Savile Street	via Newhall Road	
Crookes	5.10		6.30(2), 6.31, 6.58
Holme Lane	5.20, 5.22, 5.25, 5.38		5.52, 6.30, 6.31, 6.45
Hillsborough			6.30
Nether Green via Hunters Bar		5.10	
Hunters Bar	5.15		6.30(2)
Millhouses	5.10	5.10	6.30, 7.00
Woodseats	5.10, 5.15		6.21, 6.22, 6.25, 6.45, 7.00
Handsworth	5.25		
Darnall			6.50
City Centre (augmenting above services except Handsworth and Darnall)	6 cars between 5.20 and 6.10	3 cars between 5.30 and 6.05	22 cars between 5.20 and 7.50

In addition, there were cars from the City at 6.35 to Woodseats and to Millhouses, at 6.10 and 6.35 to Crookes, at 6.04 to Hillsborough, between 5.08 and 7.40 ten cars to Holme Lane, at 4.50 to Intake and at 5.45 to Darnall. There was a car from Firth Park to Twelve o'Clock junction (returning at 6.00) and from Hawke Street to Firth Park at 6.06.

Balancing workings ran in the opposite direction to all the above services but not necessarily returning to the same starting point nor via the same route.

There was no service on the Nether Edge, Walkley, Malin Bridge, Owlerton and Petre Street routes, nor on the sections between Nether Green and Crookes Junction, Banner Cross and Hunters Bar, and Middlewood and Hillsborough. Passengers from Intake to the East End departing at 5.10 had to change cars in the City.

Appendix H(3)

Ordinary off-peak weekday service, 1939

Route	First Car		Off-peak Service Intervals (Minutes)	Last Car	
	From City	To City		From City	To City
Templeborough	4.25	5.13	5	11.30	11.29
Rotherham	4.25	5.00	5	11.20	11.16
Wadsley Bridge	4.30	4.50	5	11.32	11.58
Sheffield Lane Top via Pitsmoor	4.35	4.58	10	11.32	12.00
Middlewood	4.40	5.06	4	11.31	11.30
Intake	4.40	5.10	8	11.30	11.50
Millhouses	4.41	5.01	4	11.32	12.00
Crookes	4.42	5.03	4	11.32	11.20
Walkley	4.42	5.00	4	11.35	11.53
Handsworth	4.43	5.08	5	11.31	12.00
Brightside via Savile Street	4.44	5.04	10	11.30	11.25
Tinsley	4.45	4.15	3	11.30	12.15
Ecclesall	4.50	5.10	4	11.32	11.55
Meadowhead	4.51	4.56	6	11.35	11.58
Firth Park via Attercliffe	4.55	5.13	10	11.30	11.50
Nether Green via Hunters Bar	5.00	5.20	5	11.30	12.02
Darnall via Elm Tree	5.05	5.20	8	11.31	11.46
Elm Tree via Darnall	5.09	5.25	8	11.27	11.43
Heeley via Shoreham Street	5.11	5.28	8	11.32	12.09
Malin Bridge	5.26	4.22	5	11.30	11.47
Fulwood via Hunters Bar	5.46	6.17	10	11.30	11.58
Heeley via Queen's Road	5.50	6.07	8	11.19	11.56
Millhouses via Woodseats	6.00	6.20	10	11.30	11.52
Woodseats via Millhouses	6.08	6.26	10	11.32	11.50
Woodseats via Shoreham Street	6.47	7.12	8	11.32	11.56
Woodseats via Queen's Road	9.23	9.47	8	11.19	11.43

Appendix H(4)

Departure times of postal cars, 1939

Mondays to Fridays (bank holidays excepted)

Abbey Lane	10.00 pm each way, Millhouses 10.06, Woodseats 10.08
Brightside	10.05 pm
Crookes	10.00 pm
Ecclesall	10.06 pm Hunters Bar 10.10
Fulwood	10.00 pm Nether Green 10.05
Middlewood	10.04 pm Hillsborough 10.05
Sheffield Lane Top	10.05 pm Firth Park 10.08
Handsworth	10.05 pm
Intake	10.00 pm
Malin Bridge	10.02 pm
Meadowhead	10.00 pm
Elm Tree	9.54 pm via Darnall (No service in opposite direction)
Templeborough	10.06 pm
Tinsley	10.05 pm
Wadsley Bridge	10.02 pm
Walkley	10.06 pm

There was no service via Queen's Road, Shoreham Street,
nor via the Upwell Street–Newhall Road route.

Appendix H(5)

Examples of tramcar duties

All times quoted in this Appendix relate to departures.

(1) *Mondays to Fridays* (Before 3rd October 1959)

	am	
Tenter Street Depot	6.18	via Bridge Street, Haymarket
Pinstone Street	6.28	via The Moor
Woodseats	6.50	via The Moor, Angel Street, Bridge Street
Flat Street	7.23	via Queen's Road
Woodbank Crescent	7.39	via The Moor
Leopold Street (reverse)	7.59	via The Moor
Meadowhead	8.24	via The Moor
Snig Hill	8.49	via The Moor
Tenter Street Depot	8.52	In operation 2½ hours approximately

(2) *Saturdays* (Before 28th March 1954)

	am	
Holme Lane Depot	5.22	
Langsett Road (reverse)		
Hillsborough	5.27	via Bridge Street
Brightside	6.05	via Bridge Street, Snig Hill
Angel Street	6.25	
Ecclesall		
Middlewood	pm	and 12 return journeys in the period 6.25 am to 11.30 pm
Middlewood	11.10	
Angel Street	11.30	
Ecclesall	11.55	
Tenter Street Depot (entrance)		
	am	
Angel Street	12.30	(Sunday)
Ecclesall	12.55	
Midland Station (reverse)	1.25	
High Street	1.30	
Beauchief	1.55	
Snig Hill	2.20	
Holme Lane Depot	2.30	approximately. In operation over 21 hours

(3) *Saturdays* (From 14th April 1956 to 12th April 1958)

	am	
Shoreham Street Depot	4.10	
Fitzalan Square	4.15	via Darnall*
Elm Tree	4.43*	
Fitzalan Square	5.15	via Darnall
Elm Tree	5.43	via Darnall
Fitzalan Square	6.15	and 18 return journeys in the period 6.15 am to 12.15 am next day
	am	
Fitzalan Square	12.15	(Sunday)
Shoreham Street Depot		In operation over 20 hours.

*This car was required to make three connections: (1) on the outward journey at Staniforth Road junction with the 4.08 am tram from Sheffield Lane Top to City via Attercliffe, (2) at Elm Tree with the 4.35 am bus from Intake to Walkley, and (3) at Staniforth Road junction on its return journey with the 4.50 am tram from City to Tinsley.

(4) *Sundays* (Until 28th April 1957)

	am	
Crookes Depot	10.57	
Midland Station		via Commercial Street
Flat Street	11.22	
Wadsley Bridge / Woodseats		via Shoreham Street 4 return journeys
Flat Street	5.22	
Wadsley Bridge / Meadowhead / Wadsley Bridge		via Shoreham Street 4 return journeys
Meadowhead	11.21	via Shoreham Street, Sheaf Street, Commercial Street
Church Street	11.46	
Crookes Depot		In operation 13 hours approximately

Appendix J

1. Fares

The basic pattern of fares throughout the tramway era in Sheffield was that of single fares between the City centre and suburban termini. There were never through bookings between suburban termini via the City centre. The dominant feature of Sheffield tram fares was their cheapness.

During the inter-war years the fare charged for the whole journey between City centre and suburban termini (referred to in this appendix as the standard fare), averaging about three and a half miles and up to a maximum of just over five miles, was cheaper for similar distances than on any other tramway undertaking in the country, as were children's fares. The short stage fare of about a mile was not particularly cheap compared with other systems; it was about the same as on the extensive London tramways.

The Company fares at the time of the Corporation takeover were 2d or 3d and they remained at these amounts for some time. However in response to a petition from Brightside residents the Tramways Committee decided on 22nd December 1896 to reduce the full journey fare to 2d with a centre point at Brown's Bridge (Carwood Lane) for a penny fare.

With the opening of additional horse car routes 2d became the standard fare with some 1d intermediate stages and one of ½d at Brightside. An exception was Walkley (Harcourt Road) where the charge for the outward uphill journey was 2d, but only 1d for the return.

No additional fare was charged when the cross-City line between Moorhead and Lady's Bridge was opened.

When the routes to Tinsley and Nether Edge were electrified the fare on all routes was reduced to 1d, but when the following route extensions were opened in 1901-1902 a standard fare of 2d was charged:

Broomhill–Ranmoor–Nether Green
Hunters Bar–Hangingwater Road
Manor Lane–Intake (Woodhouse Road)

and 1½d when the extension from Bannerdale Road to Millhouses Lane came into use.

However, on 14th October 1902 the Tramways Committee resolved to reduce the standard fare to 1d (equivalent to 0.42 pence in post-1971 coinage) on all routes except Intake where the outer part of the route was beyond the City boundary.

Upon the opening of the Malin Bridge route and the extension from Hunters Bar to Banner Cross in 1908, a higher standard fare of 1½d was charged. This applied also in the case of the extension of the Pitsmoor route to Firth Park (Bellhouse Road) in 1909. The extension from Darnall to Handsworth (Finchwell Road) in the same year attracted standard fares of 1½d to Shelfhanger Road (just outside the City boundary) and 2d to the terminus just over three quarters of a mile beyond.

In keeping with the similar action of 1902, from 9th January 1913 fares on the new or extended routes of 1908 and 1909 were reduced to conform with those charged on all other routes excepting Intake and Handsworth where the fares were reduced only to 1½d. These fares did not come into complete conformity with those on other routes until the Urban District of Handsworth became part of the City of Sheffield in 1921.

The 1d fare remained current until rising costs brought about by the First World War made necessary an increase, so that on 2nd March 1919 the standard fare was raised to 1½d and on 22nd December to 2d, excepting Petre Street which remained at 1½d.

Following an experiment on the three routes to Woodseats early in 1923, fares covering two consecutive 1d stages for 1½d became available on all routes from 1st July of that year but this fare lapsed when the standard fare was reduced in 1930.

At no time until 1st April 1947 did the standard fare exceed 2d and between 1st June 1930 and 1st November 1941, during which period routes had reached their maximum length, the fare was 1½d and ½d for children. During these years the short stage fare was 1d, but an odd exception which did not conform to the normal fare stages was the unadvertised 1d fare between Church Street and the Midland Station.

Standard fares applied on the circular routes as follows:

Between City and Beauchief via Woodseats
City and Woodseats via Beauchief
Woodbank Crescent and Springfield Road via Beauchief
City and Darnall via Elm Tree
City and Elm Tree via Darnall
Staniforth Road junction and Cemetery Gates via Elm Tree.

Details of fares charged on "cross-country" routes have not been traced, but it is known that in 1928 the standard fare of 2d applied between Intake and Brightside or Vulcan Road.

On 1st April 1947 the standard fare rose to 2½d, equivalent to one penny in current coinage. The inflationary trend in currency following the Second World War caused fares to rise steeply to 3d in December 1950, 4d in March 1952, 6d in February 1955, 7d in January 1957 on the longer routes, and to Beauchief 7½d in May 1960.

There were always one stage fares, in general at ½d to May 1917, 1d to 1947, 1½d until 1952 and 2d thereafter, but for a reduced distance during the period 1st April 1947 to 19th February 1955 inclusive. On 20th February 1955 midday fares were introduced and enabled passengers to travel between 10 am and 4 pm on Mondays to Fridays for 1d less on fares of 4d or over. The concession was abolished on 28th January 1957.

Children's fares for those between the ages of five and fourteen, or over for children still at school, were normally one half or less than the corresponding adult fare, as illustrated below for the period 1925-1960:

From 30th March 1925	½d maximum
On 1st April 1947 when the standard fare became 2½d	1d
On 20th February 1955 when the standard fare became 6d	2d
but on adult fares up to 4d	1d

A Tramways Committee meeting on 22nd September 1925 agreed that school children travelling to playing fields and parks between 2.45 and 4.30 pm should be granted a return fare of ½d instead of ½d each way. It is not known how long this concession lasted.

There were a few exceptions to the above pattern of fares the principal ones were as follows:

Central Fares (From 1923)

On 22nd October 1923 "central fares" were introduced

on through routes. These fares were available for two consecutive one penny stages—one on either side of the City terminus, at a charge of 1½d. As transfers were never permitted in Sheffield in normal conditions, central fares were available only on a limited number of journeys. In 1939 these fares were available as follows:

Between:

Ecclesall junction and Kelvin Grove on services between Ecclesall and Middlewood Fulwood and Malin Bridge

Ecclesall junction and Burngreave Vestry Hall on services between Woodseats* and Firth Park*

Ecclesall junction and Norfolk Bridge on services between Millhouses* and Tinsley or Templeborough

Cherry Street and Clarkson Street on services between Woodseats via Shoreham Street and Crookes

Cream Street and Clarkson Street on services between Woodseats via Queen's Road and Crookes

Fitzwalter Road and Weston Street on services between Intake and Walkley.

*or beyond

Zone Fares (From 1935)

In the early 1930s there was public pressure for the abolition of the traditional City termini, to be replaced by a central zone in which passengers could board at any stopping place without extra fare. These proposals were resisted by the General Manager on grounds of loss of revenue. However, on 15th September 1935 zone fares were introduced on through routes at a charge of 2d. This arrangement enabled passengers to travel a short distance not exceeding about a quarter of a mile beyond a City terminus, or to board cars at about the same point before the City terminus. The distance involved varied partly because of the overlapping of all City termini on the through routes, an arrangement in which Sheffield may have been unique.

One example was Millhouses–Market Side–Tinsley
Tinsley–Pinstone Street–Millhouses.

The zone stages were Moorhead and Wicker (Nursery Street/Blonk Street) in both directions.

The zone stages were fixed, for all through services which passed the under-mentioned points, at Moorhead, West Street at Westfield Terrace, West Bar at Corporation Street, Wicker at Nursery Street/Blonk Street (later extended to Wicker Arches), Commercial Street bottom (later extended to Duke Street bottom or Midland Station).

Return fares (1908-1913 and 1919-1941)

Return tickets first appeared at the same time as the higher than normal single fares introduced on the extended routes to Malin Bridge and Banner Cross in 1908 and to Firth Park and Handsworth in 1909. In the case of Malin Bridge and Banner Cross an all day return ticket at a fare of 2d (single fare 1½d) became available only on 'to City' cars. The Handsworth extension attracted an all day return of 3d (single fare 2d), together with an intermediate return fare of 2d between Shelfhanger Road and the City in the 'to City' direction only. The corresponding children's fares were 1½d and 1d respectively. No return fare was made available on the Firth Park route.

All return fares were abolished on 9th January 1913 when single fares were standardised on all routes except Intake and Handsworth; but on 1st May 1919 return tickets were reintroduced for issue before 9 am on all routes at a fare of 3d (single 1½d, increased to 2d on 22nd December 1919), subject to the sole exception of Petre Street where an all day return of 2½d (1½d single) became available.

On 26th February 1924 the Tramways Committee decided to reduce the price of return tickets on the short Nether Edge and Walkley routes to 2½d.

Return fares lapsed finally with the November 1941 fare increases.

Sheffield–Rotherham joint service

When the Rotherham route to Tinsley was opened in 1903, a through single fare of 3d to or from Sheffield was introduced, 2d being Rotherham Corporation's share. When Sheffield took over the section from Tinsley to Templeborough on 1st January 1926 the standard Sheffield fare was adopted for the extended journey to Templeborough. By that time the through fare between Sheffield and Rotherham had risen to 5½d but from that date it was reduced to 4d and by 1939 it had been further reduced to 3d. The through fare was increased on 2nd November 1941 to 3½d and finally on 1st April 1947 to 4d until closure of the joint service in December 1948.

The effects of the Sheffield fares policy

Whilst the cheap standard maximum fare policy of the City Council was a benefit to the tramcar travelling public, it had a serious disadvantage in that it inhibited route extensions. Mr. Fearnley was always opposed to schemes which necessitated extra mileage being worked without any significant increase in revenue. This situation led to a number of outlying suburbs being served by buses (at higher fares) with consequent duplication of services by trams and buses over some sections. Had tram fares been charged on a pro rata to mileage basis those suburbs would probably have been more economically served by extension of existing tram routes, resulting in a better integrated public transport system.

2. Tickets

Originally, separate series of tickets were issued for each route, the route name being printed on the tickets, but after 1912 when routes had been given code letters, these replaced the route name. Tickets continued to bear route letters to the end of tramway operation, long after they had ceased to identify a particular route. A single letter was in general use but 'Central' tickets carried two. The same route letter was used for every route in the City until the stock (in ten thousand lots) had been exhausted, when a new letter would be introduced. Moreover tickets of different values issued on the same tram could have shown a different route letter. It follows that the route letters of the later years could have been more appropriately described as serial letters.

Stage point numbers were in general use on tickets. However, tickets showing the geographical locations of stage points, which had been used some years earlier, were reintroduced for standard fare stage points on the Abbey Lane and Prince of Wales Road routes.

Appendix K

Accidents

Damage to tramcars by collision with other vehicles was fairly frequent and repairs of accident damage were a continuing operation at the Works. The incompatibility of manoeuvring motor traffic with tramcars guided by their tracks all functioning on the same carriageway inevitably led to conflict. Nonetheless, the tramway safety record in Sheffield was good and no fatal accident to a passenger has been traced where the passenger was not at fault.

Because records of the multiplicity of mishaps are incomplete it is practicable to refer to a very limited number of incidents. In general, if the number of the tram(s) is not known accidents are referred to only if there was some feature of particular interest.

In the earlier years tramcars which sustained damage were invariably restored and returned to service but in the years following the Second World War structural damage usually led to permanent withdrawal.

The first notable accident occurred on 27th March 1902 when single deck car No. 156 ran out of control from the Intake terminus at Manor Lane, became derailed at Granville Road junction and crashed into the low wall and railings of the forecourt of house No. 284 City Road. Double track points had already been installed for a proposed line (never constructed) to The Moor at Ellin Street. Although the car was full of passengers no-one was injured. The accident was attributed to the negligence of the crew and both driver and conductor were dismissed.

What might have been Sheffield's most destructive accident occurred a year later. The extended line from Woodbank Crescent to Chantrey Road (then called Norton Woodseats) had been opened only a few days when on the afternoon of Good Friday, 11th April 1903, open-topped car No. 63 returning to the City overran the passing loop at Smithy Wood and collided with No. 133 of similar type which was coming up round the left hand curve towards the loop. No. 63 was derailed and ran into a telegraph pole which prevented its going down over the precipice into the valley below. The retaining wall and railings had not at that time been erected.

On 5th July 1915 a tram running from Tinsley to Millhouses ran backwards while ascending Waingate, crashed into one following, and together both ran into a third car. It was reported that the first two cars were badly damaged and that Mr. Fearnley was quickly on the scene and personally obtained a spare car from Fitzalan Square which he used to drag the two leading damaged cars to Queen's Road Works. Delay to services was reported to have been only twelve minutes.

During 1918 (said to have been in early December), short canopied car No. 71 was involved in a collision with a railway locomotive at the works level crossing of Vickers Limited in Brightside Lane.

Several trams in the original fleet were so extensively rebuilt as the result of damage in accidents that they became almost unrecognisable except by their numbers. In February 1919 by the negligence of the crew, one of the fifteen open platform and canopy cars built by the Corporation in 1912, No. 290, ran down the one in nine gradient of Nether Green Road from the terminus, left the track and crashed into a shop in Oakbrook Road at the corner of Hangingwater Road. This car was rebuilt as a fully enclosed one but retained the bulkheads and sliding doors on both decks.

It is believed to have been an accident, of which there were several during the previous twelve months, which led in December 1927 to the even greater change in the appearance of No. 228, as described in chapter eight.

At the end of the morning rush hour on 15th May 1924 open platform and canopy car No. 18, returning empty to the City via Attercliffe, came into collision at the site of the future Firth Park Library with a Corporation steam roller which moved out into the track travelling in the same direction. Extensive damage was done to the side of the tram and the saloon was filled with steam. The front roller of the steam roller was torn away. At the same location in the afternoon of 19th April 1933 Standard car No. 63 and Brush car No. 430 came into collision. The latter was the only Brush car destroyed in the air raid on 12th December 1940.

Not far away a steam lorry crashed into a tram at the bottom of Bellhouse Road on 17th December 1928. The lower panels of the saloon were ripped off and seven passengers were injured. The car involved is believed to have been one of the three re-seated earlier in the year.

A destructive form of accident to car bodies was the collision between trams, particularly when they converged on one another at junctions due to drivers' errors or faulty equipment. Such was the case at the entry crossing to Millhouses turning loop when on 7th October 1948, just as Standard car No. 9 was approaching the crossing from Beauchief, Brush car No. 419 from the City (which should have continued towards Beauchief) incorrectly turned right into the loop and crashed into the front corner of No. 9. Four passengers were injured and it is believed that neither tram ran again.

During the evening rush hour on 26th June 1930 two trams collided at Ecclesall Road junction. A tram bound for Woodseats turned on to the Nether Edge track in error and ran into a tram from Woodseats. Both cars were derailed and severely damaged. Over one hour elapsed before re-railing was completed and serious dislocation of services resulted. Queues of cars formed back to the Town Hall, and on the tracks from Nether Edge, Millhouses and Woodseats.

A similar type of accident of no severity occurred on 23rd September 1935 when Brush car No. 450 to Tinsley was run into by Standard car No. 203 to Nether Green at the Fargate–Leopold Street junction.

Nineteen people were injured on 20th January 1946 when two cars collided in the single line controlled by signals at Broad Oaks, Staniforth Road. Cravens car No. 493 never returned to service and was the first of the large post-1918 cars to be withdrawn from duty. The other car involved, No. 81, returned to service after repairs, with sliding vents to all lower saloon side windows.

On 24th July 1953 Brush car No. 397 ran out of control and collided with another Brush car No. 434 which it was following closely on the falling gradient towards Intake terminus. Both cars were scrapped as a result. The same fate overtook the Improved Standard cars Nos. 133 and 263 when they collided on 26th August 1957 near Norfolk Bridge. The driver of the latter car had dozed off at his controls. He was fined and demoted to conductor.

"Preston" car No. 345 received end damage in 1947 and soon afterwards No. 348 of the same type was similarly damaged. The sound end of No. 345 was used to restore No. 348 and No. 345 was accordingly scrapped.

In several cases end damage resulted in cars being restored so that the two ends ceased to be identical. For the last few years of their term of service which ended in the Autumn of 1934 the open balcony cars Nos. 124 (renumbered 203 in January 1933) and 200 were in this form. In the former case the headlamp was in the lower position at each end but a flat lamp glass was fitted at one end only—believed to be the only such case in the entire passenger fleet at that period. No. 200 had the headlamp in the old position at one end and below the number at the other.

In the Standard car production programme, commencing with car No. 213 in 1935, the headlamp position was raised clear of the lower blue band. During the next three years three of the Standard cars in the old livery, Nos. 71, 100 and 119, received this later pattern dash at one end. Subsequently several other Standard cars were similarly dealt with. In the old livery the raised lamp left insufficient space for the old type numerals so that smaller gilt Gill Sans type were used. Cars Nos. 100 and 119 were destroyed in the air raid on 12th December 1940. When, as reported in chapter twelve, car No. 71 was overhauled and received a simplified form of lining-out, Gill Sans numerals were added to the undamaged dash, although there was adequate space for the old type numerals.

From time to time accidents occurred between trams and buses. In the evening of Easter Monday, 5th April 1920, open balcony car No. 190 was waiting at the "to City" stopping place at the bottom of Carterknowle Road when it was overtaken on the off-side by a charabanc[1] returning from Matlock. The tram restarted and it seems that the charabanc was caused to pull over sharply to avoid a tram approaching from the City, whereupon No. 190 ran into the rear of the motor vehicle.

On 11th December 1930 Brush car No. 448 collided with a bus on the Dewsbury service in Firth Park Road, and Cravens car No. 447 crashed into a Yorkshire Traction bus near Osgathorpe Road on 7th September 1948. A collision occurred at Ickles on 19th September 1940 between a lorry and car No. 217, which received severe platform damage. This is the only known reported case of an accident to a Sheffield tramcar on Rotherham track and moreover is believed to be the only reported case of a traffic accident involving a Sheffield car during the 1939-45 war.

In addition to those already mentioned, there were other cases of runaway trams. At about 10.30 am on 26th October 1920 the Brush open balcony car No. 336 descending the hill between Bute Street and Coombe Road became derailed and crashed into the kitchen of No. 40 Crookes. The tram sustained minor damage but the house was wrecked. On the same route on 14th June 1919 a runaway car in Northfield Road crashed into another car awaiting clearance of the single line at Crookes terminus.

On 19th June 1952 Standard car No. 209 became derailed following a collision with a coal lorry and ran into the front of shop No. 927 Chesterfield Road, Woodseats. Among other collisions with lorries were: No. 50 returning from Wadsley Bridge on 26th November 1948, and No. 442 descending Barnsley Road on 28th July 1928.

An accident caused by the weather occurred at Sheldon Road (Abbeydale) at about 11 o'clock at night on 19th February 1920 when a tram already halted by a blizzard was run into by another tram. In much better conditions on 10th April 1937 the Improved Standard car No. 258 was run into in the rear by another tram at Ecclesall Church. Three people were injured. This car was also involved in an accident in Holme Lane on 26th July 1939 when one platform was badly damaged.

There were a number of tramcar fires, usually caused by electrical faults. The Brush open balcony car No. 306 sustained fire damage on its way to Hillsborough on 10th March 1915 and the large Brush car No. 437 caught fire on The Moor on 11th October 1922. The ex Newcastle car No. 312 was damaged beyond repair, by fire, in Tenter Street Depot on 29th May 1947 some three years before the rest of the class was withdrawn from service. The fire was believed to have been caused by a burning cigarette which was not detected by the staff when the car entered the depot. The first fire to occur on a Roberts car was on No. 502 on 3rd July 1950, only seven and a half weeks after entering service. This car was very fully loaded on its way to Intake when the rear fuse box ignited and six people required hospital treatment. This first all-metal tram thus taught a lesson and the electrical apparatus was rearranged on this car and all subsequent cars of the class. Nonetheless, No. 513 caught fire at Beauchief on 8th August 1957 and a similar incident brought the first and premature withdrawal of one of these cars when 520 was damaged by fire on Attercliffe Common in 1959.

There was a serious accident on 17th July 1950 when a runaway lorry emerged from the foot of Derbyshire Lane and crashed broadside into Brush car No. 438 bound for Sheffield Lane Top, which overturned and was damaged beyond repair. It was stated that forty-three years had elapsed since a tram overturned, but no such incident in 1907 has been traced. The driver's platform of a tram had been damaged by a lorry at the same point at Derbyshire Lane on 21st August 1926.

A fitting location at which to conclude this subject is the end of the line at Nether Edge where electric traction in Sheffield commenced, and the only place where the lines ended directly facing buildings. It was here on 4th October 1927 that a tram ran off the end of the terminal stub and stopped just short of entering the grocer's shop on the corner of Nether Edge Road and Machon Bank Road.

[1]Open topped motor coach.

Acknowledgements

Sincere thanks are due to the many friends and associates who have helped in their various ways to enable me to complete this history and work of reference.

My father, Ernest Gandy, was a member of the City Council from 1926-1935 which gave him access to information and facilities which in later years proved to be most useful. In particular, his associates the late Aldermen T. Garnett and H. Keeble Hawson were very helpful, as were the staff at Queen's Road Works. Unfortunately I do not have the names of several depot employees to whom I am also indebted for relevant material.

Most of all, however, my thanks are due to John W. Richmond, a life-long resident of Sheffield, without whose extensive local tramway knowledge and devoted services it would have been impossible to complete this history. His diligent, painstaking searches and investigations and his assistance in many ways have been of essential and inestimable value.

The unstinting and willing help of Mr. J. M. Olive and his staff at the Sheffield Central Library, Local Studies Department, in making available a variety of relevant documents over a period of thirteen years contributed greatly to the achievement of my programme. In addition, I gratefully acknowledge the courteous guidance of Mr. J. C. Pyle concerning publication. His practical assistance in the final stages of my work is much appreciated. Thanks are also due to Jill Leeming, the Library's Graphic Designer, for designing the finished article.

Valuable assistance in the selection of illustrations and checking of information was given by Edward P. Marshall. Others whose help was much appreciated were Michael Gandy (maps and general advice), John Barrie and F. K. Farrell for making available early periodicals of the Light Rail Transit Association, H. B. Priestley for route details, R. Benton, C. W. Clough and B. C. Sexton for general assistance.

I also acknowledge the information supplied by Miss E. M. Willmott (Bradford) and A. Betteridge (Calderdale) about tramway depots in their respective districts.

I am indebted to Messrs. A. W. Brotchie, I. L. Cormack, H. G. Dibden, C. C. Hall, G. S. Hearse, R. Mercer and R. J. S. Wiseman for the assistance obtained from their articles on rolling stock, and to Charles Roberts Engineering Ltd. for authorising the inclusion of part of their specification for the tramcars built by the Company for service in Sheffield.

The following have generously consented to the use of their photographs: R. Brook, T. Elliott, P. Lazonby, J. H. Meredith, M. J. O'Connor, A. D. Packer, the late J. G. Parsons, H. B. Priestley, D. Robins. J. L. Smith (Lens of Sutton), the late D. Tate, D. A. Thompson, C. C. Thornburn, G. Whitehouse, P. N. Williams, Mrs. A. R. Wiseman and R. J. S. Wiseman. The illustrations of Bamforth & Co., the City Museum, Cravens Railway Carriage & Wagon Co. Ltd., the Science Museum, Sheffield Central Library, South Yorkshire Passenger Transport Executive, the Tramway Museum Society and Valentines are acknowledged with thanks, as is the permission of the Director General, Ordnance Survey to reproduce maps subject to copyright.

I am most grateful to Sylvia Fry, Gillian Rouse and my wife Sybil for their generous help in typing letters and/or the manuscript, and to R. W. Packham for indexing correspondence.

Finally, grateful thanks are due to Sybil and Barbara Sheerman-Chase for their valuable services in checking the typescript and proofs.

Thanks and apologies are due to those helpers who may inadvertently have escaped mention above or whose identity is not known to me.

Bibliography

Pool, A. G., *A survey of transport in Sheffield.* 1933

"Kennington", *London County Council Tramways handbook.* 1974

Young, Andrew D., *100 years of Leeds Tramways.* 1970

Walton, Mary & Lamb, J. P., *Raiders over Sheffield.* 1980

Cormack, Ian L., *Seventy-five years on wheels.* 1960

Sheffield Transport Department, *Sheffield municipal transport 1896-1946.* 1946

Hall, Charles C., *Sheffield transport.* 1977

Hawson, H. Keeble., *The growth of a city 1893-1926.* 1968

Hearse, George S., *The tramways of Gateshead.* 1965

Sheffield Transport Department, *The tramway era in Sheffield.* 1960

Bett, W. H. & Gillham J. C., *The tramways of South Yorkshire and Humberside.* Edited Price, J. H. 1975

Periodicals:

"Civic record". City of Sheffield Information Service

"Leeds & district transport news". R. Mercer

"Scottish Tramlines" (No. 11). Scottish Tramway Museum Society

"The modern tramway" (numerous issues). Light Rail Transit Association

"The tramway review" (Nos. 5, 16, 27, 56-58, 68 and 69). Light Rail Transit Association

"Trams" (Nos. 1, 4, 6, 8 and 24). Tramway Museum Society.

Index

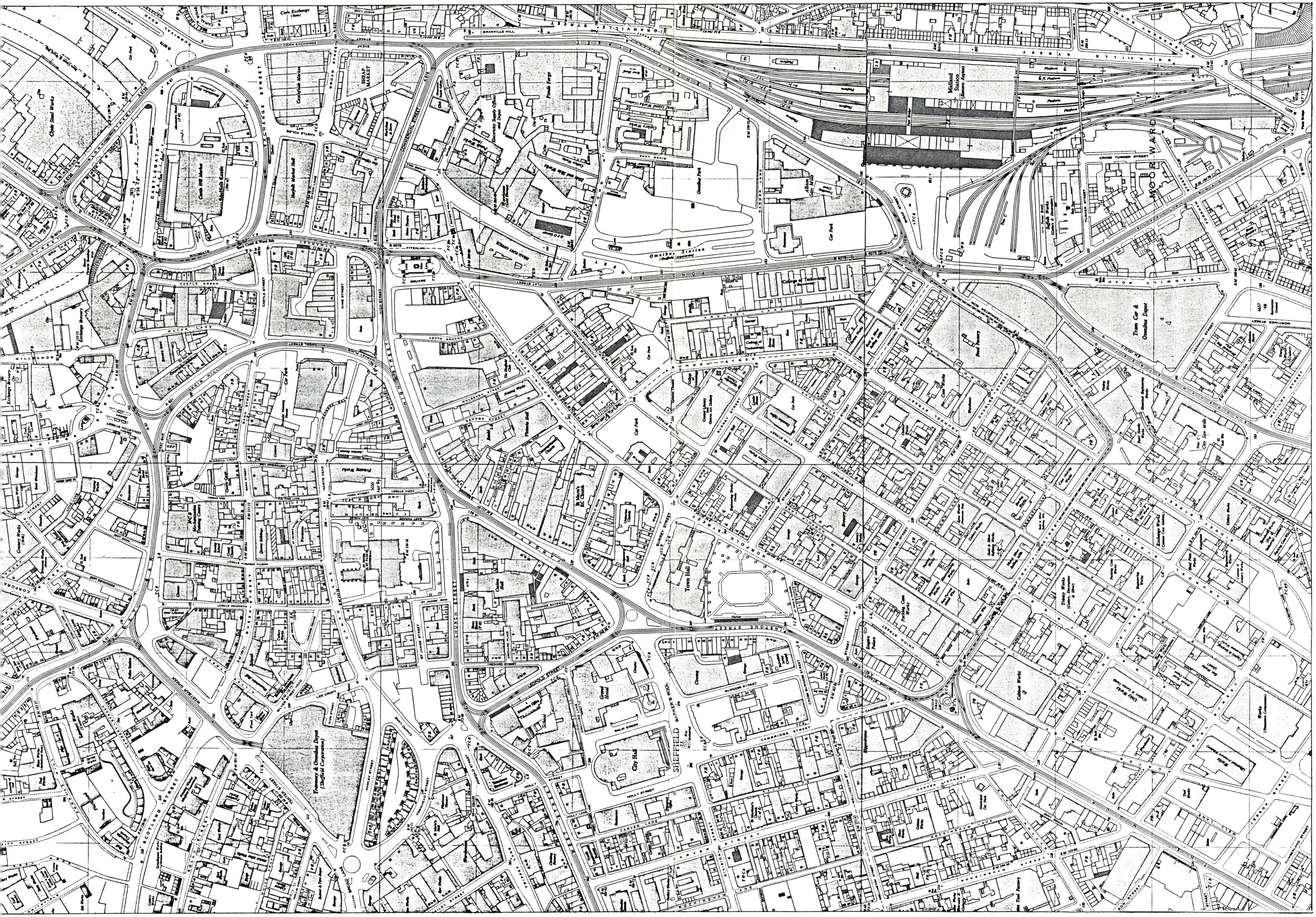

THE CENTRAL AREA IN 1954

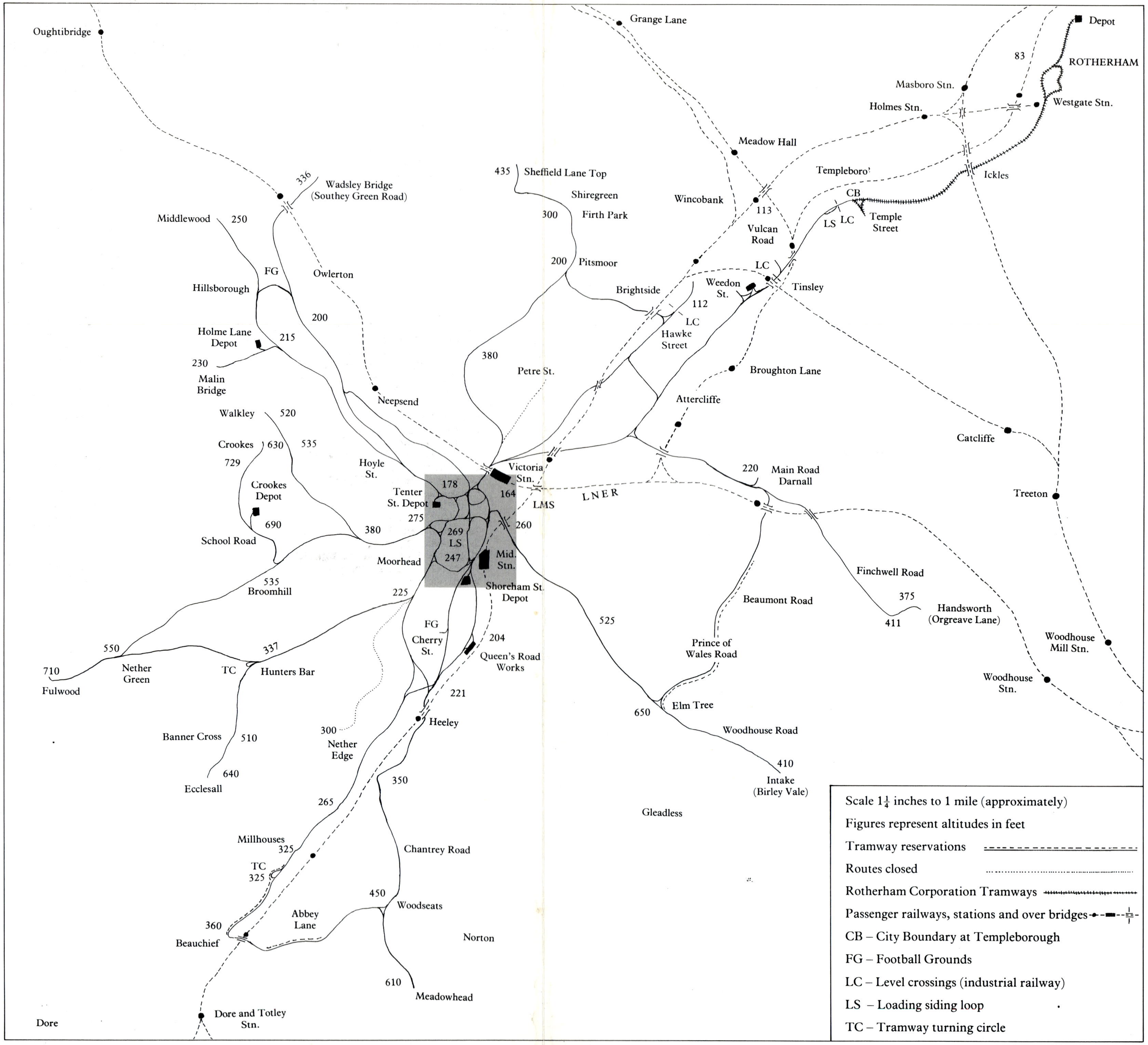

The Tramway System at 31st March 1936